THE STARS OF

COUNTRY MUSIC

Publications International, Ltd.

Contributing Writers:

Lydia Dixon Harden is managing editor of *Music City News* in Nashville. She has authored a Dolly Parton biography and has written for the program book for the Academy of Country Music Awards.

Dave Hoekstra is the country music writer for the *Chicago Sun–Times*, where his features and columns on country music, entertainment, and popular culture have appeared since 1981.

Michael McCall is a Nashville–based country music writer whose credits include a biography of Garth Brooks and articles in *US*, *Billboard*, the *Los Angeles Times*, the *Nashville Banner*, and *Pulse Magazine*.

Janet Williams has served as associate editor of *Close Up*, the magazine of the Country Music Association. Previously, she served as an associate producer of USA Network's *Night Flight.*

Kimmy Wix is a Nashville country music writer, associate editor of *Music City News*, and a former editor of *Cash Box* magazine, where he covered the country music industry.

Editorial Assistance: Don Roy, Shawn Williams

Photo Credits

Front Cover: Paul Natkin/ Photo Reserve Inc.

Greg Allen: 73; Archive Photos: 20 (bottom), 44; Frank Driggs Collection: 20 (top); 22; Frank Edwards/Fotos International: 117 (left); Miranda Shen/Fotos International: 219 (left); **Atlanta Records: 161; Celebrity Photo: 171 (left);** Tammie Arroyo: 49, 56 (left), 85, 86, 128 (top), 140 (right), 148 (left), 159, 173, 185, 174 (bottom), 220 (right), 231, 234; Greg DeGuire: 207; Scott Downie: 112 (left), 124 (bottom), 215; Janet Gough: 127 (right); Victor Malafronte: 182; John Paschal: 51 (left), 52, 60, 67, 91, 96, 97, 102, 110, 116, 125, 130, 140 (left), 154, 157, 163 (left), 176, 181, 187, 190, 202 (right), 227, 228; Bob Scott: 90, 164 (right); Miranda Shen: 169; **Chris Carroll/ Epic Records: 139; Globe Photos: 45 (top), 47 (bottom), 63,** 64, 180; John Barrett: 171 (right), 179, 213; Joseph Delvalle: 128 (bottom); Ralph Dominguez: 87, 175, 209; Michael Ferguson: 57; Beth Gwinn: 224; Mann & Greene: 146; Lynn McAfee: 120; NBC: 80 (left); Bob Noble: 113 (bottom), 147 (right), 225; Gary Null/NBC: 92, 101; Gary Null: 192; Lisa Rose: 65, 94, 201; Ada Scull: 111; Gavin Smith: 70; Stephen Trupp: 54, 58, 118 (top), 158 (right), 239; **Hank Jr. Fan Club: 27 (top), 28; Les Leverett: 10 (top), 24, 38, 40 (left),** 80 (right); Libby Leverett–Crew: 124 (top); WSM Photo: 32 (right), 40 (right); **Liberty Records: 220 (left); Jim McGuire/ MCA Records: 100, 198 ; Paul Natkin/Photo Reserve Inc.: 43, 46** (right), 50, 51 (right), 98, 114, 142, 150, 166, 186, 218; **Onyx:** Max Aguilera-Hellweg: 122; Edie Baskin: 62; Rob Brown: 156;

Mark Jenkinson: 148 (right); Aaron Rapoport: 143; Brian Smale: 210; **RCA Records:** 55, 164 (left), 204; Jim McGuire: 222; Don Putnam: 174 (top); **Sony Records:** 184; Sony/Columbia: 188 (right); **Retna LTD.:** 48; John Atashian: 56 (right), 129; Nancy Barr: 217 (right); Jay Blakesberg: 152; Larry Busacca: 88; David Denenberg: 226; Steve Eichner: 104; Gary Gershoff: 74 (bottom), 82, 100; Beth Gwinn: 47 (top), 72, 84, 106, 112 (right), 113 (top), 126, 131, 136, 138, 165, 200, 206, 212, 214, 219 (right), 232, 236; Andrew Kent: 105, 217 (left); Chris Kraft: 108, 163 (right); Janet Macoska: 160; Eddie Malluk: 68, 233; Robert Matheu: 76, 238; Van Osdol: 168; Susan Rutman: 118 (left); Barry Schultz: 178; Bill Schwab: 162; Charles Steiner: 74 (top); Angie Wagner: 153; **Roy Rogers Collectors Association: 21; Hot Schatz: 223; Southern Folklife Collection/the University of North Carolina at Chapel Hill, Chapel Hill, NC:** 9, 10 (bottom), 11, 13, 14, 16, 17, 18, 19, 23, 25, 31 (bottom), 32 (left), 33, 34, 36 (bottom), 37, 41, 46 (left), 121, 167; **Courtesy of Showtime Archives:** 8, 12, 31 (top), 35 (bottom), 36 (top), 39, 42 (bottom), 77 (left), 123, 147 (left); Colin Escott: 6, 15, 27 (bottom), 29, 42 (top), 77 (right), 78; Colin Escott/George Merritt: 26; Lynn Russwurm: 30; Glenn Smith: 35 (top); **Shooting Star:** 79, 144; Charles Williams Bush: 45 (bottom), 202 (left); Mark Charles: 118 (right); Ron Davis: 127 (left), 155, 158 (left), 230; Diana Lyn: 208; Marc Morrison: 71, 89, 172, 188 (left), 194, 195, 196, 216; S. Nannarello: 109.

·CONTENTS·

·COUNTRY ROOTS·

The world of country music has been shaped by an extraordinary galaxy of luminaries. The participants have been unassuming, pretentious, profane, sweetly likable, predictable, and unpredictable. Country is indeed the correct label for these artists, because their voices call out from every corner of America—from the Texas panhandle to the Tennessee River, from a bar in Bakersfield, California, to a New York honky-tonk. Country music is a glorious hybrid of American musical influences.

Country music is a hybrid of musical influences and genres. Throughout its history, commercial country music has absorbed and integrated various popular styles. Even in the pure country sounds of Hank Williams the echo of the blues can be found.

Country musicians inherited their ragged-but-right independence from descendants in rural folk music. Free of any commercial obligation, rural folk artists were adventurous and untamed. Texas fiddle player A.C. "Eck" Robertson is regarded as being the first to bring rural folk into a country landscape with his 1922 recording of "Sallie Gooden." Robertson's playing was fluid and fierce— a Texas comet burning across tight traditional strings. The Texan was also the first musician to wear full western regalia while performing.

The early years of country music were amazingly fertile, and Eck Robertson was not the only game in town. At the same time as Robertson's success, another Texan, Vernon Dalhart, was determined to take the rural sound uptown. Dal-

hart had moved to New York City and was singing country music in churches and vaudeville houses. Some observers called Dalhart's style "Tin Pan Alley country." The simultaneous yet quite different careers of Robertson and Dalhart established a country-music axiom that remains valid today: For every action there is a reaction. Eck Robertson was a hick; Vernon Dalhart was slick.

Country music has always been a music of response. In other words, one approach inspires another. The success of Robertson and Dalhart influenced the establishment of the style of country that came to be known as hillbilly music.

The sophisticated style of Patsy Cline represents country music's tendency to emulate the smooth sounds of pop music. This tendency can be traced back to the 1920s when Vernon Dalhart's "Tin Pan Alley Country" was all the rage.

Popular music was riding a wave of nostalgia in the mid-1920s. The ragtime of the Gay Nineties was enjoying a revival. Country musicians knew most of those songs because in the rural South they probably never went out of style. In 1925, Okeh Records executive Ralph Peer recorded a North Carolina string band in New York City. The musicians jokingly described themselves to Peer as hillbillies in the big city. Peer then named the group the Hill Billies, despite some reservations on the part of some band members.

With the name "Hill Billies," country music picked up its first mass-culture identity. The term has since been used derisively by detractors and adoringly by fans. Some country fans and artists refer to themselves as hill-billy singers as a matter of simple description; others resent the term, particularly when used by outsiders, as a denigration of country music and the way of life it represents.

Country music's evolution has not always been easy. Many performers have had to struggle to break preconceived notions about what country music should be. When the hillbilly sound was superseded by honky-tonk in the 1940s, some people were shocked by honky-tonk's introduction of electric guitars, piano, and drums. Lyrics reflected the new, bawdy sound, and many songs were clearly addressed to the culturally and socially disenfranchised. Vast numbers of poor Southerners finally had a "voice."

Country music's evolution continued, and the infectious din of honky-tonk was drowned out by the melodramatic slickness of the Nashville Sound. Smooth, calculated, swelling with lush string arrangements, the Nashville Sound defined country music for years—at least until rockabilly roared up as a rebellious response.

Today, country music is an amalgam of the best of what has come before, combined with a contemporary spin that makes the music as fresh and as popular as it has ever been.

Many country performers have been brought up to believe that anyone can make music in any environment—on the front porch, in the family room, in a rural church, in a honky-tonk, and, maybe someday, in a fancy studio in Nashville. The legends examined in the following pages—Roy Acuff, Johnny Cash, Patsy Cline, Merle Haggard, George Jones, Ernest Tubb, Hank Williams—all became country artists as an expression of their rural tradition. But today's country musicians come from a more sophisticated American culture that permits them the freedom to choose whichever musical course they wish. And they are a generation who chose country music. That is the ultimate tribute.

The music of the legendary Ernest Tubb, like that of other classic country performers, is an expression of America's rural traditions.

Pioneers: The 1920s and 1930s

As the 1920s began, several musicians across the South were making decent livings at civic gatherings and fiddle contests performing old-style folk songs and rustic versions of Tin Pan Alley hits. In Texas, for example, fiddler Eck Robertson and his guitar-strumming friend Henry Gilliland were having a fine time performing at political functions and in theaters during the showing of silent films. The two were willing to travel to find new audiences, and in the summer of 1922 they decided to journey to a Civil War reunion in Virginia, figuring they could pay for the trip with money picked up from the huge crowds expected to attend.

The Virginia trip went so well that the two enterprising instrumentalists decided to go on to New York and look into the new business of making phonograph recordings. When they showed up at the offices of Victor Records, Robertson was dressed as an Old West cowboy and Gilliland wore a Confederate uniform. The Victor executives were reportedly amused by these bold characters and took them into the studio.

Fiddlin' John Carson was recorded by Ralph Peer in 1923, but the well-known fiddler had been a major presence in Georgia for 40 years. He played at political campaigns as well as at various social functions.

Robertson and Gilliland didn't intend to enter into history or into a long-running debate about the origin of the first country music recordings. However, the two cut several songs, including Robertson's solo rendition of the fiddle tune "Sallie Gooden." Many music historians have referred to these Victor sessions as the first country music recordings and to "Sallie Gooden" as one of the best examples of an old-time fiddle tune on record.

There were other country-music pioneers. Fiddlin' John Carson was a popular radio performer on WSB in Atlanta, and Okeh Records executive Ralph Peer recorded Carson's "Little Old Log Cabin in the Lane" in June of 1923. George Banman Grayson and Henry Whitter were a duo who, like Robertson and Gilliland, traveled to New York without an invitation but ended up recording several songs now considered country music standards, including "Handsome Molly" and "Little Maggie."

No one referred to these tunes as country songs at the time. The genre of mountain music and folk blues from Southern rural whites gained its first name when Ralph Peer asked that North Carolina string band he had just recorded what they wanted to be called. "Call us anything you want," answered a band member. "We're just a bunch of hillbillies from Virginia and North Carolina." The phrase was soon transformed into a one-word adjective and used to describe this developing genre of hill country tunes.

By 1924, country music had its first million seller, "The Prisoner's Song" by Vernon Dalhart, a Broadway performer who had appeared in a Gilbert & Sullivan production before seeing a career opportunity in performing for the growing rural record market. The growth had been pushed along by the increasing influence of radio, which gave the rural population a chance to hear and enjoy music that once had been accessible only to urban audiences.

Radio station WBAP in Fort Worth fueled the growing Southern folk music boom in early 1923 by presenting a barn-dance program that inspired a great listener response. Chicago's WLS followed with the *National Barn Dance*, and a few years later WSM in Nashville began its own variety barn-dance hour that would turn into a three-hour program known as the *Grand Ole Opry*. There, a jovial banjo picker named Uncle Dave Macon and an African-American harmonica player, DeFord Bailey, built an audience that expanded tremendously after Roy Acuff came along in the 1930s to become the *Opry*'s first superstar.

At first, country music didn't sell as well as opera, classical, or the popular Tin Pan Alley hits, but it was inexpensive to produce and it helped the young recording firms reach a previously untapped audience. The sales of country records increased after Ralph Peer stumbled upon country music's first superstar, Jimmie Rodgers. Peer recorded Rodgers in Bristol, Tennessee, while on a trek through the Southeast in the summer of 1927. On the same trip, Peer also cut the first records of the Carter Family, thereby launching two of country music's most significant acts within days of each other.

One of the Grand Ole Opry's *most popular performers in the 1920s was DeFord Bailey, who played country harmonica blues.*

Uncle Dave Macon, another original star of the Grand Ole Opry, *embellished his banjo-picking with spirited whoops and hollers. His son, Dorris, often accompanied him.*

Rodgers was a rambling, gambling man who liked to drink, carouse, and live life to the fullest. Known as "the Father of Country Music," Rodgers was the first entertainer to prove that blending a hodgepodge of different Southern musical styles could successfully attract listeners all across America. He was the first country music star, selling an estimated 20 million copies of recordings made in the last six years of his short life.

Musically, Rodgers borrowed sounds from African-American blues and jazz and combined them with mountain music to create a style uniquely his own. He also perpetuated many of country music's primary themes: He sang about drinking and rambling, lasting love and yearning for home, mother and country, cowboys

Recording scout/folklorist Ralph Peer discovered Jimmie Rodgers, country music's first major star. Seated left to right: Rodgers, Mrs. Peer, Peer, and Mrs. Carrie Rodgers. Seated below: Rodgers's daughter, Anita.

and prairies, loose women and one-night stands, and rivers and gambling. He wrote overtly sentimental songs and bawdy double entendres. With his music, he helped popularize the notion of referring to a town, state, or region with great reverence and pride, while his songs and image helped promote the escapist myth of living life as a ramblin' rounder.

Rodgers was born on September 8, 1897, in Meridian, Mississippi. His father worked as a foreman for the Mobile & Ohio Railroad. His mother had been infirm for most of her adult life, dying of tuberculosis when her only son was seven years old. Both his father's occupation and his mother's health would loom large in the Rodgers legend.

At age 14, Rodgers landed a job in the railroad yard, thanks to his father. He was a water carrier, a laborious job usually performed by African-Americans. Rodgers was surrounded by coworkers who sang black spirituals and old slave songs, and he became fascinated by those who could pick the guitar, banjo, ukelele, mandolin, or other instruments.

Throughout his life, Rodgers worked a variety of jobs for the railroads, including stints as a flagman and as a baggage master. He also worked as a brakeman, a premiere job on the railroad line, which accounted for his nickname "the Singing Brakeman." While riding the trains, he began mimicking the long, lonesome wail of a train whistle, transforming it into a kind of blue yodel that brought a moaning, plaintive quality to the familiar Swiss yodel. He turned it into a vocal trademark that would be endlessly imitated.

Though Rodgers would later romanticize his employment with the railroads, he was probably more interested in pursuing a career as a performer than riding the rails. While still just a teenager, he ran away from home to join a medicine show. An early marriage disintegrated because, according to his first wife, he couldn't make a decent living by "plunking on some old banjo or guitar."

In April 1920, he married his second wife, Carrie Williamson, the seventh daughter of a preacher, whose strict, refined upbringing was the opposite of Rodgers's rough, rowdy lifestyle. They lived in poverty, and their second child died

Jimmie Rodgers's style of yodeling was based on the long, lonesome moan of a train whistle. It was called simply "blue yodel."

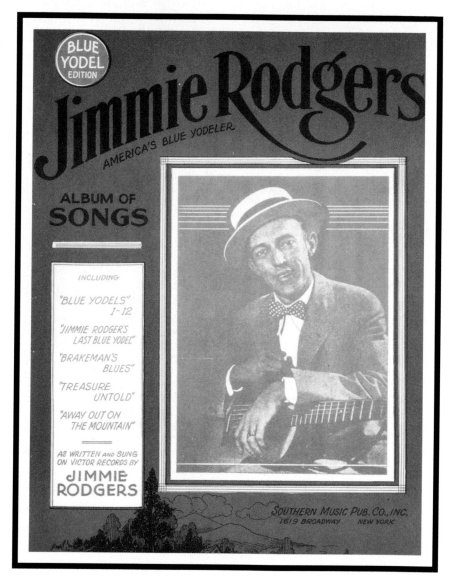

Rodgers enjoyed success for only six years before he died from tuberculosis, an affliction he cursed in the autobiographical song "TB Blues."

in infancy. Rodgers also began to struggle with the heavy coughs and colds that had beset his mother. In 1925, he was diagnosed with tuberculosis and advised to give up the hard-working railroad life. To make money, Rodgers performed as a minstrel singer in blackface and later was hired by a medicine show that took him to Tennessee and Kentucky.

In 1927, he formed the Jimmie Rodgers Entertainers in Asheville, North Carolina. He read a newspaper account of auditions being held by Victor Records executive Ralph Peer in Bristol, Tennessee, and convinced his three partners to audition with him. However, once in Bristol, his partners auditioned as a trio without telling him. Rodgers convinced Peer to give him a shot as a solo artist. One of his two songs, "Soldier's Sweetheart," gained enough radio play to persuade Rodgers to move his family to Washington, D.C., near both RCA and Victor's New Jersey recording center.

One of his first sessions in Camden, New Jersey, included "Blue Yodel No. 1," also known as "T for Texas," the song that established Rodgers as a major American recording star. Within months, he was earning $2,000 a month on the vaudeville circuit, moving almost instantaneously from itinerant worker to wealthy celebrity.

By 1930, Rodgers's jaunty country blues and sentimental songs put him at the forefront of American musical performers. He was also suffering increasingly debilitating bouts of tuberculosis. In 1931, at the height of his fame, he recorded "TB Blues," which stated with gutsy directness: "I've been fighting like a lion, looks like I'm going to lose, 'cause there ain't nobody ever whipped the TB blues." To help him perform, he sipped a mix of honey and lemon, followed by a shot or two of rye whiskey, before going onstage.

He spent a month in a San Antonio hospital in 1933, where he had moved his family. Discovering he had spent most of his wealth on medical bills and various consumer goods, he set up a prolonged recording session with Victor Records in New York. He left Texas in May 1933 to cut 24 songs with Peer in New York, perhaps understanding he needed to add to his legacy as quickly as possible. His disease had progressed to a point where he had to rest on a cot between songs, and his last session took place on May 24. He rallied the next day and felt well enough to visit Coney Island. However, upon his return to his room that evening, he began to hemorrhage. Rodgers died the next morning, less than six years after his initial recording.

In contrast to Jimmie Rodgers's preference for music that focused on high times, hard drinking, and fast living, the Carters were devoutly religious and domestic people who preferred songs about family and faith. They stuck closely to the traditional musical styles of their native mountain home throughout their entire careers.

The Carter Family became country music's first commercially successful traditional act. They performed songs that were as old as the communities in the Clinch Mountain area where A.P., Sara, and Maybelle Carter had been raised. The trio set their mountain folk songs to a string band sound, and they slowly grew into one of America's most popular singing groups as well as one of country music's most endearing and enduring recording acts.

The Carter Family began performing together on the front porches and in the living rooms of family members and neighbors. The original members—A.P., Sara, and Maybelle—stopped performing as a group in 1943.

Alvin Pleasant "A.P." Carter, the oldest member, was born in December 1891 in a log cabin in the mountains near Maces Spring, Virginia. He married Sara Dougherty, a resident of Copper Creek, located on the other side of Clinch Mountain. Her younger cousin, Maybelle Addington, married A.P.'s brother Ezra shortly after her 16th birthday in 1926.

In 1943, Maybelle went on the road with her three daughters—June (left), Anita (with accordian), and Helen (with bass). They were billed as Mother Maybelle and the Carter Sisters.

A.P., Sara, and Maybelle shared a love for music, and they began performing together on front porches and in living rooms around Maces Spring. Sara played the autoharp and sang in a husky, compellingly beautiful voice. Maybelle played guitar in an accomplished two-finger style, her thumb providing the melody on the bass strings while her fingers strummed the rhythm on the tenor strings. A.P. sang bass and acted as the group's leader. He also collected songs, hunting down traditional folk tunes in old hymnals and sheet music and transcribing lyrics from informants and fans. A.P. not only disseminated traditional rural music, he also preserved it.

In 1927, Victor Records executive Ralph Peer traveled to their area seeking local talent. On August 1, Peer recorded the Carter Family's first songs. At Victor's encouragement, the Carters traveled to Camden, New Jersey, for a recording session that resulted in "Wildwood Flower" and "Keep on the Sunny Side," two of their best-known hits. Their songs became well known throughout the South, but the austere, simple-living Carters did not earn the fortunes acquired by Rodgers. The Carters worked the family farm and maintained other jobs, traveling only sporadically to nearby states until 1938, when they moved to Del Rio, Texas. There, they performed regularly on Mexican border station XERA, which had a 50,000-watt signal that reached across the West, Midwest, and South.

A.P. and Sara had separated in 1932 and divorced in 1938, yet the trio continued to record and perform. In the group's later years, Sara's daughter, Janette, and Maybelle's daughters, Helen, June, and Anita, joined the group. In 1943, A.P. and Sara retired from music, while Maybelle continued to perform with her daughters as Mother Maybelle and the Carter Sisters.

The Carter Family sang about an America of simple, rural values and agricultural traditions that had virtually disappeared by the time of their success, giving their music a hint of melancholy that still pervades traditional styles of country music.

Peer's two discoveries represented the diversity that would remain a hallmark of country music for decades. The rambling music of fast-living Jimmie Rodgers and the mountain tunes of the Carter Family provided a broad base for the next generation of country performers to build on.

Classics: The 1940s

In the late 1930s, several important factors pointed country music toward its future as a prominent entertainment form. The NBC radio network began a national broadcast of a portion of the *Grand Ole Opry* each Saturday night, taking the sound of Nashville and the rural South into millions of homes. Gene Autry sauntered onto the American landscape as a film star by portraying a solid, heroic figure of the Old West who dressed in fancy cowboy duds and crooned romantic, wistful songs about open spaces and long-lasting love. And, the jukebox popularized dance halls and juke joints as social gathering places where the music needed to be loud enough to be heard over a crowd and rhythmic enough to keep dancers moving.

The *Opry*'s 30-minute time slot on national radio was a major step in establishing this legendary program as an American institution. Throughout the Depression, the Opry organization had worked hard to attract musicians from all over the country to widen the program's appeal. The Vagabonds from Chicago and the Delmore Brothers from Alabama joined the roster, but it was the addition of Roy Acuff and Bill Monroe that helped turn the *Grand Ole Opry* from a radio show into a home for country music stars.

In the 1930s, Alton (left) and Rabon Delmore helped lead the Grand Ole Opry toward an emphasis on vocal performers.

The most important day in the career of Roy Acuff was February 19, 1938. He was 34 years old, thin, solemn, and determined. He was also more nervous than he'd ever been in his life. He was making his debut on the *Grand Ole Opry* that evening. In previous years, he had auditioned several times, always failing to gain an invitation to appear on the show. But he and his band, the Crazy Tennesseans, had made a name for themselves on a Knoxville radio station, which developed into his opportunity to appear on the *Opry*.

He made several mistakes on the two fiddle tunes he chose to perform first. Then the band began to play "The Great Speckled Bird," a traditional hymn that he sang and didn't have to play. Even though Acuff had trouble remembering the words, he performed it with complete conviction, letting his unadorned, plaintive voice soar with intensity. The crowd roared its approval.

Acuff returned to Knoxville. Two weeks later, he received a letter inviting him to become a regular. WSM, which broadcast the live *Opry* show, had been inundated with fan mail following his performance.

Acuff soon proved just as important to the Grand Ole Opry organization as it was to him. Opry management encouraged him to change the name of his band from the Crazy Tennesseans to the Smoky Mountain Boys. It then made Acuff the core of a promotional blitz designed to increase ticket sales for Opry package concerts across America. The campaign worked: the *Grand Ole Opry* became the premiere radio program in the South, and Acuff became one of country music's biggest attractions in the early 1940s.

A true country music pioneer, Roy Acuff molded the Grand Ole Opry into the star-studded showcase that it is today. He also helped turn Nashville into Music City, U.S.A., by establishing a prominent music publishing company there in 1942.

Born on September 15, 1903, in Maynardville, Tennessee, Acuff's original ambition was to become a professional baseball player. He earned an invitation to try out for the New York Yankees, but a series of sunstrokes ended his sports career and forced him to spend much of his time indoors regaining his strength.

Acuff had worked as a callboy in railroad yards, where he had learned to mimic the blast of the train whistle. This strengthened his voice and provided him with a vocal technique that would serve him well in the years ahead. He began to pursue music with a vengeance, and he was soon hired to go on tour with a neighbor who headed a medicine show. By 1933, he had formed a band and gained a regular job as a live performer with a Knoxville radio station.

Roy Acuff and the Crazy Tennesseans made their first recordings for the American Record Corporation in 1936. "The Great Speckled Bird" was recorded at that time, as was "The Wabash Cannon Ball," a Carter Family song now closely identified with Acuff. The 1936 version of "Cannon Ball" features Crazy Tennessean band member Sam "Dynamite" Hatcher on vocals. Though Acuff performed the song from the time he first joined the *Grand Ole Opry*, he didn't record it as a vocalist until 1947.

In 1939, when NBC Radio decided to air a half-hour segment of the *Opry* each Saturday night, Acuff and the Smoky Mountain Boys played the opening and closing numbers, giving them national exposure just as radio was expanding across America. The singer made the best of the opportunity, blending humble comments and warm introductions with devout mountain gospel songs and passionate tales of love and heartbreak. His duties as host of the *Opry* made him a bona

Hollywood courted several entertainers with a country flair during the 1930s. Roy Acuff appeared in his share of low-budget B-musicals with Southern themes and characters.

fide star, garnering him recognition and stature across the country. Acuff remained the host of the *Opry* for the rest of his life. He died in 1993.

Bluegrass legend Bill Monroe joined the Grand Ole Opry in 1939, giving the Opry another major star. Monroe's debut performance featured his first famous song, "New Mule Skinner Blues."

There are few country music figures who can legitimately claim to have popularized or revived a particular style of music, but only Bill Monroe can take credit for *creating* a distinct musical form. When Monroe is called "the Father of Bluegrass Music," it's not an overstatement. He forged an individual musical style out of an amalgam of old-time mountain music, Holiness Church gospel, blues, and jazz that attracted a school of imitators and inspired a new genre of music. It came to be known as bluegrass because Monroe called his band the Bluegrass Boys, after a famous aspect of his native state, Kentucky.

In developing the style of music known as bluegrass, Bill Monroe used the mandolin as an aggressive, even percussive, instrument, which could hold its own in a large band. Prior to bluegrass, the mandolin was mainly a gentle parlor instrument.

Bill Monroe was born in 1911 on a farm near Rosine in western Kentucky. His poor eyesight led to a reclusive devotion to music, and he developed into an expert player of the mandolin, fiddle, and guitar. His mother, an old-time fiddler, died when Monroe was ten. His father died six years later, and the young Monroe moved in with his uncle, Pendleton Vandiver, an accomplished musician.

In the late 1920s, Bill joined with his older brothers Charlie and Birch to play at square dances during their spare time. When full-time radio work was offered in 1934, Birch left the group, leaving Bill and Charlie as the Monroe Brothers duet. The pair found success in radio and as recording artists with Victor Records between 1936 and 1938. The brothers split in 1938, with Charlie forming the Kentucky Pardners and Bill organizing the first version of the Bluegrass Boys.

At that point, Bill Monroe set out to create a more aggressive, hard-driving sound. He pushed the mandolin, banjo, and fiddle into lead instruments, demanding that his musicians excel at nimble ensemble playing and flashy, improvisational solos. Later, during the 1940s, his *sound* became a musical *style* as younger musicians began to emulate his vocal stylings and instrumentation.

Patsy Montana became the first solo female country star by adopting a cowgirl persona and singing western-style music.

The popularity of Gene Autry on a Chicago radio program called the National Barn Dance *led to a Hollywood contract. It was also responsible for turning the phrase "hillbilly" music into "country-western."*

Aside from the prominence of the *Grand Ole Opry*, country music's popularity expanded because of the influence of western themes and sounds during the late 1930s. With Gene Autry, America found an image on which to focus its long-running fascination with the mythical life of the free-roaming, valiant cowboy. His popularity fed the imaginations and musical ambitions of thousands of youngsters. More importantly, Autry's picturesque but well-groomed look provided a commercial vision for other Southern-based performers, many of whom ditched their overalls and exaggerated rural costumes for the nicely tailored cut of the western outfit as conceived by Hollywood. With the popularity of Autry, the term "hillbilly music" gave way to "country-western."

Though most think of Autry as the premiere western singer from this period, Patsy Montana's career was also shaped by romanticized notions of the West. She began her career by forming a trio known as the Montana Cowgirls, taking the name from Monty Montana, a world-champion roper and cowboy. In 1933, she joined the Prairie Ramblers, a male quartet who performed on the WLS *National Barn Dance* in Chicago. She was the first solo female country music star, and her 1935 hit "I Wanna Be a Cowboy's Sweetheart" was the first million-selling record by a woman. She and the Prairie Ramblers remained major touring and recording stars until 1951. She also appeared in a couple of western serials with Gene Autry.

Before galloping across the big screen, Roy Rogers was part of a western-style singing group called the Sons of the Pioneers. The Pioneers were famous for their smooth harmonies and finely crafted songs.

By the 1940s, several other western singing stars roamed the Hollywood prairies. Foremost among them was Roy Rogers ("the King of the Cowboys") and his early musical partners, the Sons of the Pioneers. The latter group is widely considered the epitome of western music as an art form, and Rogers was the soloist who went on to the widest national fame. There were others: Tex Ritter, Johnny Bond, Jimmy Wakely, Elton Britt, Stuart Hamblen, and Rex Allen also sang of tumblin' tumbleweeds and yodeled their way into the hearts of Americans.

The jukebox, meanwhile, nurtured a more raucous, harder-edged style of country music, and the nightlife that it encouraged brought with it new topics for songwriters. Wurlitzer introduced the jukebox in 1928, and the machine's popularity grew as the Depression and Prohibition began to fade away. By 1940, more than 300,000 portable jukeboxes were in operation. With the jukebox, the beat of Southern music picked up its tempo, and the piano, the string bass, the electric guitar, and the steel guitar joined the fiddle as primary country music instruments.

The louder music and new lifestyles broadened the topics for lyrics, too. In addition to God, family, and home, songwriters explored in depth the insecurities of love, the varying levels of guilt, and the joys and dangers of drinking, rambling, and other means of escape.

Two musical styles emerged in country music during the 1940s: gritty, lyric-driven honky-tonk and freewheeling, instrumentally daring western swing. Both forms produced pioneers and heroes. In western swing, the list is headed by Bob Wills and His Texas Playboys, Milton Brown and His Musical Brownies, and Spade Cooley. In honky-tonk, they included Ernest Tubb, Hank Williams, Floyd Tillman, Moon Mullican, and Ted Daffan.

Bob Wills remains country music's greatest bandleader, as well as one of its most innovative, progressive musical visionaries. He didn't exactly create the musical style called western swing, though he was among a community of musicians who forged this new, lively blend in the early 1930s. But one fact is indisputable: Wills and his band, the Texas Playboys, are responsible for making western swing a popular American musical style.

Born in 1905 in Kosse, Texas, Wills was a wild, restless youth. His father was an accomplished breakdown fiddler, and young Bob often joined his father at barn dances and house parties. Wills traveled Texas as a hobo in the 1920s, working odd jobs. He spent time as a farmer and a barber before leaving home for good after an arrest for public rowdiness. He joined a medicine

Bob Wills liked to dress the part of a stylish uptown Texan. He had grown up in West Texas but spent most of his adult life in more sophisticated surroundings.

show, where he gained a wider exposure to blues, swing, Dixieland, and other musical styles.

In Fort Worth in 1929, Wills hooked up with guitarist Herman Arnspiger. Along with another friend, singer Milton Brown, Wills and Arnspiger found work on a radio show. Because they plugged Light Crust Flour for boss W. Lee O'Daniel—who later was elected governor of Texas—Wills and his band became known as the Light Crust Doughboys.

Milton Brown left the group in 1932 to form Milton Brown and His Musical Brownies, credited by some as the first western swing band. Wills departed the following year with singer Tommy Duncan to form a new band. Unfortunately, each time they found employment at a radio station, O'Daniel would see to it that they were fired. So Wills, Duncan, and the others moved to Tulsa, Oklahoma, to take a job with 50,000-watt KVOO. It was the best move Wills ever made.

Wills dubbed his band the Texas Playboys, and from 1934 to 1941 the group performed daily on KVOO, then entertained dance crowds nightly at the expansive Cain's Academy ballroom in downtown Tulsa. In 1935, Wills hired Smokey Dacus,

Wills, guitarist Herman Arnspiger, and singer Milton Brown first performed together on a radio program that was sponsored by Light Crust Flour. Their band was called the Light Crust Doughboys.

making him the first drummer in a major country music outfit. He then added a horn section. From that point on, Wills increasingly emphasized dance rhythms and swinging, hot musicianship.

Wills's own fiddle playing drew on the traditional breakdown style he learned in his youth. When he blended that sound with the swing and Dixieland jazz sweeping the United States, he created a bopping style unique to the Southwest. Wills liked the blues of Bessie Smith, the smooth pop of Bing Crosby, the swing of Tommy Dorsey and Benny Goodman, and the rhythmic drive of Count Basie and

Earl "Fatha" Hines. He incorporated these styles with the polkas and waltzes of the German immigrants in Texas and with the pulse of Tex-Mex accordion music. It was a swinging hodgepodge that Wills was clever enough to temper with the supple baritone of Duncan.

Wills led his band with an entertaining charisma and bawdy dynamism. He strutted across the stage during concerts dressed as a stylish uptown Texan and chomped on a cigar as he pointed to musicians for their solos. Despite his cavalier presence, he attracted top musicians and demanded originality and innovation. He also gave them room to play and allowed them to take part in arranging the music.

Wills and His Texas Playboys recorded their most famous work between the late 1930s and early 1950s, though he continued to record periodically into the 1960s. His last studio appearance came during a 1973 reunion of the Texas Playboys. About that time, Wills suffered a stroke and slipped into a coma. He died in 1975.

Like Bob Wills, Ernest Tubb was a trailblazer, as well as a congenial and generous mentor to scores of musicians and country artists. He was an architect of what became known as the honky-tonk sound, partly because he was among the first country stars to use an electric guitar as a musical focal point. He had made the move in 1941 when a nightclub owner complained that jukebox records couldn't be heard once a crowd grew animated. He added a drum in 1950 on his recordings, another rarity for a *Grand Ole Opry* performer at the time.

Ernest Tubb didn't always hit the right notes, but he struck a deep chord in listeners, proving that a singer with a limited vocal range could achieve unlimited success in country music. His remarkable baritone was warm, earthy, and thoroughly natural, and he used it to intimately communicate his lyrics.

Tubb was born in 1914 on a farm near Crisp, Texas, and he decided to become a singer at age 14 after hearing Jimmie Rodgers. In 1933, Tubb moved to San Antonio and, while working for the WPA, talked his way into a singing job on radio station KONO. The next year he met Carrie Rodgers, his idol's widow. She landed Tubb a contract with Victor Records and made him a present of her husband's valuable guitar.

Following a tonsillectomy that severely affected his voice, Tubb joined Decca Records in 1940, and the following year he

Ernest Tubb was a distinctive song stylist who overcame the limitations of his baritone by singing with warmth and heart. He was a tremendous influence on subsequent country artists, including Hank Williams.

An influential and innovative guitarist, Merle Travis made his mark as an actor. Unlike other country musicians, Travis lived on the West Coast for much of his life.

recorded his breakthrough hit, "Walking the Floor Over You." He made it to the Grand Ole Opry two years later and appeared in two western movies with star Charles Starrett.

Tubb was the first major country music artist to record regularly in Nashville, thereby helping establish the city as a leading recording center. His insistence on recording in Nashville also led Decca Records to open a branch office in that city. When other companies followed, the foundation was set for what is now known as Music City, U.S.A.

Merle Travis, an exponent of the West Coast honky-tonk sound, is perhaps best remembered as an innovative, groundbreaking guitarist. But the versatile Kentucky native also was an accomplished songwriter and singer who mastered honky-tonk, western swing, and folk music with style.

Travis was born in 1917 in the small town of Rosewood in the coal-mining area of Muhlenberg County, Kentucky. He began playing guitar as a youngster, and by adulthood he had perfected a regional style of picking that used the thumb to play rhythm on the bass strings and the index finger to play the melody on

A talented songwriter, Travis wrote everything from novelty tunes such as "So Round, So Firm, So Fully Packed" to the mournful miner's lament "Dark as a Dungeon."

the treble strings. It has become a frequently emulated style known as "Travis-pickin'."

After recording with Grandpa Jones and the Delmore Brothers in Cincinnati, Travis moved to the West Coast, where Capitol Records offered him a recording contract after he played on a Tex Ritter session. Travis's earliest solo recordings were folk-based tunes done at the request of Capitol, and they included the original versions of such Travis compositions as "Sixteen Tons," "Dark as a Dungeon," and "I Am a Pilgrim." These songs later became better known through versions by other singers. He also wrote "Smoke, Smoke, Smoke That Cigarette."

As a performer, Travis moved on to record his most famous solo country hits, including "Divorce Me C.O.D.," "So Round, So Firm, So Fully Packed," "Sweet Temptation," "Three Times Seven," and "Fat Gal." These witty novelty tunes featured the unusual touches of trumpet and accordion, as well as fiddles and guitars.

An actor, author, and even cartoonist, as well as a singer/songwriter, Travis was a multitalented indivivual. He continued to tour and to play small roles in films until his death in 1983.

Hank Williams will forever represent the essence of country music. He grew up poor in rural Alabama, yet he rose to become the biggest star of his generation. He couldn't write a literate letter, yet he composed classic songs. He climbed far beyond his dreams, yet he lived a tortured existence racked with pain, sorrow, and guilt. His music was loved by millions, yet at age 29 he died of a drug and alcohol overdose in the backseat of a Cadillac driven by a stranger.

Alabama teenager Hank Williams at a time when he performed on the streets of Montgomery and Greenville.

Williams was an overwhelmingly charismatic performer, both on record and in concert, and he sang with a passionate conviction that splintered the artifice on which most entertainers rely. His songs used everyday language to communicate intensely personal emotions, and they set standards for musical expression in the way he transformed his own anxieties into simple, colorful verse that articulated the concerns and obsessions of working people everywhere.

He was born Hiriam Williams on September 17, 1923, on a tenant farm outside of Mount Olive, Alabama.

Though Hank and Audrey Williams look happy in this family portrait, their relationship was turbulent. Baby Randall Hank bounces on his father's knee while Audrey's daughter Lycrecia sits between them.

Tortured by physical and emotional pain, Hank Williams was unable to reconcile his internal struggles with his financial success. Seeking relief, he turned to drugs and alcohol, which killed him; seeking solace, he expressed himself in the lyrics of his songs, which are his legacy.

His father, Elonzo Williams, was a fragile man who suffered a nervous disorder attributed to shell-shock from World War I battle experience. His mother, Lillian "Skipper" Williams, was an imposing, domineering woman who left her husband and ran a dreary, hard-knocks boarding house in Montgomery, Alabama. Williams hated the name Hiriam, a misspelling of the biblical King Hiram, and preferred Hank as soon as he had an opinion.

He learned guitar as early as age eight, but he cites his early teen experiences with a black street singer named Tee-Tot (Rufe Payne) as the seasoning that taught him to put feeling into his music. Williams dogged Tee-Tot on the streets of Greenville, Alabama, giving him money he made from shining shoes to learn blues chords and old folk songs.

At age 17, he left for Texas to pursue his other romantic preoccupation, rodeo bronc riding. But he was born with a bad back, and a throw from a horse aggravated his condition, so he quit the sport. He never lost his allegiance to the cowboy myth, however. He called his band the Drifting Cowboys, even though his songs had little connection to cowboy music. And he always cited the Texas honky-tonk sound of Ernest Tubb as an overriding influence. The keen rhythms of Lone Star swing, combined with the stark emotionalism of Southeastern country music, formed the foundations of the Hank Williams sound. Back in Montgomery, he auditioned for WSFA radio and soon became a featured singer on the Montgomery radio station. His radio station position led to broader concert bookings, and while performing in Banks, Alabama, he met his future wife, Audrey. At the time, she was married to a soldier stationed in Europe.

Meanwhile, his reputation grew. He performed as the local opening act for the Opry's package tours in Alabama, meeting Roy Acuff and selling a song he wrote to Opry star Pee Wee King. He was also building a reputation as a problem drinker who wasn't always reliable.

He married Audrey in 1944 at a filling station in Andalusia, Alabama. His wife stoked his ambition and encouraged him to go to Nashville, just as the stars he met had suggested. Fred Rose of Acuff-Rose had shown interest in his songs, and after the first Nashville trip in 1946, Rose signed Williams to a song publishing contract. Early the next year, Williams recorded for Sterling Records, backed by the Willis Brothers.

His second recording session for Sterling yielded the self-composed "Honky Tonkin'." Its success led to interest from MGM Records, and in April 1947 he recorded "Move It on Over" for the nationally distributed MGM.

Williams was on his way. He joined the *Louisiana Hayride* radio show in Shreveport in August 1948. Though the program had only started in April, it was broadcast on a clear-channel station that reached a weekend audience throughout the South and Midwest, and it hooked Williams up with such acts as Kitty Wells, Johnny Horton, Johnny and Jack, and the Bailes Brothers.

In February 1949, Williams released "Lovesick Blues," a song

Hank, Sr., holds Randall Hank Williams, who later changed his name to Hank Williams, Jr. But, Hank, Sr. preferred to call him Bocephus.

from a 1922 musical he first heard on a Rex Griffin record. It was Hank's first number-one record, and one of country radio's biggest hits of all time. In May, while the record was entrenched at number one, Randall Hank Williams was born. Two weeks after his son's birth, Williams accepted an invitation to join the Grand Ole Opry.

As his fame accumulated, his personal life deteriorated. In 1952, he left Audrey and moved into a home with young Ray Price, then a struggling newcomer. Their home became famous for its wild parties. Williams grew more erratic and unreliable, and the Opry dropped him from its ranks in August 1952. He then married Billie Jean Jones, who was supposedly on a date with Faron Young when Williams met her. Their wedding took place three times, once with a justice of the peace and twice before sold-out audiences in New Orleans.

Williams spent Christmas of 1952 visiting his mother in Montgomery and his father in southern Alabama. His last performance took place on December 28 at the Elite Cafe in Montgomery in a benefit for the local American Federation of Musicians union. He died on January 1, 1953, on his way to a New Year's Day show in Canton, Ohio. He had been heavily medicated and had been drinking for days. He was found slumped over in the backseat of a Cadillac by a driver hired the previous day.

During the 1950s, the cast of the Grand Ole Opry *included the best entertainers that country music had to offer. The Opry organization paid only minimum fees to performers, but membership on its roster meant better bookings and more prestige.*

The week before he died, his song "I'll Never Get Out of This World Alive" made its debut on the charts. Eventually, the song reached number one. After his death, his hits continued: "Kawliga," "Your Cheatin' Heart," "Take These Chains from My Heart," and "I Won't Be Home No More" were released after his death.

Williams's legacy of music, created in such a short period of time, spans a remarkable breadth of styles. He wrote religious songs, mother songs, party songs, and rambling songs. Some of his tunes can be seen as precursors of rockabilly, and the smooth versions of his tunes by such pop crooners as Tony Bennett and Joni James set the tone for the cosmopolitan country that followed. His blend of blues rhythms and Appalachian angst remains a bedrock of traditional country music, as does his combination of fiddles and slap bass with electric guitar and pedal steel.

More importantly, his lyrical images of the lonesome sound of a distant train whistle or of a moon slipping behind a cloud to cry will eternally serve as reflections of the despair hidden in the human heart.

Nashville Sounds: The 1950s

Meanwhile, as country music broadened its horizons and expanded its popularity, the means of marketing, distribution, and personal appearances expanded as well. WSM's *Grand Ole Opry* was the largest of the many live radio shows that beamed country music into homes across America. As the program's influence grew, an invitation to join the Opry's performance roster became an important career step for any ambitious country music singer set on national stardom. With the talent flocking to Nashville because of the Opry, several astute WSM performers and radio executives decided to branch out into recording, song publishing, and concert booking. Thus, Nashville began its rise as the capital of country music.

Expanding from the WSM base, Roy Acuff and veteran New York songwriter Fred Rose started Nashville's first major music publishing company. Acuff-Rose became the first successful company to concentrate solely on publishing country music songs. Two other country music publishing companies, Cedarwood and Tree, were also started by former WSM employees.

Three former *Opry* engineers opened Nashville's first professional music studio. *Opry* stars—including Acuff, Tubb, Williams, and Foley—quickly found that scheduling time at Castle Recording Company was infinitely more convenient than traveling to New York or Chicago. Then Decca prudently decided to produce country music records in the city where the country music stars were centered. After Decca hired Owen Bradley to produce records by Tubb and Foley, RCA followed suit by hiring a young guitarist named Chet Atkins in 1952 to serve as their recording director in Nashville.

Atkins knew many of Nashville's sessions musicians who had migrated to the city because of the recent proliferation of

Chet Atkins was largely responsible for the development of the Nashville Sound, a pop-influenced style that downplayed fiddles and steel guitars in favor a more commercial sound.

Jim Reeves began his career singing in the honky-tonk style that dominated the early 1950s. Later he turned to a velvet-toned, pop-influenced sound with the help of his friend Chet Atkins.

Eddy Arnold consistently pursued a pop direction throughout his career. The country crooner was dubbed the Tennessee Plowboy, though there was little about his style that suggested the backwoods.

recording studios and song publishing companies. These musicians, who became legendary for their talent, versatility, and improvisational skills, were permanently based in the city. Using the talents of many of these sessions musicians, Atkins deliberately tried to develop a pop-influenced sound for country music. Fiddles and steel guitars were downplayed in favor of a smoother, more commercially appealing sound.

The development of "the Nashville Sound" paralleled the rise of Nashville as America's country music center. The Nashville Sound caused significant changes in the instrumentation and vocals of country music, while Nashville's identity as Music City, U.S.A., turned country music into a billion-dollar industry. Purists grieved over the loss of traditional rural sounds and styles, but the influence and lure of pop music had always been lurking on the edges of country music. The Nashville Sound was the manifestation of the pop leanings of country music, and it produced some of country's most sophisticated performers and song stylists.

Jim Reeves rose from deeply rural roots in the thickets of East Texas to become one of the smoothest, most universally popular country singers of the late 1950s and early 1960s. While he maintained his country origins, Reeves managed to appeal to pop music audiences with his mellow style.

He was born James Travis Reeves in 1923 in Panola County, Texas, and was just ten months old when his father died, leaving his mother to raise the infant and eight older siblings.

A promising minor-league baseball career was cut short by injury, and Reeves moved into radio announcing. He dabbled in performing while working in Texas in the early 1950s and later had an unexpected top-ten success with "Mexican Joe,"

recorded on the Abbott Records label. Reeves's bosses at KWKH in Shreveport, Louisiana, quickly installed him as a member of the *Louisiana Hayride*, which was broadcast from the station.

Several more hits led to a contract with RCA Records. Reeves moved to Nashville, and when Chet Atkins encouraged him to lower his voice, the results were two of Reeves's best-known songs, "Four Walls" and "He'll Have to Go."

The singer toured Europe and Africa in 1962, initiating a following that later led to his status as one of country music's most successful international recording stars. In July 1964, as Reeves was enjoying his thirty-third top-ten hit, he was killed in a private plane crash just outside of Nashville. So great was his popularity, however, that he notched 19 posthumous top-ten hits, including five number-one records and a 1981 duet with another deceased star, Patsy Cline.

Crooner Eddy Arnold and his soft, smooth ballads also benefitted from the popularity of the pop-flavored country music that emerged during the 1950s. Arnold, one of the first country singers to "cross over" to the pop charts, drifted away from more traditional rural sounds during the 1940s. And, during the 1950s, he began using orchestras and choruses on his recordings, which helped him gain wider acceptance by pop audiences. Other country artists who flirted with pop stylings during the 1950s included Ferlin Husky and Faron Young.

Ray Price etched his mark into country history with two distinctively different but equally successful styles. He bopped through the late 1950s with a swinging, hard-edged honky-tonk sound centered on a shuffle rhythm that came to be known as the Ray Price Beat. Then, in the mid-1960s, he lowered his voice, traded the fiddles and steel guitars for a violin section and muted guitars, and became a successful country-pop crooner.

Price was born in 1926 in Perryville, Texas, and grew up in Dallas. In 1949, he quit his studies in veterinary medicine to pursue music full time. In 1951,

Ray Noble Price quit his studies in veterinary medicine in 1949 to pursue a career in country music. Price continued to chart records into the 1980s and continued to perform regularly into the 1990s.

Ray Price became a member of the Grand Ole Opry in 1952 with the help of his friend Hank Williams.

after two years on the *Big D Jamboree* radio show, Price signed with Columbia Records and moved to Nashville. He joined the Opry roster in 1952 with help from his friend and roommate, Hank Williams.

Price scored his biggest early hit in 1956 with "Crazy Arms," which introduced his shuffle beat. But by 1967 he devoted himself to a lusher style, starting with a recording of "Danny Boy" that featured a 47-piece orchestra. He continued to have success with this pop-inspired sound into the 1970s.

Despite the influence of country-pop and the Nashville Sound in the 1950s, several country performers representing a variety of styles flourished during that decade. Kitty Wells, for example, became country music's first major female solo star by singing about honky-tonk angels in a rural-based style. Her success helped open the door for more women performers in a male-dominated industry.

One of the few country music stars actually born and reared in Nashville, Wells came into the world on August 30, 1919. Born Muriel Deason, Wells's stage name was an invention of her husband, Johnny (born Johnnie) Wright, who took the name from the old folk song "Sweet Kitty Wells." Wells grew up in a fundamentally religious family and began singing in church early in her life. At age 14, she learned to play acoustic guitar so she could accompany herself while performing hymns.

Kitty Wells helped advance the commercial possibility of women as country music soloists by conveying an image as a wholesome family woman whose songs chastised unfaithful men.

She was 16 when she met Wright, and along with Wright's sister, Louise, they began performing on Nashville radio station WSIX as Johnnie Wright and the Harmony Sisters. In 1937, Wells and Wright were married. That same year, Wright hooked up with singer Jack Anglin, eventually forming the duo Johnny and Jack. Wells joined the two on the road as their "girl singer," a familiar role in many touring bands of the time. Wells helped out with harmonies and performed a few songs of her own during the group's shows.

In 1948, Wells joined the *Louisiana Hayride* with Johnny and Jack. A beneficiary of the group's spreading fame, Wells signed a solo contract with RCA Records. But her songs received scant attention on country radio, and Wells continued to be known primarily as a subordinate member of Johnny and Jack.

In 1952, however, Wells switched to Decca Records, where company president Paul Cohen suggested she work with popular musician and arranger Owen Bradley.

Wells's first single on Decca was a song she wrote in response to Hank Thompson's "The Wild Side of Life," which had opened with the line "I didn't know God made honky-tonk angels."

Wells's song, "It Wasn't God Who Made Honky-Tonk Angels," emphasized male culpability in illicit romances, and it became the first record by a woman performer to reach number one on *Billboard* magazine's charts after the trade

Kitty Wells was part of the singing act that included her husband Johnny Wright and friend Jack Anglin (right). Roy Acuff (left) welcomed Wells to the Opry in 1944.

sheet initiated the country music charts in 1944. It also introduced Wells's plaintive, unpretentious voice to a large audience. While the song was perched at number one, Wells, Wright, and Anglin were offered an invitation to join the Grand Ole Opry.

Following "It Wasn't God Who Made Honky-Tonk Angels," Wells continued to record songs that responded to assertions made in hit songs by men. Her second hit, "Paying for That Back Street Affair," followed Webb Pierce's smash "Back Street Affair." Then came "Hey Joe," which provided a feminine answer to Carl Smith's hit of the same name.

After "Hey Joe" Wells's hits stood on their own merits. Her songs of love, anguish, and quiet resignation competed on the charts with releases by male stars

Canadian Hank Snow was originally billed as the Yodeling Ranger. After he joined the Grand Ole Opry, Snow called himself the Singing Ranger.

Resplendent in a wide variety of custom-made outifts, Snow has been one of country music's most colorful dressers.

in a way no other female singer equalled until Loretta Lynn began hitting the top of the charts in the mid-1960s.

Wells scored over 30 top-ten hits from 1952 to 1965, including such landmark country songs as "Cheatin's a Sin," "Release Me," "Makin' Believe," "Searching (For Someone Like You)," "I Can't Stop Loving You," "Mommy for a Day," "Amigo's Guitar," "Heartbreak U.S.A.," and "Will Your Lawyer Talk to God." She was also a frequent presence on country radio as a duet performer, attaining hits with Red Foley, Webb Pierce, and Roy Drusky.

The course of her career suggested to record companies and radio stations that country music fans were ready to embrace female solo performers. Most of the other successful women country singers of the 1950s performed with their families or as part of a group, as with Wilma Lee Cooper, Molly O'Day, Rose Maddox, June and Anita Carter, Martha Carson, and Texas Ruby. Although Wells did not always perform alone, her solo career was a milestone in the evolution of country music.

Hank Snow displayed an ability to create memorable music in a variety of styles, ranging from the insistent boogie of "I'm Movin' On" to the tender sentiment of "(Now and Then, There's) A Fool Such As I" to the western lilt of "Yellow Roses."

Born Clarence Eugene Snow in 1914 in the Canadian province of Nova Scotia, Hank watched his parents go through a divorce when he was eight years old. He spent a few troubled years with his grandparents before eventually moving in with his mother and her new husband, who beat him brutally and regularly. Around the age of 12, Snow ran away to join the Merchant Marine as a cabin boy. While at sea, Snow broke the boredom by learning to play the harmonica. After hearing the music of Jimmie Rodgers, he

bought his first guitar for $5.95 and learned to play the country music that he loved.

Snow imitated Rodgers in his early years, billing himself as Hank, the Yodeling Ranger. At age 22, he gained his first recording contract with RCA Records in Canada. Eight years later, determined to crack the American music market, he began traveling across the border into the States. By 1946 he was performing on radio station WWVA in Wheeling, West Virginia.

Three years later, Snow persuaded RCA Records to give him a chance in the United States. That same year, he met Ernest Tubb, who convinced the Grand Ole Opry to hire the talented, eager Canadian. Snow then changed his billing to the Singing Ranger. Shortly after joining the Opry, he enjoyed his first number-one hit, the smash "I'm Movin' On," which spent 21 weeks at the pole position of the country charts.

The Louvin Brothers recorded for MGM in the early 1950s but moved to Capitol Records in 1952. They continued to chart hits up through 1962.

Charlie (left) and Ira Louvin flank one of their idols, Opry legend Roy Acuff. The traditional-sounding Louvin Brothers joined the Grand Ole Opry in 1955.

Snow quickly piled up a stack of similarly memorable songs, and his resonant baritone brought authority to up-tempo country boogies and a gentle wistfulness to ballads. He also was an accomplished guitarist and the first to record an instrumental duet with Chet Atkins.

Snow recorded 41 top-ten songs in the 15 years following his first hit, and he continued to hit the number-one position as late as 1974. Snow was inducted into the Country Music Hall of Fame in 1979.

During the 1950s when commercial country tunes were moving toward harder-edged honky-tonk or smooth pop, the Louvin Brothers performed chillingly powerful, old-time mountain music. Though considered anachronistic by some of their contemporaries, Ira and Charlie Louvin have grown in stature over the years. Their emotionally stirring high harmonies, sparse instrumental blend, and reverent lyrical style are now considered timeless examples of pure, traditional country music at its best.

The brothers' family name was Loudermilk; Ira was born in 1924, and Charlie followed three years later. They grew up in the small town of Henegar in Northeast Alabama, and their first professional work came in 1942 after winning first place in a talent contest in Chattanooga, Tennessee.

World War II briefly interrupted their partnership, but the two reunited in Memphis, where they performed gospel music at a local radio station. They released one song on Decca Records in 1949, and a few more on MGM in the early 1950s. War separated the brothers for a second time when Charlie went to fight in Korea. Shortly after his return, the Louvins hooked back up with Capitol Records, whom they had signed with shortly before the Korean tour, and released their first big hit "When I Stop Dreaming." In 1955, the brothers joined the Grand Ole Opry.

The Louvins continued to chart hits through 1962, though their popularity had slipped prior to the start of the new decade. In 1963, they decided to split and pursue solo careers. Ira was killed in an auto accident in 1965; Charlie continues to perform as a member of the Grand Ole Opry.

During the 1950s, the term "country music" encompassed a wide variety of styles. There were the pop leanings of Eddy Arnold, Chet Atkins, Slim Whitman, Ferlin Husky, Sonny James, and Jim Reeves; the traditional sounds of the Louvin Brothers, Kitty Wells, and Roy Acuff; and the honky-tonk of Ray Price, Lefty Frizzell, Webb Pierce, and Hank Snow. Despite the diversity, it was the sounds of honky-tonk and country-pop that proved to be more commercially durable than traditional rural styles.

Webb Pierce was among the group of country stars creating hard-edged honky-tonk music when other country performers were drifting toward pop and rock 'n' roll.

Crossroads: The 1960s and 1970s

Like a pair of faithful blue jeans, the Nashville Sound started to come apart at its Southern seams in the 1960s. Older generations of country stars had aged during the 1950s, and their star power diminished. Some of the performers who had been established in the 1950s seemed conservative and prone to a country-pop sound that became bland with repetition. Also, Nashville could no longer afford to distance itself from other musical influences, particularly rock 'n' roll.

The seeds of change were sown during World War II, when many country listeners moved to such northern industrial centers as Chicago, Detroit, and Cleveland in search of jobs in the burgeoning wartime economy. They didn't move back.

No one pinpointed the essence of the migration better than Johnny Cash. When his majestic career was featured in a Country Music Hall of Fame exhibit that opened in 1988, Cash was quoted as saying, "The cities were looking for something and I think they found it in country music. It's realism and truth—something some music doesn't have."

But the grind of city living gnawed away at "realism and truth." Country songwriters began to deal with the wicked allure of the city, which gave birth to raunchy honky-tonk and rockabilly.

Patsy Cline conveyed the essence of country music—its sincerity and heartfelt emotion—to a mainstream audience through her warm, rich voice.

By the late 1950s, the children of Northern transplants were growing up on rock 'n' roll, while the country music capitol was still captivated by the mellow stylings of the Nashville Sound. Though some country-pop performers were prone to homogenization and blandness, others were true artists whose careers and styles remain lasting influences on subsequent generations. Patsy Cline remains an everlasting echo of the best qualities of the Nashville Sound.

Cline was born Virginia Patterson Hensley on September 8, 1932, in Gore, Virginia, though she was raised in nearby Winchester. At 16, she was noticed by a member of a Grand Ole Opry touring troupe who had stopped in Winchester. Cline auditioned and won a guest spot on the local billing. Encouraged by this attention, she made a trip to Nashville, though she returned to Winchester when time and money ran out.

In the early 1950s, a bandleader suggested she come up with a first name that sounded "country," so she amended her middle name to Patsy. "Cline" was the result of her marriage to Gerald Cline, whom she had wed in 1952. As Patsy Cline, she was signed by Four Star Records in 1954. A distribution deal with Decca led to her first recordings with arranger and producer Owen Bradley, who had also worked with Kitty Wells.

Cline's first career break came in January 1957, when she was a winner on *Arthur Godfrey's Talent Scouts*, singing "Walkin' After Midnight" and Hank Williams's "Your Cheatin' Heart." Decca Records subsequently released "Walkin' After Midnight" as a single; it became a hit on the country charts and reached number 12 on the pop charts. Ironically, Cline had not wanted to record "Walkin' After Midnight," feeling it was not country enough. The year 1957 was filled with career breaks and new starts for Cline. That year, she divorced Gerald Cline and married Charlie Dick.

Since Cline's death in 1963, her music has grown in popularity making her one of the best-selling artists in the history of MCA Records.

Patsy Cline and a very young Jimmy Dean pose with an industry executive. Though Cline successfully crossed over to the pop charts, she had reservations about removing too much "country" from her style.

Because of Cline's country conviction, she found it difficult to follow up the immediate crossover success of "Walkin' After Midnight." Decca forced the pop issue, eliminating fiddles and steel guitar in favor of polish and backing vocals. But, Patsy did not return to the pop charts until 1961 when "I Fall to Pieces" and Willie Nelson's torch ballad "Crazy" were released.

By this time, Cline's voice had developed a stunning sophistication that mixed with the understated commercial charm of Patti Page. Cline enjoyed several country hits in 1962, including Harlan Howard's "When I Get Thru With You (You'll Love Me Too)," and "She's Got You," whose dramatic narrative texture created another pop breakthrough.

On March 5, 1963, one month to the day after she recorded "Sweet Dreams (Of You)," Cline was killed in a plane crash. She had performed at a benefit in Kansas City, Kansas, two nights before. Along with fellow country stars Lloyd "Cowboy" Copas and Hawkshaw Hawkins, Cline was flying back to Nashville in

a private plane piloted by her manager. After a refueling stop in Dyersberg, Tennessee, the plane encountered bad weather and crashed, killing all aboard.

When Cline died, she and Kitty Wells were the top women stars in country music. Loretta Lynn's career was just beginning. Tammy Wynette and Dolly Parton were waiting in the wings.

By the early 1960s, the Nashville Sound lost its specificity, and the phrase was soon applied to any commercial style coming out of the country music capitol. Other musical influences, including urban folk music as well as rock 'n' roll, began to affect the styles and sounds of country-western and to attract the attention of new audiences in nontraditional venues. In 1962, Patsy Cline became the first country star to appear in Las Vegas, in a two-week booking at the Mint Lounge. Marty Robbins followed her to the gambling city in 1963.

Marty Robbins paid little attention to musical formulas or boundaries. His clear, romantic, mellifluous voice proved flexible enough to encompass everything from traditional cowboy ballads ("El Paso") to rockabilly ("That's All Right Mama") to middle-of-the-road balladry ("My Woman, My Woman, My Wife"), and his wide range helped him enjoy one of country music's longest-spanning careers.

The western lore that was part of Robbins's image came naturally to the native of Glendale, Arizona. His father played harmonica, and his grandfather was a storyteller and a traveling barker with a medicine show who collected and

Marty Robbins excelled at singing a variety of country styles, ranging from cowboy ballads to Hawaiian love songs to rockabilly.

Marty Robbins toyed with an acting career, among other pursuits. He appeared in the westerns The Gun and the Gavel *and* Buffalo Gun.

performed old cowboy songs. Like many youngsters his age, the young Robbins became enthralled with Gene Autry and other cowboy movie stars. He later told stories of picking cotton all day to make enough money to pay to see an Autry movie on the weekend.

At age 19, he joined the Navy, where he learned guitar and began to appreciate the country music performed by sailors from the South. When he returned home, he performed in Phoenix nightclubs, changing his name to hide his musical activity from his mother. Soon he began hosting a radio show. One of his guests, Opry star Little Jimmie Dickens, praised his voice and recommended him to Columbia Records in Nashville.

Robbins's first Columbia single, "I'll Go On Alone," spent two weeks at number one in early 1953. He joined the Opry cast a few months later, but he didn't achieve a second number-one record for four years, when a change in direction led to the rock-influenced hit, "Singin' the Blues."

Marty Robbins joined the Grand Ole Opry in 1953. A fan favorite, he was often the last performer on the program so that he could keep singing for the audience after the radio broadcast ended.

Robbins spent the end of the 1950s directing songs toward the burgeoning teen market. Then in 1959, a shift in style led to another enormous hit, the great Spanish-influenced story ballad, "El Paso." He went on to star in 15 low-budget films, including the classic *Ballad of a Gunfighter* in 1963.

Robbins maintained a high profile on the charts in his second and third decades as a performer, achieving 17 top-ten hits in the 1960s and 15 more in the 1970s. He also led a colorful, adventurous private life: An interest in stock car racing resulted in his earning a berth in the competitive NASCAR circuit until a series of serious accidents convinced him to give up participation in the sport. He suffered a heart attack in the early 1970s and became the fifteenth person to undergo a bypass operation. Robbins was inducted into the Country Music Hall of Fame in October 1982. Two months later, on December 8, he died of a heart attack.

Other venues opened up to country performers during the 1960s, including national television, adding to the commercial viability of country music. Affable

Jimmy Dean proved a country performer could host a successful prime-time variety show when he was given his own series in 1963. By showcasing pop stars as well as country acts, Dean attracted a broad enough audience to stay on the air until 1966. Based on the popularity of Dean's show, Roger Miller was asked to host a variety series in 1966. *The Johnny Cash Show* followed, airing from 1969 to 1971, as did *The Glen Campbell Goodtime Hour,* running from 1969 to 1972; at the same time, Buck Owens and Roy Clark headed the ensemble cast of *Hee Haw,* which was a country version of the irreverent *Rowan and Martin's Laugh-In. Hee Haw* lasted just two seasons on a major network, but it enjoyed a wildly successful rebirth after segueing into syndication in 1971. Although the show trafficked in hillbilly stereotypes and cornball humor, it nevertheless brought country music to a mass audience.

Buck Owens guest-starred on The Jimmy Dean Show *in the mid-1960s. Dean's TV variety series featured both mainstream pop entertainers and top-rated country acts in order to appeal to the broadest audience possible.*

Though best known to the general public as the cohost of *Hee Haw,* Buck Owens made considerable contributions to country music. He helped introduce arresting percussion to a once-stoic country music form. Owens's elevation of the drum into a position of prominence alongside the steel guitar helped establish open space for the 1980s country rock movement spearheaded by Dwight Yoakam.

Alvis Edgar Owens was born August 12, 1929, in Sherman, Texas. His father, a sharecropper, moved the family to Mesa, Arizona, when Owens was eight years old. Owens remained in Arizona until he was 22, when he went to Bakersfield, California, and joined his first band.

Owens played electric guitar as part of the Bill Woods Band's rhythm-soaked shows between 1951 and 1958 at the Blackboard Lounge in Bakersfield. Many times the band performed as long as 11 consecutive hours. His entertaining was done at

Roy Clark (right) cohosted the long-running syndicated TV variety series Hee Haw. *The program made Clark a favorite with rural audiences, but it obscured his virtuosity as a musician.*

clubs and VFW halls where people wanted a rhythm they could dance to. This compelled Owens to make use of drums.

Bakersfield became the perfect environment for experimentalists such as Owens and Merle Haggard. Their invigorating and jazzy strain of country music became more expressive and less repressed than if they had been playing in Nashville. And Owens's syrupy tenor sounded more distinguished in Bakersfield than it would have in a more polished Nashville.

Owens formed the Buckaroos in 1960, and the following year, the band raced up the charts with one of their first big hits, "Act Naturally." The drumbeat caught the ear of Ringo Starr, and the Beatles covered the tune a short time later. In 1965, Owens and the Buckaroos released their best-known hit, "I've Got a Tiger

By the Tail." With the beat and drive of rockabilly and the hard edge of honky-tonk, Buck Owens and the Buckaroos hammered their way through 19 number-one songs to become a truly dominant presence in the mid-to-late 1960s. Owens's later stint on the cornball *Hee Haw* often overshadows his earlier musical accomplishments.

The success of country music on the small screen gave sudden credence to a new style of performer—crossover country artists such as Glen Campbell and Kenny Rogers, who used country music sentiments and conventions as a springboard for a more accessible, countrypolitan sound. Campbell and Rogers had both dabbled in rock 'n' roll: Campbell played backup for the Beach Boys during a summer tour while Rogers was the lead singer for the rock group the First Edition. Their brand of country music did not reflect the harsh rural flavorings of traditional sounds and was more acceptable to the mainstream audiences of the late 1960s and 1970s.

Other country performers perfected styles and sounds that would also prove highly commercial, including country crooner Conway Twitty. While Campbell

Buck Owens shared cohosting duties with Roy Clark on Hee Haw. *The series kept Owens in the public eye, but his many successful business ventures made him a wealthy man.*

and Rogers carried a crossover appeal with their rock-tinged country-pop, Twitty remained strictly country. Ironically, Twitty had begun his career performing rock 'n' roll after hearing Elvis Presley's version of "Mystery Train" in 1955.

Twitty was born Harold Jenkins on September 1, 1933, in Friars Point, Mississippi, a few chords away from the Delta region that shaped the country-blues of Robert Johnson. As a youngster Twitty was exposed to the primitive guitars and

As a young performer, Conway Twitty was strongly influenced by Elvis Presley's rockabilly hits from Sun Records. Twitty's experiences at Sun, however, proved less than successful.

raw harmonica of the rural blues movement. Twitty always maintained that the blues made more of a difference in his development than listening to the *Grand Ole Opry* on the radio.

Twitty was four years old when he began playing guitar, picking up songs from his father, who was a ferryboat pilot on the Mississippi River. When he was ten, Twitty's family moved to Helena, Arkansas, where another blues connection

was made. Twitty formed the Phillips County Ramblers, a country-blues band that landed a weekly gig on KFFA, the same radio station that broadcast "King Biscuit Time" with blues legend Sonny Boy Williamson.

Twitty also excelled in sports, especially baseball. After being discharged from the Army in 1957, the center fielder was offered a contract with the Philadelphia Phillies. Twitty turned down the offer to follow the Sun—particularly the rockabilly sound that was coming out of Sun Studios in Memphis. Sun owner Sam Phillips worked with Twitty in the studio, but Phillips was unhappy with the results. Nothing was released.

Twitty rebounded by finding a manager that encouraged him to continue to play rock 'n' roll. The manager also suggested a snazzier stage name than Harold Jenkins, so the young singer turned to a map. He found Conway, Arkansas, and Twitty, Texas.

In 1958 Twitty scored his biggest hit, "It's Only Make Believe," a dramatic ballad that echoed with the sexuality of Elvis Presley. The song soared to number one on the pop charts. He continued to sing penitent pop ballads until 1968, when he crossed over to country. Twitty's early 1970s success in dueting with Loretta Lynn gave him exposure to a wide country audience.

Duets have always been a staple of country music. One of the most potent vocal combinations to ever share a microphone was Loretta Lynn and Conway Twitty.

Though Conway Twitty was a versatile performer, his romantic ballads made him a country music superstar.

Twitty's specialty was singing country ballads with blatantly sexual lyrics to female audiences. His fans were intensely loyal, and while some of his songs sparked controversy, his gentlemanly demeanor offset the overt lyrics. More versatile than his crooner image might suggest, Twitty mastered almost every type of country song over the course of his career. By his death in 1993, he had racked up 63 top-ten hits on the *Billboard* country charts, including a string of 20 number-one country songs in the 1970s.

The great commercial expansion in the 1960s and 1970s lured performers who tore away at the white male unanimity of country music. Talented female singer/songwriters, including Loretta Lynn, Tammy Wynette, Dolly Parton, and Barbara Mandrell, had opened doors for other women, while ethnic performers such as Doug Kershaw, Freddy Fender, and Johnny Rodriguez enjoyed success and popularity. The performer who did the most to open the minds and hearts of country artists was Charley Pride.

Pride was a baseball player before he was a country singer. In the mid-1950s, the twilight years of baseball's Negro Leagues, Pride was a member of the Memphis Red Sox. After a two-year stint in the service, Pride joined a semi-pro team in Helena, Montana, in the summer of 1960. One night he sang between the games of a doubleheader. The response to his efforts was so strong that Pride got a part-time engagement at a local country club.

Pride went on to become the first successful black singer in country music history, just as his hero Jackie Robinson was the first successful black player in major league baseball history.

Born on March 18, 1938, in Sledge, Mississippi, Pride was the only one of ten brothers and sisters who was interested in music. He started listening to Hank Williams records, and by the time Pride was 14 he had saved up enough money from working in the cotton fields to buy his first guitar, a Sears Silvertone.

For all his rugged rural roots, Pride's baritone has always been slick, due in great part to the smooth technique of Nashville producer Jack Clement. Clement's understated approach shaped Pride's biggest hits—"All I Have to Offer Is Me," "Just Between You and Me," "Snakes Crawl at Night," "Kiss an Angel Good Morning," and "Is Anybody Goin' to San Antone?"

Pride settled in Dallas, Texas, where he returned to his original inspirations—sports and Hank Williams. Two of his 1980s recordings were a cover of Williams's

Charley Pride grew up listening to Hank Williams, who became a major influence on Pride's style. In 1980, Pride payed homage to his musical hero with "There's a Little Bit of Hank in Me."

The Academy of Country Music honored Charley Pride with its Pioneer Award in 1994 in recognition of his career achievements and his influence on other performers.

Singers such as Waylon Jennings, whose hard-edged musical style had been influenced by rock 'n' roll, instigated the "outlaw movement" during the 1970s.

Bob Dylan's flirtation with country music during the early 1970s established a fertile ground for country-rock bands to flourish.

Williams's "Honky-Tonk Blues" and a rollicking tribute to the local football team, "Dallas Cowboys." In recognition of his career significance, the Academy of Country Music honored Pride with its Pioneer Award in 1994.

A direct response to the slick sounds emanating from Nashville during the 1960s as well as television's easygoing interpretation of country was the outlaw movement, which began in 1973 when Waylon Jennings recorded *Honky-Tonk Heroes*, an album of stark, uncompromising songs by Texas songwriter Billy Joe Shaver. Then in 1976, Willie Nelson hit the outlaw trail with a take-no-prisoners

cover of Lefty Frizzell's "If You've Got the Money, I've Got the Time" at the Country Music Association awards show. Country's collective jaw dropped.

The mixture of outlaw, countrypolitan, and crossover artists overshadowed the once-glittering legends of Patsy Cline, George Jones, Chet Atkins, and Merle Haggard, all of whom had been at their commercial peak in the early 1960s.

By the end of the 1970s and through the 1980s the old-liners had fallen out of fashion, but they each had at least one identifiable descendant. Dire Straits's Mark Knopfler's understated guitar licks reflected the gentle tones of Atkins. Singer k.d. lang mimicked the drama of Cline's vocals. Randy Travis sang in Haggard's forever forgiving echo. And, Jones's tense, authoritative vocals influenced everyone from Elvis Costello to Bob Dylan.

Dylan had sparked an entire subcategory of country rock with his 1966 double album *Blonde on Blonde* and 1969's *Nashville Skyline*, which featured Charlie Daniels as a sideman and Johnny Cash in a duet. Both albums were recorded in Nashville. On *Blonde on Blonde*, Dylan introduced rock guitar and dramatic keyboards to the Nashville studio scene while using such traditional sessions men as Charlie McCoy and Hargus Robbins.

Dylan's foray into Nashville helped take the twang out of country and established a fertile landscape for country-rock bands such as the Flying Burrito Brothers, who debuted in 1969 with bassist Chris Hillman and vocalist Gram Parsons, formerly of the Southern California folk-rock group the Byrds. Others followed, including the radio-ready Eagles (who featured ex-Burrito Brother Bernie Leadon) and in the late 1980s, the Desert Rose Band, anchored again by Hillman.

The Eagles enjoyed perhaps the greatest success of any group at straddling the boundaries of country and rock. Joe Walsh (left), Don Henley (center), and Glenn Frey were three of the band's most prominent members.

The stage was set for country music's biggest commercial explosion since the Nashville Sound—an accessible style created by a new breed of stars who not only incorporated rock 'n' roll musical influences, but also used rock 'n' roll themes, theatrics, and arenas to reach more people. Country music had always celebrated the past. As the 1980s began, it was finally ready to confront the future.

New Breed: 1980s and 1990s

Country music witnessed more dramatic change between 1980 and 1990 than in any previous decade. The 1980s were ushered in with the calculated glitter of the Urban Cowboy movement. The 1990s began more honestly, with the sincere promise of a new breed led by Garth Brooks, Mary Chapin Carpenter, Clint Black, and Reba McEntire.

Country music has always prospered in times of economic recession, and America's fortunes were on the downslide in both 1980 and 1990. Yet the catalysts that sparked the changes in country music for each of these decades were decidedly different. The 1980 film *Urban Cowboy* was a Hollywood concoction that existed almost independently of country music, while the roots of the new country styles spawned in the 1990s were firmly planted in country tradition.

The Urban Cowboy fad died out because the songs that resulted from it were too calculated, lacking a lasting appeal. Still, Nashville took its cue from Hollywood, at least for a while, and produced overly accessible records with an emphasis on string sections and saccharine pop rhythms. It was in such an arena that Crystal Gayle, Kenny Rogers, Olivia Newton-John, and other slick country-pop artists flourished in the early 1980s.

Crystal Gayle's country-pop stylings were well suited to the slick, polished sounds flowing from Nashville in the early 1980s.

Musical conformity continued to define Nashville in the middle of the decade. Barbara Mandrell popularized country pop in Las Vegas, while Lee Greenwood—a former Vegas blackjack dealer—brought Las Vegas to country. Country music hardly seemed "country" at all, and the music lacked the passion that had characterized it in earlier years.

But something interesting was bubbling beneath the glitzy surface: a "cow-punk" movement that opened the doors for younger acts that played country

Disgusted with Nashville's slick conformity during the 1980s, "cowpunker" Dwight Yoakam moved to the West Coast to make his music. His success helped steer country music away from the polished country pop that dominated that era.

music in a rock 'n' roll landscape. Those musicians included Jason and the Nashville Scorchers, Steve Earle, Dwight Yoakam, and Marty Stuart.

Sparked by the cowpunkers in the late 1980s, Nashville record companies shifted progressive artists from country to pop divisions. That left fertile space for such acts as Garth Brooks, Clint Black, Alan Jackson, Vince Gill, Trisha Year-wood, Pam Tillis, and Kathy Mattea. These performers represent a new breed who were raised on a variety of musical influences—but who chose country.

The other significant reason for the rise of the new country artists is that they proved to be highly marketable—they excited listeners and sold a lot of records. Even better, they led cosmopolitan yet squeaky-clean lives. Clint Black does not allow his entourage to drink before shows; Garth Brooks studied advertising in college; K.T. Oslin learned the showbiz ropes while a singer on Broadway. Country music has changed—just ask rowdy redneck Hank Williams, Jr.,

Kathy Mattea represents one of the new breed of country performers who have been influenced by other styles, such as folk music, but channel those influences into a recognizable country style.

who was CMA Entertainer of the Year in 1987 and 1988, but who was not even nominated in 1991.

Thanks largely to this new direction, country music weathered the difficult recession of the early 1990s better than any other form of popular music. Mass-audience awareness of country music remained high, yet seemed to run deeper than in the early 1980s.

It is clear that the country shuffle of the 1990s has considerably more substance than it did during much of the 1980s. Country's new breed seems intent upon shaping the future of the music while maintaining the integrity of its past. By any measure, it will be a pleasurable and fascinating evolution.

Alan Jackson exploded onto the country music scene during the early 1990s with his traditional-based country sound and state-of-the-art stage show.

· ALABAMA ·

P erhaps it's the captivating nonconformist outlaw image, but throughout the history of country
music, rugged solo artists have overshadowed
most duets and groups. At least that was the case
until Alabama burst on the scene and forever

*Alabama, the ACM's Artist of the Decade (1980s), has
won more awards than any other country group.*

changed the way that country music bands would be
viewed.

The band has been honored many times by the Country Music Association (CMA) and the Academy of Country Music (ACM). The CMA presented them with the prestigious Entertainer of the Year award in 1982, 1983, and 1984, while the ACM named them Entertainer of the Year from 1982 through 1986. Alabama has won a couple of Grammy Awards and from 1980 to 1987 notched 21 consecutive number-one singles.

Alabama came together in Fort Payne, Alabama, a valley village of about 12,000 people at the foot of the Lookout Mountains. Socks, not music, had been Fort Payne's best-known product until Alabama rose to fame. Lead singer Randy Owen, keyboardist and lead guitarist Jeff Cook, and bass guitarist Teddy Gentry are cousins, but they didn't start playing together until 1969. Their first band was the ZZ Top-inspired Wild Country. Another cousin, Jackie Owen, was the group's first drummer. In 1973, he was replaced by Mark Herndon, a nonrelative. Alabama's earliest shows were at Canyonland amusement park outside of Fort Payne.

In March 1973, Alabama left Fort Payne for Myrtle Beach, South Carolina. Thanks in part to the rapid turnover rate of the resort crowds, Alabama was able to perform an eclectic repertoire, including covers of rock hits by Bachman Turner Overdrive and Van Morri-

son, as well as rocking versions of country hits by George Jones and Merle Haggard.

By 1980, the group was leaning more heavily on original material and had established its trademark polished harmonies. Randy Owens's lead vocals, reminiscent of Glenn Frey of the Eagles, caught the ear of several record companies. Eventually, Alabama signed with RCA Records, and in 1980 their first album, *My Home's in Alabama*, was released to great popular success.

Alabama sold 45 million records in the 1980s, partly because of the band's youth appeal. By the time the 1990s rolled in, the group sounded more like a pop-rock band than a country band, especially in the acoustics of the big arenas in which they played. No longer as novel as they once were, Alabama has seen some of its rock-oriented appeal diminished by the advent of solo acts like Garth Brooks and Clint Black, who utilized rock 'n' roll-style lighting, staging, and songs to cross over from country in search of a wider audience.

Alabama continues to attract fans who enjoy their close harmonies and relate to their songs about the pains and joys of working-class life. As a country group that has been enormously successful, Alabama has set a standard for other groups—from Shenandoah to Confederate Railroad—to follow.

ALABAMA

REAL NAMES: Randy Yeueil Owen, Jeff Alan Cook, Teddy Wayne Gentry, Mark Joel Herndon

FIRST HIT: "My Home's in Alabama" (1980)

OTHER NOTABLE HITS: "I'm in a Hurry (And Don't Know Why)" (1992); "Pass It on Down" (1991); "Southern Star" (1989); "The Closer You Get" (1983); "Mountain Music" (1981); "Tennessee River" (1980)

BEST ALBUMS: *Southern Star* (1989); *Roll On* (1984); *The Closer You Get* (1983); *Mountain Music* (1982); *Feels So Right* (1981); *My Home's in Alabama* (1980)

AWARDS INCLUDE: Grammy, Best Country Performance by a Duo or Group with Vocal (1983, 1982); Academy of Country Music (ACM) Artist of the Decade (1989); ACM Vocal Group of the Year (1986, 1985, 1984, 1983, 1982, 1981); ACM Entertainer of the Year (1986, 1985, 1984, 1983, 1982); ACM Album of the Year (1985, 1984, 1982); Country Music Association (CMA) Entertainer of the Year (1984, 1983, 1982); CMA Vocal Group of the Year (1983, 1982, 1981); CMA Album of the Year (1983)

ACHIEVEMENTS: 21 consecutive number-one singles, 1980-1987; 37 number-one singles

PERSONAL: Alabama hosts an annual "June Jam" in their hometown of Fort Payne, Alabama, which draws top-name performers and raises money for various local charities.

· CLINT · BLACK ·

Exploding onto the country scene in 1989 with his first album, *Killin' Time*, Clint Black has dazzled hard-to-please music critics and hard-core country fans alike with his rich, expressive vocals and a songwriting ability that rings with

Clint Black became an instant success in 1989 with his debut album, Killin' Time.

a wisdom beyond his years. Black wrote or cowrote all of the songs on this finely crafted debut album.

The fourth son of a musical family, Black remembers becoming fascinated with the harmonica and swiping one from an older brother. By age 15, he was proficient enough on the guitar and bass to join his brothers' band, which was playing in clubs around Houston. Black was encouraged by his close-knit family to embark on a musical career by performing at all-night backyard barbecues around the neighborhood.

"When my brothers took a break, I'd sit on a stool in the middle of the yard and keep going," Black reminisced. "I'd do the same thing at Bear Creek Park west of Houston, where I'd go from picnic table to table, just to sing to anybody who'd listen."

Black was soon fully committed to a country music career. Playing solo engagements in and around Houston, he slowly built up a following. At one gig, the singer met Hayden Nicholas, another young and aspiring songwriter/musician. The two Texans forged a songwriting partnership that is highly regarded in Nashville today.

Though born in New Jersey, Clint Black grew up in Texas. He began performing his honky-tonk music around Houston.

Recording their own songs on an eight-track machine in Nicholas's garage, the pair put together enough material to catch the eye of Bill Hamm, the legendary and powerful manager of the rock group ZZ Top. Sensing Black's potential to become a country superstar, Hamm arranged a meeting and audition with RCA Records executive Joe Galante. A deal was soon inked.

Under the guidance of producers Mark Wright and James Stroud, Black recorded *Killin' Time*, a startling debut album that went platinum in eight months and yielded five number-one country singles, including the Black/Nicholas title tune and "A Better Man." Clearly influenced by Merle Haggard, Black showed he had a good feel for classic country sounds with his authentic honky-tonk style. Black's clear, expressive voice,

Black appeared on the Roy Rogers Tribute album, showing his respect for country tradition.

Black received ACM honors for Best New Male Artist and Male Vocalist of the Year in 1989, the first time both awards had been given to the same performer.

dimpled good looks, and natural charm proved a winning combination as he vaulted to prominence in 1989.

The young singer's style was more traditional than that of Garth Brooks, whose career skyrocketed shortly after Black's. Brooks's crossover appeal and his tendency to grab the media spotlight at times overshadowed Black's more conservative audiences and low-key manner. Yet Black's success has been no less significant than his crossover counterpart's in terms of the revitalization of country music in the 1990s.

Black was unruffled by the enormity and speed of his success, perhaps because he was prepared for it. From the time of his debut single, he willingly met with radio-station representatives and pressed flesh with record retailers—whatever it took to ensure that he would not be just another one-album wonder. A careful career planner, Black proved he was serious about his music, considering his songwriting and performing to be his profession. "I don't look on this as a party," he has told entertainment reporters.

The singer was summoned to the podium at virtually every awards presentation after the success of *Killin' Time*. He was named Best Male Vocalist by the Country Music Association, the Academy of Country Music, and the Music City News Country Awards on the strength of his initial effort.

Not one to succumb to sophomore jitters, Black followed up *Killin' Time* with *Put Yourself in My Shoes*, which featured more of Black's Texas honky-tonk. Traditional country themes, such as the highs and lows of contemporary romance and the ongoing struggle of the working man, were explored through Black and Nicholas's compositions.

Capitalizing on his newfound clout in the music industry, Black decided to record a tune with the legendary King of the Cowboys, Roy Rogers.

Rogers had been a longtime idol of Black's since childhood. The pair teamed up to make a charming video to accompany their "Hold on Partner" duet, which they performed at the 1991 CMA Awards.

As the singer/songwriter's fame continued to soar, his personal and professional life grew more complicated. Considered one of country's most dashing and eligible bachelors, Black was linked with such glamorous women as *Entertainment Tonight*'s Leeza Gibbons and pop music singer Paula Abdul. He broke more than a few hearts when he announced his surprise engagement to actress Lisa Hartman. In October 1991

Lisa Hartman Black

On October 20, 1991, Clint Black and former *Knots Landing* star Lisa Hartman exchanged wedding vows in a family-only service held on Black's 180-acre farm outside Houston. The two met backstage at a New Year's Eve concert Black was headlining in Houston (hometown to both Black and Hartman). From that encounter came a dinner in Los Angeles, an on-location visit in Toronto while Hartman was filming a TV movie, and a romantic vacation in Hawaii. Though Black was madly in love, his marriage proposal on a casual walk in Utah took even him by surprise. "I don't know if it was the environment or what," he said. "It seemed like the first time that we really had to stop the world from spinning and look around at the mountains and just talk. We had talked about what we both wanted for ourselves, and I just popped the question. I told her we were both nuts!" The couple works hard to balance their careers and spend as much time together as possible. Hartman often accompanies Black when he tours, and both consider time spent together relaxing in their four-bedroom house in L.A.'s Laurel Canyon precious. Says Black, "Married life is the best life I know."

The pairing of Black and Wynonna Judd resulted in the 1993 "Black & Wy" tour and a hit duet.

the couple wed in a simple, private ceremony on Black's farm outside Houston.

Shortly after the wedding and on the premiere of *The Hard Way*, rumors circulated that the relationship between the singer and his manager, Bill Hamm, had gone sour. Black subsequently fired Hamm, then issued a sharply worded press release accusing his former manager of a variety of business misdeeds. The two became embroiled in a bitter lawsuit.

Black released *The Hard Way* in 1992 after a self-imposed ten-month hiatus from music making. He had taken nearly a year off from recording in order to write songs and make the album the way he wanted to, resulting in his most critically acclaimed work yet. On this album, Black's songs delved more deeply into love's mysteries and took an unflinching look at the pitfalls. Several singles, including "We Tell Ourselves" and "When My Ship Comes In," found their way to the top of the country charts.

Black titled his fourth album *No Time to Kill*, doubtless a play on the name of his career-making debut disc. Between the time he signed his record deal and the release of his first album, *Killin' Time*, Black had been in a holding pattern, trying to put an album together. He truly had a lot of time on his hands. By 1993, the opposite was true. Enjoying a high point in his career, Black had little time to waste. Aside from a collection of vivid, keenly penned tunes from Black and Nicholas, *No Time to Kill* features a collaboration between Clint and Jimmy Buffet called "Happiness Alone." A major single from the album, "A Bad Goodbye," was originally written by Black as a solo, but teaming up with Wynonna Judd on the highly touted "Black & Wy" tour resulted in the two singing it as a high-powered duet.

When Black burst onto the country scene in 1989, he was considered one of the "hat acts"—those performers whose music and image echoed the traditions of country-western music. Black usually wore a starched shirt and a black cowboy hat both on and off the stage, reflecting his country roots. Recently, he has been photographed wearing different styles of dress, and he sports his black hat on stage only. The press and some fans have speculated that he may be moving away from his country image. But, Clint Black's continued explorations into the themes and sounds of traditional country music disprove these misgivings. As Black proudly proclaims, "If people are wondering where I'm going—listen to my music. It's what it's all about. I use fiddles and guitars. I don't have any synthesizers. I'm intent on staying with country music. It's what's drawn me all my life."

CLINT BLACK

REAL NAME: Clint Patrick Black

BORN: February 4, 1962, in Long Branch, New Jersey

FIRST HIT: "A Better Man" (1989)

OTHER NOTABLE HITS: "State of Mind" (1993); "A Bad Goodbye" (with Wynonna, 1993); "We Tell Ourselves" (1992); "Loving Blind" (1991); "Where Are You Now" (1991); "Put Yourself in My Shoes" (1990); "Nobody's Home" (1989); "Killin' Time" (1989)

BEST ALBUMS: *No Time to Kill* (1993); *The Hard Way* (1992); *Put Yourself in My Shoes* (1990); *Killin' Time* (1989)

AWARDS INCLUDE: Country Music Association (CMA) Vocal Event of the Year (with George Jones, et al., 1993); CMA Male Vocalist of the Year (1990); CMA Horizon Award (1989); Academy of Country Music (ACM) Top New Male Vocalist (1989); ACM Top Male Vocalist (1989); Single of the Year (1989); ACM Album of the Year (1989)

ACHIEVEMENTS: Grand Ole Opry member (1991)

PERSONAL: Black is married to actress Lisa Hartman.

· SUZY · BOGGUSS ·

With her charming smile and winsome ways, Suzy Bogguss comes across as the girl next door. She's devoid of the psychological problems that hobble some performers, and she takes all the commotion and pandemonium that surrounds a successful career in stride. Bogguss jokingly refers to it as the Mary Tyler Moore syndrome. "I would hate for people to think that I was just so sweet," she muses. "I definitely have a wilder side to my personality."

Her all-American upbringing in the small town of Aledo, Illinois (population 3,000), suits her wholesome, engaging image. Bogguss, the youngest of four children, enjoyed a childhood of openness and trust. She was a lifeguard, a Girl Scout Cadet, and a homecoming queen.

Bogguss always exhibited a flair for performing, whether in church or high school productions. When she realized there was more to the world than

Award-winner Suzy Bogguss performs folk-influenced country that often reflects issues of modern women.

her hometown, Bogguss headed to Illinois State University, where her horizons expanded. Instead of performing in her previous venues, the young coed hit the local coffee-houses and nightclubs. She still has a tape of her first solo performance, though the memory of it makes her wince.

By the time she graduated with a degree in metalworking, Bogguss had become a one-woman show. She usually booked her own performances and then took off in her camper. While she often traveled with friends and accompanists, many times her "entourage" consisted entirely of her dog Duchess and her cat Chaucer. During a five-year span, she traveled and worked from Canada to Mexico.

In 1985 Bogguss headed for Music City, U.S.A., to try her luck. She made her way by performing in a restaurant and singing on songwriter demos. At the studio, she met her future husband, Doug Crider, a songwriter working as a recording engineer. Though it seemed like the two were too busy for much conversation, something obviously clicked because Crider kept hiring her to do demos of his songs, and she kept coming back to sing them. The couple married and continued collaborating on songs.

In 1986, Bogguss landed a recording contract with Capitol Records (now Liberty) after a talent scout heard her singing at Dollywood. Unfortunately, her first two albums were not soaring successes. Believing her recording contract could be in jeopardy, she served as coproducer of her third album, *Aces*. In selecting songs, she turned toward her folk-country roots and away from the contemporary Nashville tunes that dominated her previous efforts. The decision was based on Bogguss's own musical interests and strengths, having been influenced by such folk-flavored rock artists as Linda Ronstadt, Emmylou Harris, and James Taylor. The collection included Cheryl Wheeler's "Aces," Nancy Griffith's "Outward Bound," and the folk-rock classic "Someday Soon."

With her later albums, *Voices in the Wind* and *Something Up My Sleeve*, Bogguss continued in this direction. She coproduced these critically acclaimed works, and the song selection included such tunes as "Drive South" by country-rock songwriter John Hiatt for *Voices in the Wind* and "Hey Cinderella" by Bogguss, Matraca Berd, and Gary Harrison for *Something Up My Sleeve*.

Suzy Bogguss, along with Mary Chapin Carpenter, helped launch the wave of female country performers in the 1990s whose influences were more in line with Judy Collins and Linda Ronstadt than with Loretta Lynn or Patsy Cline. These young performers have updated the image of female country singers and injected more thought-provoking ideas into their lyrics. Suzy Bogguss's music offers a modern woman's perspective on the roles of men and women in relationships without resorting to outdated stereotypes.

SUZY BOGGUSS

REAL NAME: Susan Kay Bogguss

BORN: December 30, 1956, in Aledo, Illinois

MUSICAL INFLUENCES: Linda Ronstadt, James Taylor, Emmylou Harris

FIRST HIT: "Aces"

OTHER NOTABLE HITS: "Hey Cinderella" (1993); "Just Like the Weather" (1993); "Drive South" (1992); "Letting Go" (1992); "Outbound Plane" (1991); "Someday Soon" (1991); "Somewhere Between" (1987)

BEST ALBUMS: *Something Up My Sleeve* (1993); *Voices in the Wind* (1992); *Aces* (1991)

AWARDS INCLUDE: Country Music Association Horizon Award (1992); Academy of Country Music Top New Female Vocalist (1988)

PERSONAL: Bogguss has a degree in metalworking from Illinois State University and makes her own jewelry; she also designs her own line of leather clothing, The Suzy Bogguss Leather Collection.

·GARTH· ·BROOKS·

Garth Brooks, arguably the most explosive property in country music, is credited with boosting country-western to its highest level of popularity in decades. While such observations may be true, they only scratch the surface. In a couple of years, Brooks's career skyrocketed in a way never before seen in country music. His career-defining

Garth Brooks's top-selling albums, sell-out concerts, and numerous awards have made him a country music phenomenon.

album *Ropin' the Wind* debuted in the number-one position on *Billboard*'s pop chart, nudging out such heavyweight contenders as Metallica and Michael

Jackson. His albums have sold more than 35 million units as of 1994, leaving many established pop artists in his retail wake.

Brooks's universal popularity is reflected by the diverse audiences who attend his no-holds-barred live concerts, which blend rock 'n' roll theatrics with his country-flavored music. Men and women, fans of rock music and country-western, and a cross section of young adults from various economic levels make up the fans in Brooks's audiences. His concerts routinely sell out in minutes. Seats for his 1992 L.A. Forum show, for example, were filled in a scant 14 minutes.

Brooks made history when he walked away with six Academy of Country Music awards in April 1991. He also received trophies from every other awards organization that year, including the Country Music Association, the TNN Music City News Awards, the *Billboard* Music Awards, and the Grammy Awards.

Despite the attention, Brooks has maintained a humble, self-deprecating manner so seemingly genuine that few doubt its sincerity. At the "Night of 100 Stars" benefit in 1990, Brooks modestly observed, "It was more like 99 stars and me." In an industry where battle-hardened veterans are the norm, the

Brooks is the biggest crossover star in history, with both pop and country fans claiming him as their own.

chorus of praise for Brooks's generosity and earnestness seems unanimous.

Brooks has also gained notoriety for his outspoken support of civil rights, as well as other contemporary and often controversial issues. The video for his single "The Thunder Rolls," from the *No Fences* album, was the first to be banned by The Nashville Network and Country Music Television for what was deemed

Garth's live concerts do not disappoint. He has a professional stage show incorporating theatrical lighting effects and props.

unsuitable content; it is a disturbing look at domestic violence. His video for the song "We Shall Be Free," from *The Chase*, is a star-studded extravaganza that encourages Americans to abandon their prejudices and accept others. "We Shall Be Free" was named Video of the Year at the 1994 Academy of Country Music Awards.

The youngest of six children, Brooks was reared in a household short on material comforts but long on loving kindness. His father, Raymond, was an oil company engineer and his mother, Colleen, a country singer on the Capitol Records label. At one time she performed on television with Red Foley's *Ozark Jubilee*, but she quit to raise a growing family.

A high school athlete, Brooks headed to Oklahoma State University on a track scholarship, working on a marketing degree by day and playing music by night. A devoted fan of such rock artists as James Taylor, Journey, and Dan Fogelberg, he soon found himself developing an appreciation for such country stalwarts as George Strait and George Jones.

To support himself, the beefy Brooks took a job as a bouncer in a Stillwater nightclub. One evening he was told to break up a ruckus in the women's restroom. There he met future wife Sandy Mahl, who had put her fist through the wall in a dispute with another woman. Sandy turned out to be a fellow student, and the two embarked on a sometimes turbulent relationship that is regarded as one of the most devoted—and most publicized—in the music world.

Brooks, bolstered by his growing fame in and around his hometown, ventured to Nashville to try his luck at country music stardom. Convinced that Music City would be anxiously awaiting his arrival and that his name would be plastered on every water tower in town, Brooks soon came face to face with reality. After less than 24 hours in town, he was on his way back to Oklahoma with nothing to show for it. Humiliated and embarrassed, Brooks retreated to his parents' home, where he stayed for two weeks before showing up at his nighttime haunts.

A short time later, Brooks and Sandy, now his wife, returned to Nashville. This time, he was fueled by a fierce determination to make his mark on the country music scene. The couple worked at a local boot store to put food on the table while Garth played at various

"What's in a Name?"

Garth Brooks and wife Sandy (Mahl) became parents for the second time on May 3, 1994, the evening Brooks was named Entertainer of the Year at the 29th Academy of Country Music Awards. Given their parents' penchant for choosing unusual names, it is unlikely that the Brooks children will be confused with their classmates when they reach school age. The Brookes's first child, Taylor Mayne Pearl, was born on July 8, 1992. She is named after James Taylor, the state of Maine (where she was conceived), and Minnie Pearl. The Brookses named their second child, also a daughter, August Anna—after the month in which she was conceived and Garth's grandmother. Following the birth of his second daughter, Brooks announced he would devote most of his energies to his wife and children.

Although he toured in Asia and Europe, he did not tour extensively in the States. As loyal and hungry for his music as Brooks's fans are, his decision to lighten his schedule was a daring one.

writer's nights, hoping he would get noticed for his powerfully intimate vocal style and his insightful songs.

While playing at a showcase for ASCAP (American Society of Composers, Authors and Publishers), Brooks impressed a Capitol Records (now Liberty Records) executive, which led to a recording contract in 1989.

Brooks soon distinguished himself with such career-defining hit singles as "The Dance" and "Friends in Low Places," which helped propel him to a level of success unknown to any country artist. By creating music that related directly to the problems and passions of everyday people in an energetic, pop-flavored style, Brooks launched a career that leapfrogged to a bona fide phenomenon.

However, the superstar singer paid a price for his white-hot fame. In the early days of his success, Brooks and his wife quarreled over the singer's infidelity on the road, and Sandy eventually left him. A turning point in their marriage and Brooks's life, her departure caused him to mature into a solid family man. Brooks is quite open about the subject, and the well-publicized lows and highs of his marriage have helped construct his image as a sincere performer who prefers hearth and home to the bright city lights. After the birth of each of his daughters, in 1992

and 1994, Brooks lightened his schedule significantly to spend time with them at home.

Brooks has established a reputation as one of the most philanthropic stars in recent memory. He works with Feed the Children, an international nonprofit Christian organization that provides food, clothing, medicine, and other necessities to disaster victims. He persuaded Liberty Records to contribute one dollar for every copy of his Christmas album that sold. Putting his money where his mouth is, Brooks also personally donated one million dollars toward rebuilding South Central Los Angeles following the 1992 riots.

While pop music fans cross over to enjoy the music and on-stage antics of Garth Brooks, country fans still claim him as one of their own. Both audiences savor his emotional subject matter—whether it is a plea for universal tolerance or a lesson on the preciousness of love and life—as well as his easy-listening style that is a step removed from traditional country sounds. His occasional rocking, rollicking barroom songs, such as "Friends in Low Places," keep his repertoire from becoming too heavy.

As the popularity of country music indicates no sign of losing steam, the phenomenon of Garth Brooks continues to grow, intriguing and inspiring millions along the way.

GARTH BROOKS

REAL NAME: Troyal Garth Brooks

MUSICAL INFLUENCES: George Jones, George Strait, Merle Haggard, Billy Joel, Dan Fogelberg, James Taylor, KISS

BORN: February 7, 1962, in Tulsa, Oklahoma

FIRST HIT: "Much Too Young (To Feel This Damn Old)" (1989)

OTHER NOTABLE HITS: "Ain't Goin' Down (Til the Sun Comes Up)" (1993); "Learning to Live Again" (1993); "We Shall Be Free" (1992); "What's She Doing Now" (1992); "The Thunder Rolls" (1991); "Friends in Low Places" (1990); "The Dance" (1990); "If Tomorrow Never Comes" (1989)

BEST ALBUMS: *In Pieces* (1994); *The Chase* (1992); *Ropin' the Wind* (1991); *No Fences* (1990)

AWARDS INCLUDE: Grammy, Best Country Vocal Performance (1991); Academy of Country Music (ACM) Entertainer of the Year (1993, 1992, 1991, 1990); ACM Top Male Vocalist (1991, 1990); Country Music Association (CMA) Vocal Event of the Year (with George Jones, et al., 1993); CMA Entertainer of the Year (1992, 1991); CMA Horizon Award (1990)

ACHIEVEMENTS: Grand Ole Opry member (1990)

PERSONAL: Brooks and his wife Sandy (who writes under her maiden name, Mahl) have collaborated on "I've Got a Good Thing Going" and "That Summer"

BROOKS · & DUNN

Success stories in country music seem to be countless, but there are those acts that shine a bit brighter than most. Sheer talent is a must, but when the chemistry is right and an unexpected magic develops, a successful country act emerges. Such talent, chemistry, and magic joined forces in the award-winning duo of Brooks & Dunn.

Brooks & Dunn's crowd-pleasing single "Boot Scootin' Boogie" became a dance club sensation.

Kix Brooks and Ronnie Dunn grabbed hold of the chemistry, welcomed the magic, and soared straight to the top with their fire-and-brimstone hillbilly music and high-powered stage show.

Dunn drove their first three singles to number one on the country charts, snagged a gold album for their debut project *Brand New Man*, and landed the opening-act spot for Reba McEntire. Beginning with an Academy of Country Music award for Top Vocal Duet in 1991, the pair has chalked up a series of honors and awards over the last few years that has given them a high profile in the industry. After they released the dance-club classic "Boot Scootin' Boogie," the duo followed up with a second successful album, *Hard Workin' Man*. When Brooks & Dunn hit the touring circuit to showcase that album, they broke attendance records at fairs and music halls across the country.

Brooks & Dunn were named the ACM's Top Vocal Duet in 1991, 1992, and 1993.

Brooks, the "hat man" of the twosome, is known for charging on stage with scorching energy. Dunn strolls on with a more conservative demeanor—most often dressed down in basic black. Despite their differences, including the high tenor of Dunn vs. the gutsy baritone of Brooks, the two clicked from their first meeting and launched one of the most successful duo acts in country music history.

Within a year of forming the partnership, Brooks &

The pairing of Brooks and Dunn was a match made in Nashville heaven. The artists, hoping for solo deals, hadn't known each other for very long before becoming a duo act. It was through a songwriting collaboration that they developed a relationship. Arista Records' Nashville president, Tim DuBois, brought the pair together one day in 1990. Over enchiladas, DuBois asked Brooks and Dunn to begin writing together. They thought the record executive's plans were for them to write material to be recorded by Alan Jackson or some other artist. The two joined forces and came up with "My Next Broken Heart." The song was submitted, but after DuBois heard them singing together, he decided they should work as a duo. Brooks and Dunn were signed to Arista.

Leon Eric Brooks, who hails from Shreveport, Louisiana, picked up his first instrument, a ukulele, when he was only six. By the time he was 12, he was already playing with a band. In college, he began to focus seriously on his music, and he was soon playing every music hall he could get into. About this time, he penned his first song, a catchy little tune about a dog called "Tucker's Got the Mange!"

After several jobs in different cities, Brooks ended up in Nashville in 1981. The ambitious young entertainer's first break in the country music business came when he was introduced to producer Don Gant, who had recently started his own publishing company. From Gant, Brooks learned the craft of songwriting, Nashville style. This led to a cut on the Oak Ridge Boys' million-selling album, *Bobbie Sue*. The artist's progressive songwriting style was soon noticed, and he signed a recording contract with Capitol Records in the late 1980s.

A 1989 album did little for Brooks's career as a performer, but he continued to churn out songs for other artists. Brooks has penned several number-one hits for other performers, including John Conlee's "I'm Only in It for the Love," the Nitty Gritty Dirt Band's "Modern Day Romance," Highway 101's "Who's Lonely Now," and McBride & the Ride's "Sacred Ground." In addition to writing or cowriting many of the songs he records with Dunn, Brooks has written for Sawyer Brown, Ricky Van Shelton, and Holly Dunn.

Ronnie Dunn was born in Coleman, Texas, and his father was in the pipeline business, just like Brooks's father. After playing bass guitar in different bands and singing in gospel groups, Dunn discovered he couldn't focus on school and be in a band at the same time. While studying to become a minister, Dunn was caught playing in a local honky-tonk and dismissed.

Dunn moved with his parents to Tulsa, Oklahoma, where he became friends with people who worked in the music business. He was briefly signed with MCA/Churchill Records.

In 1989, close friend Jamie Oldacker entered Dunn's name in the annual Marlboro Talent Search. Though convinced he didn't stand a chance, Dunn sent the contest officials a tape. He managed to win the finals, and for his prize he was given the opportunity to participate in a recording session. Dunn's recorded vocals from this session led to his next career step, meeting Kix Brooks.

The commercially sizzling sounds of Brooks & Dunn have provided country music with a swagger and a beat reflected in the party-like atmosphere of their concerts. The duo offers a rugged fusion of hip country sounds and traditionalism designed to make their audiences get on their feet and scar up those hardwood dance floors.

BROOKS & DUNN

REAL NAMES: Leon Eric (Kix) Brooks; Ronnie Gene Dunn

BORN: May 12, 1955, in Shreveport, Louisiana (Brooks); June 1, 1953, in Coleman, Texas (Dunn)

MUSICAL INFLUENCES: Hank Williams, Johnny Horton (Brooks); his father, Jesse Eugene Dunn (Dunn)

FIRST HIT: "Brand New Man" (1991)

OTHER NOTABLE HITS: "Hard Workin' Man" (1993); "That Ain't No Way to Go" (1992); "Boot Scootin' Boogie" (1992); "Neon Moon" (1992); "My Next Broken Heart" (1991)

BEST ALBUMS: *Hard Workin' Man* (1992); *Brand New Man* (1991)

AWARDS INCLUDE: Academy of Country Music (ACM) Top Vocal Duet (1993, 1992, 1991); ACM Album of the Year (1992); ACM Single of the Year (1992); ACM Top New Vocal Group or Duet (1991); Country Music Association (CMA) Vocal Duo of the Year (1993, 1992)

◆ MARY CHAPIN CARPENTER ◆

Mary Chapin Carpenter was born in Princeton, New Jersey, the third of four daughters. Her father, Chapin, was an executive with *Life*; her mother, Bowie, worked at a private school. The family relocated in 1969 to Japan when Carpenter's father was named to head the magazine's Asian bureau. Her stay in the Far East as a youngster has had

Mary Chapin Carpenter's songs have a folk flavor that appeals to a wide audience.

a lasting effect: She once greeted a Japanese reporter in his own language at a press conference. Carpenter holds a degree in American civilization from Ivy League Brown University. Her eclectic and broad-based background is considered atypical for a country singer, a point that the press has magnified out of proportion. While the mainstream press likes to refer to her style as "intelligent country," Chapin rebuffs the insult to country music that that phrase implies and calls herself simply "a singer/songwriter."

Carpenter's songs have widened the spectrum of what is considered country music and expanded its audience. Influenced by folk and rock music, Carpenter is one of the new wave of female country performers who write and sing about modern women who are not defined by the actions of men. Her material ranges from reflections on a familiar object ("This Shirt") to the *joie de vivre* that music can inspire ("Down at the Twist and Shout") to broken-heartedness ("Never Had It So Good"). Her writing has also shown a vein of humor: "Girls with Guitars," which appears on Wynonna Judd's second album, *Tell Me Why*, tweaks the noses of those who think women can't be serious contenders in the music world. Carpenter's songs have also found a home on alternative or college radio stations.

Carpenter and the other new female artists have also changed the

Carpenter has been called ultra-serious because of the introspective lyrics of her songs.

With her top-selling albums and crossover appeal, Carpenter has helped change the perception of women in the country music industry.

Carpenter's successful albums are the result of a longtime partnership with producer John Jennings.

industry's perception of women in country music. It's been a long-time axiom of country music that while female singers may add to the performance bill, they're a liability because their record sales are lower. Women are the majority of record buyers, and (so the thinking goes) they only want to hear male singers. To the contrary, Carpenter has seen *Shooting Straight in the Dark*

certified gold and *Come On Come On* go double-platinum, just as the sales of other female artists have also skyrocketed.

Carpenter danced to a cajun beat in front of President George Bush at the 1991 Country Music Association Awards, but when election time rolled around a year later it was obvious from her Clinton/Gore button that Carpenter supported the Democratic party ticket. Equally apparent was her support of AIDS research via the now-famous red ribbon. She has donated her talent and time to a variety of causes, from cleaning up the Chesapeake Bay area, to recycling, to women's issues, to children's advocacy.

The idea that her music has captivated people on a national scale is still mind-boggling to Carpenter. For several years, Carpenter was a hometown musical hero in the Washington, D.C., area, and her music did not spread beyond the D.C. area for years.

Mary Chapin Carpenter got her start by playing guitar for a captive audience—herself, alone in her bedroom. While still in school, she got up enough nerve to perform at "open mike" nights at clubs during summer breaks. At 19, she had a regular gig at a bar called Gal-

lagher's. It took a while for Carpenter—then so shy she could barely look at the audience—to mix in original material with the cover tunes.

By the time Carpenter was in her mid-20s, the club scene had lost its charm. She was performing other artists' songs and entertaining people who much preferred to talk and drink. Alcohol had also become a problem, and she had lost some of her creative energy. It was a time of insecurity, self-doubt, and crisis.

Carpenter overcame her alcohol problem and decided to go to work in the real world. She was offered a job as a researcher

Carpenter has recorded such light-hearted songs as "The Bug" and "I Feel Lucky," which revealed to fans her sense of humor.

for a Washington consulting firm, but she turned it down in a moment of panic. Later, she took a job with a small philanthropic organization that offered her the flexibility she needed to perform during off hours. Her vacation days were spent traveling and making music. Having a job gave her the stability she needed as well as such practical benefits as health insurance.

She set out once again to break into the music scene, this time determined to do *her* music. She met producer John Jennings in 1982, and slowly they began committing her songs to tape. As soon as she would get a little money together, she would cut another song in Jennings's basement studio.

After a time they had enough songs for a tape to sell at Carpenter's club shows. That

Mary Chapin Carpenter's awards include two Grammys for Best Country Female Vocal Performance.

tape caught the attention of Rounder Records. She was on the verge of signing with Rounder when she discovered that a major label, Columbia Records, was also interested. She signed with Columbia instead, and the folk-based album *Hometown Girl* was released in 1987.

Though initial sales were not strong, Carpenter made a name for herself. Columbia had enough faith in the determined singer/songwriter to provide the budget for a second album, *State of the Heart*, which featured her first chart success, "How Do." When "Down at the Twist and Shout," from the *Shooting Straight in the Dark* album, won a Grammy, Mary Chapin Carpenter found herself on the path to stardom. Other hits followed, including "Never Had It So Good," "You Win Again," "Right Now," "Quittin' Time," "Going Out Tonight," and "Passionate Kisses."

"Down at the Twist and Shout" aside, *Shooting Straight in the Dark* was basically a collection of serious, introspective songs about love and life. Though written from a woman's perspective, Carpenter dislikes the implication that her songs are "women's songs." "People say I write for women," she says. "But I [believe] men and women feel the same kinds of things."

After the seriousness of *Shooting Straight in the Dark*, Carpenter lightened up a bit with *Come On Come On*. The album featured a cover of Dire Straits's "The Bug" and a song called "I Feel Lucky," in which the singer wins the lottery and then gets to flirt with country cowpunkers Lyle Lovett and Dwight Yoakam in a bar. To further explode her image as a brooding, serious performer, Carpenter surprised fans and industry insiders by taking part in Dolly Parton's video for her song "Romeo." In this good-natured video that pokes fun at the roles of men and women, Carpenter, Parton, Kathy Mattea, and Tanya Tucker take turns ogling Billy Ray Cyrus. "I've had this image—for better, for worse—of being sort of ultra-serious," Carpenter said. "Clearly, I think you have to have a sense of humor to be singing that song or being in the video."

As she began winning awards and falling into the media spotlight, the questions, the scrutiny, and the need to categorize her music occupied the press. Was it country? Was it alternative? This desire for music critics to pigeonhole artists has been a source of exasperation for Carpenter. She admits that her music straddles the line between country and other genres, but fans of country music in the 1990s are accustomed to crossover artists and are not concerned with labels.

Country, folk, rock, what difference does it make? Mary Chapin Carpenter gets to the heart of life with her music. In the process, she has attracted many new fans to country, helped change the attitude of the industry toward female entertainers, influenced a number of young performers, and updated the image of female country singers.

MARY CHAPIN CARPENTER

BORN: February 21, 1958, in Princeton, New Jersey

FIRST HIT: "How Do" (1989)

OTHER NOTABLE HITS: "I Feel Lucky" (1992); "He Thinks He'll Keep Her" (1992); "Passionate Kisses" (1992); "Down at the Twist and Shout" (1991); "Right Now" (1991); "Quittin' Time" (1989); "Never Had It So Good" (1989); "Something of a Dreamer" (1989)

BEST ALBUMS: *Come On Come On* (1992); *Shooting Straight in the Dark* (1991); *State of the Heart* (1990)

AWARDS INCLUDE: Grammy, Best Country Female Vocal Performance (1992, 1991); Country Music Association Female Vocalist of the Year (1993, 1992); Academy of Country Music (ACM) Top Female Vocalist (1992); ACM Top New Female Vocalist (1989)

PERSONAL: When Carpenter was recording her *Hometown Girl* album, the song "Runaway Train" was cut in the final edit; Rosanne Cash heard the song and was so moved by it that she included it in her *King's Record Shop* album.

JOHNNY CASH

Johnny Cash is the most internationally recognized figure in country music. The Man in Black has secured more pop hits than any other country artist; and only George Jones has enjoyed more country music chart hits. Cash has been a movie actor, the host of a successful television series, and a

Johnny Cash has been part of the country music scene since the late 1950s. His distinct sound has remained virtually unchanged across decades.

best-selling author (his autobiography, *The Man in Black,* sold over a million copies). He counts among his friends such diverse people as Billy Graham, Mick Jagger, and Bob Dylan. He writes from the point of view of the common man, yet he has sat across the table from kings, dictators, popes, and presidents.

Cash was born on February 26, 1932, into an impoverished farm family in Kingsland, Arkansas. He was three years old when his parents, Ray and Carrie Cash, bought 20 acres of cotton fields near Dyess, Arkansas, with help from a government New Deal program that relocated farm families to productive land. The farm was located in a remote region, and the family home didn't receive electricity until 1946. By then, two of Cash's brothers had died.

The Cash family entertained themselves with music, with everyone joining in to sing traditional gospel and old country songs, including a heavy dose of Carter Family tunes. Johnny began writing songs by the time he reached high school.

After graduation, Cash moved to Pontiac, Michigan, to work in the Fisher Body Plant. Eventually worn down by boredom, he joined the U.S. Air Force and spent four years in Germany. While there, he taught himself to play guitar. His first performances were for crowds of soldiers on foreign military bases.

When he returned, he settled in Memphis. He met his first wife, Vivian Liberto, while attending radio announcer's school. He also met two musicians, guitarist Luther Perkins and bassist Marshall Grant, and began per-

Johnny Cash's early recordings feature just Cash and his two-man band, the Tennessee Two.

Cash's baritone vocals are instantly recognizable. His most famous recordings include "I Walk the Line" and "Folsom Prison Blues."

forming informally with them. He talked them into auditioning at Sun Records, home of Elvis Presley and Jerry Lee Lewis. Their first song was "Hey Porter." Sun owner Sam Phillips was intrigued and asked Cash to come up with something with more of a rock beat. The singer went home and wrote "Cry, Cry, Cry," which became his first country music hit in 1955 as recorded by Johnny Cash and the Tennessee Two. (A year later, when talented drummer Fluke Holland

Cash was initially signed to Sun Records. In his first year under contract, his single "I Walk the Line" hit number one.

joined, they became Johnny Cash and the Tennessee Three.)

Those initial songs featured the singular Cash sound—a walking bass and a simple, deep-toned, single-note guitar that provided a primitive but efficient backing. In search of a stark sound, Cash purposely omitted the fiddles and steel guitars that rang out on most country music of the period. Cash's music focused attention on the singer's foreboding, earthy voice, a baritone so ominous and penetrating that it commanded attention despite its limited range.

Within his first year at Sun, Cash released two of his most famous songs, "Folsom Prison Blues" and "I Walk the Line." The latter became his first number-one country hit, as well as his initial major pop hit, reaching number 17 on the *Billboard* charts. It has since been recorded by more than 100 artists.

In 1956, Cash became the first Sun Records artist to join the Grand Ole Opry, though the association was a rocky one for many years. Two years later, he left Sun because of disagreements over money and artistic control to sign with Columbia Records. His second Columbia single, "Don't Take Your Guns to Town," sold a half-million copies and continued Cash's run of success on both the country and pop charts.

During the 1960s, Cash recorded a series of folk-influenced albums on such themes as the plight of Native Americans, the forgotten working man, the oppressed migrant worker, and the unredeemed prisoner. Because of his own restlessness and struggles, he identified himself with the people in his songs. A keen-eyed observer of society's ills, the Man in Black (after the title of a 1971 antiwar song) became a voice for the disenfranchised and the oppressed.

At the same time, he descended into a well-documented period of drug use. By his own account, he cleaned himself up with the support of singer June

June Carter Cash

June Carter Cash, like husband Johnny Cash, has enjoyed a long and rich career in the country music business. June is the daughter of Maybelle Carter, one of three original members of the legendary Carter Family—considered by many to be the most influential family in country music history. June began singing with the group in its later years, but the group's emphasis on songs that evoked a simpler time and stressed traditional American values and agricultural traditions still had not changed. When the original Carter Family disbanded in 1943, June Carter continued to perform with her mother and two sisters, first as Mother Maybelle and the Carter Sisters, and then as the Carter Family. June eventually went solo and joined the Johnny Cash road show; she was later rejoined by her mother and sisters. The Carter

Family enjoyed a brief revival in the 1980s with the addition of Carlene Carter, the daughter of June Carter and Carl Smith. Carlene Carter also enjoys a successful solo career.

The Man in Black is a country music legend. His roots are traditional country, but he is also popular with mainstream audiences.

Carter and the religious faith he'd had since childhood. The couple married in 1967. The following year, Cash achieved his first number-one hit in four years with a live version of "Folsom Prison Blues," recorded during a historic concert at the California prison named in the song.

Cash hosted a TV variety series from 1969 to 1971. Here, his mother-in-law, Mother Maybelle Carter, accompanies him on the show

His new bride and her mother, country pioneer Maybelle Carter, were regular guests on the television series *The Johnny Cash Show*, which ran from 1969 to 1971. That led to a career revival that resulted in 11 top-five songs during the years that the show was on the air.

Cash continued to perform and record throughout the 1970s. As his reputation evolved into legend, country music began to change. While lauding his status, the country music industry neglected his contemporary output. In the mid-1980s, his three-decade association with Columbia ended when the record company no longer seemed interested in promoting or producing him. Cash signed with Mercury/PolyGram, releasing several albums that did not chart well. By the 1990s, Cash was up against a new Nashville full of youthful optimism and "pretty faces." He felt as much an outsider as he had in the 1950s, when his eerily sparse sound first intimidated commercially driven Nashville.

In 1993, Cash signed with a small record company called American Recordings, whose eclectic roster included rap performers, heavy metal bands, and hard rockers. Producer Rick Rubin and Cash worked together to come up with his best album in years, *American Recordings*. A return to the stripped-down style that made him a star so many years ago, the album features compositions by such diverse songwriters as Cash, Tom Waits, Nick Lowe, and heavy-metal rocker Glenn Danzig. Playing up Cash's identity as an American legend, Rubin fired up Cash's career, reestablishing him as a premier force in contemporary music.

JOHNNY CASH

REAL NAME: J.R. Cash

BORN: February 26, 1932, in Kingsland, Arkansas

FIRST HIT: "Cry, Cry, Cry" (1955)

OTHER NOTABLE HITS: "Bird on a Wire" (1994); "Man in Black" (1971); "Sunday Morning Coming Down" (1970); "A Boy Named Sue" (1969); "Ring of Fire" (1963); "Don't Take Your Guns to Town" (1959);"I Walk the Line" (1956); "Folsom Prison Blues" (1956/1968); "Hey Porter" (1955)

BEST ALBUMS: *Columbia Years 1958-1986* (1987); *The Sun Years* (1984); *Johnny Cash at San Quentin Prison* (1969); *Johnny Cash at Folsom Prison* (1968); *I Walk the Line* (1964); *Ride This Train* (1960)

AWARDS INCLUDE: Grammy, Best Country Vocal Performance by a Duo or Group (with June Carter, 1970); Grammy, Best Country Male Vocal Performance (1969, 1968); Grammy, Album Notes (1969, 1968); Grammy, Best Country & Western Duet by a Trio or Group (Vocal or Instrumental)(with June Carter, 1967); Country Music Association (CMA) Entertainer of the Year (1969); CMA Male Vocalist of the Year (1969); CMA Vocal Group of the Year (with June Carter, 1969)

ACHIEVEMENTS: Rock 'n' Roll Hall of Fame inductee (1991); Country Music Hall of Fame inductee (youngest inductee, 1980); Grand Ole Opry member (1956)

The statistics compiled by Cash during his career are staggering. He has sold more than 50 million records. He has won seven Grammy Awards. He has put 48 singles on the pop charts and more than 130 songs on the country charts. His recognition as a writer is similarly impressive. Cash has received 23 citations from the song-tracking agency BMI for radio airplay of such classic songs as "Folsom Prison Blues," "I Walk the Line," "Big River," "I Still Miss Someone," and "Get Rhythm." He's the only living performer to be honored with the Triple Crown—entrance into the Country Music Hall of Fame, the Rock 'n' Roll Hall of Fame, and the Songwriters Hall of Fame.

When the press talks about the explosion of country music during the 1990s into pop markets, they have short memories. When they rave about the current popularity of country with mainstream audiences, they have not done their homework. Though Cash is steeped in the traditions of country-western, he long ago ignored the boundaries of country music to pursue a personal style that appeals to all. Long after the current generation of pretty faces and country megastars has peaked, Johnny Cash will prevail because his music is not a commercially calculated career move but an honest reflection of the joys and pain of his life.

·ROSANNE· ·CASH·

Rosanne Cash may belong to one of country music's most famous families, but she came to country music stardom through a side door. Cash recorded her first album in Germany and her second in Los Angeles. Her hair, over the years, has changed from inky black to eggplant to light brown and back to natural black. Openly critical of the old Nashville record-

Rosanne Cash's soul-searching music is not confined to traditional country music.

ing system, Cash is one performer who has never paid attention to country music formulas.

The only woman to have a number-one country album through the early and mid-1980s, Rosanne reached the top spot with *Seven Year Ache* in 1981 and *Rhythm and Romance* in 1985. Her first number-one country song, "Seven Year Ache," hit number 22 on the pop radio charts. Since then, Cash has topped the country charts 11 times. For her part, the singer says she doesn't try to set trends, she just ignores them.

Cash was born in Memphis on May 24, 1955, just days before her father, country legend Johnny Cash, recorded his first songs at Sun Studios. At age 11, she moved with her father and mother, Vivian Liberto, to Ventura, California. Her parents divorced shortly afterward. Rosanne remained with her mother in California but maintained a close relationship with her absentee father.

After graduating from high school, Rosanne joined her father's road show, first as a wardrobe assistant and later as a backup singer. She left the band to live in England for a year, then returned to study drama at Vanderbilt University in Nashville and the Lee Strasberg Institute in Los Angeles.

In 1978, Rosanne met singer/songwriter Rodney Crowell, who had just released his solo debut album, *Ain't Living Long Like This*. She asked him to produce her demos and later traveled to Germany to record her first album for Ariola Records.

A CBS Records executive heard the album at Rosanne's father's house and signed her to a recording contract. With Crowell producing, she recorded *Right or Wrong*, released in 1979. She and Crowell were married early that year and had their first child, Caitlin, in 1980. The couple moved to Nashville and released *Seven Year Ache* in 1981, further establishing Cash as an effective vocal stylist and revealing her newfound, archly personal songwriting abilities.

Cash's next four albums—*Somewhere in the Stars, Rhythm and Romance, King's Record Shop,* and *Interiors*—often explored her turbulent relationship with Crowell, addressing the ambiguities of modern relationships with honesty, strength, and intimate insight. The couple separated in 1991.

Rosanne's musical style is nothing like that of her father, Johnny Cash. But, in honor of him, she recorded one of his early Sun hits, "Tennessee Flat Top Box," for *King's Record Shop*. Her version of the song is at once a tribute to him as an influence and an acknowledgement that she is his musical heir.

Although Cash records and tours less frequently than many country performers, devoting her energies to motherhood (she has three daughters), painting, and writing fiction, she found time to work on the landmark *Lullaby* album/video with Dionne Warwick, Carole King, Mary Chapin Carpenter, and others. She also released her eighth Columbia album, *The Wheel*, in March 1993.

"It is about transformation," says Cash. If anyone knows about turning pain and loss into personal growth and commitment, surely Rosanne Cash is that person.

ROSANNE CASH

BORN: May 24, 1955, in Memphis, Tennessee

FIRST HIT: "Couldn't Do Nothin' Right" (1980)

OTHER NOTABLE HITS: "Real Woman" (1990); "I Want a Cure" (1990); "Tennessee Flat Top Box" (1988); "It's Such a Small World" (with Rodney Crowell, 1988); "Hold On" (1986); "I Don't Know Why You Don't Want Me" (1985); "My Baby Thinks He's a Train" (1981); "Seven Year Ache" (1981)

BEST ALBUMS: *Interiors* (1990); *King's Record Shop* (1987); *Rhythm and Romance* (1985); *Somewhere in the Stars* (1982); *Seven Year Ache* (1981); *Right or Wrong* (1979)

AWARDS INCLUDE: Grammy, Best Album Package (1988); Grammy, Best Female Country Vocal Performance (1985); BMI Songwriting Award (1985)

ACHIEVEMENTS: Produced the critically acclaimed *Interiors* and wrote or cowrote all the songs

PERSONAL: Cash was married to country music singer/songwriter Rodney Crowell until 1991. She is the daughter of country music legend Johnny Cash.

MARK CHESNUTT

When Mark Chesnutt's "Too Cold at Home" became a hit in 1990, the then 26-year-old had been working on his career for so long that he was already a veteran performer. Chesnutt started out singing along with his father's Hank Williams records, then did his best to imitate George Jones. He was so committed to making a living as a coun-

Newcomer Mark Chesnutt won the Country Music Association's Horizon Award in 1993.

try performer that he quit high school in the 11th grade to devote all his time to a music career.

Chesnutt spent ten years singing nothing but country in nightclubs, making frequent trips to Nashville from

Influenced by Hank Williams, Mark Chesnutt is a country music traditionalist.

his Beaumont, Texas, home. With his father, local performer Bob Chesnutt, guiding his steps, he landed a house band job at Cutter's nightclub in 1981 and recorded the first of eight records on the Texas-based AXBAR and Cherry labels. It was Chesnutt's version of "Too Cold at Home," produced on the Cherry label, that helped land his later MCA Records contract.

Immediately after hitting the airwaves with the achingly lonely "Too Cold at Home," critical accolades began flying. "This guy is the real thing," raved Geoffrey Himes of the Washington Post. "A hard-core singer with the right voice and the right instincts."

A devotee of the classic country sound of the '60s and '70s, Chesnutt collects old country music records, and his love of the traditional is obvious from the country-to-the-bone delivery of his first two albums, *Too Cold at Home* and *Longnecks and Short Stories*, both of which have been certified gold. He released his third album, *Almost Goodbye*, in June 1993 and hit the top of the charts with "It Sure Is Monday," "I Just Wanted You to Know," and the title track.

Indicative of his growing popularity, Chesnutt surprised some and pleased many when he walked away with the highly coveted Horizon Award from the Country Music Association in 1993, perhaps the most prestigious trophy awarded to

MARK CHESNUTT

BORN: September 6, 1963, in Beaumont, Texas

MUSICAL INFLUENCES: Elvis Presley, Hank Williams, George Jones

FIRST HIT: "Too Cold at Home" (1990)

OTHER NOTABLE HITS: "It Sure Is Monday" (1993); "I Just Wanted You to Know" (1993); "Almost Goodbye" (1993); "All My Old Flames (Have New Names)" (1992); "Bubba Shot the Jukebox" (1992); "Blame It on Texas" (1991); "Your Love Is a Miracle" (1991); "Brother Jukebox" (1991)

BEST ALBUMS: *Longnecks and Short Stories* (1992); *Too Cold at Home* (1990)

AWARDS INCLUDE: Country Music Association (CMA) Horizon Award (1993); CMA Vocal Event of the Year (with George Jones, et al., 1993)

PERSONAL: Chesnutt, a collector of vintage country records, says he turns to them often for inspiration.

country newcomers. Beating out such top-selling colleagues as Tracy Lawrence, John Michael Montgomery, and Sammy Kershaw, Chesnutt's already red-hot career reached altogether new heights.

His fame escalating, Chesnutt has not shied away from tackling controversial issues, as witnessed by his participation in the "Country AIDS Awareness" campaign. The committed young singer not only lent his image to the print campaign, intoning, "AIDS ain't just some big city problem," but he also took part in walkathons to benefit area AIDS relief organizations.

In 1992, Mark Chesnutt married longtime girlfriend Tracie Lynn Motley in a private ceremony in Texas. His exotically beautiful bride costarred with him in the video for "Almost Goodbye," showcasing her impressive equestrian skills.

RODNEY · CROWELL

Rodney Crowell represents the new wave of Nashville songwriters who minimize ornamentation. His carefully selected lyrics are a response to inner emotion not external rhetoric, and he freely admits to being as influenced by rock legends John Lennon and Bob Dylan as by Merle Haggard.

Born August 7, 1950, in Houston, Texas, Crowell grew up in a musical family. He got his start playing drums in his father's band, but later switched to the guitar. A big fan of Elvis Presley and the Beatles, Crowell's first solo efforts were decidedly rock oriented. To this day, he maintains that there isn't that much difference between rock 'n' roll and country.

Crowell relocated to Nashville in 1972, where he worked as a songwriter and began absorbing the more direct songwriting styles of fellow transplanted Texans Guy Clark and Townes Van Zandt. In 1975, he moved to California to play acoustic guitar in Emmylou Harris's Hot Band, where he was pegged as the next Gram Parsons. Harris recorded several Crowell compositions, including "Bluebird Wine." In addition to being a prolific songwriter, Crowell became known as an arranger, songwriter, and producer.

Crowell struck out on his own in 1977. Warner Bros. released his debut album, *Ain't Living Long Like This*, in 1978. A year later, Crowell married Rosanne Cash, also becoming her writing partner and producer.

Rodney Crowell has earned a reputation as an influential singer/songwriter and a producer.

Crowell produced Rosanne's award-winning 1987 album *King's Record Shop*, which yielded four number-one country singles.

Many Crowell songs have been hit recordings for other artists, including Bob Seger ("Shame on the Moon") and Jimmy Buffett ("Stars on the Water"). Crowell's breakthrough as a performer in his own right didn't come until 1988's *Diamonds and Dirt*, the fifth album of his career. His most country-sounding album, it sparkled with five number-one singles, all written, performed, and produced by Crowell—a first in country music history. Crowell received the Academy of Country Music Top Male Vocalist award in 1988, and "After All This Time," a ballad from *Diamonds and Dirt*, was honored with a Grammy.

After the commercial triumph of *Diamonds and Dirt*, Crowell seemed destined for mainstream success, but subsequent albums, including *Keys to the Highway*, were not as popular. Crowell's father died in 1989, and two of the songs on *Keys*, "Many a Long & Lonesome Highway" and "Things I Wish I'd Said," stand out as commentary on this loss. Rodney's marriage to Rosanne ended in 1992. The resulting turmoil inspired some of the songs on *Life Is Messy*.

Crowell currently records for MCA, and in 1994 he released his first album for that label, *Let the Picture Paint Itself*. For this album, Crowell reunited with producer Tony Brown (who produced *Diamonds and Dirt*) to help bring out the country side to his music. In general, *Picture* was more opti-

Crowell married singer Rosanne Cash in 1979 after producing her first album. The couple divorced in 1992.

RODNEY CROWELL

BORN: August 7, 1950, in Houston, Texas

MUSICAL INFLUENCES: John Lennon, Bob Dylan, the Beatles, Elvis Presley, Merle Haggard, Hank Williams

FIRST HIT: "I Ain't Living Long Like This" (1978)

OTHER NOTABLE HITS: "Let the Picture Paint Itself" (1993); "Many a Long & Lonesome Highway" (1990); "Crazy Baby" (1989); "After All This Time" (1989); "I Couldn't Leave You If I Tried" (1988)

BEST ALBUMS: *Keys to the Highway* (1989); *Diamonds and Dirt* (1988); *I Ain't Living Long Like This* (1978)

AWARDS INCLUDE: Grammy, Best Country Song (1989)

PERSONAL: Crowell was married to Rosanne Cash, with whom he has three children.

mistic than his last few albums had been. Having exorcized his personal demons and problems in *Life Is Messy*, Rodney seemed ready to focus on what he had accomplished in his life and career.

Crowell has always intertwined his personal and professional lives. He captures his feelings about life's experiences in his lyrics, yet his observations are universal enough so that listeners can relate. An insightful songwriter and accomplished musician, Crowell is a true country music poet.

BILLY · RAY · CYRUS

Country music had never seen anything like Billy Ray Cyrus before. Cyrus exploded onto the scene in the winter of 1992, and there was no stopping this young man with the high-low haircut and wild stage antics. In just a year, Cyrus sold more than nine million copies worldwide of his *Some Gave All* debut disc, had the nation buzzing about "Achy Breaky Heart,"

Country heartthrob Billy Ray Cyrus secured instant success with his hit single, "Achy Breaky Heart."

and changed the way country music artists would be presented to the world.

Billy Ray Cyrus is certainly the product of video. In a fresh, new marketing technique, executives at Mercury/Nashville decided to release Cyrus's "Achy Breaky Heart" video to dance clubs and video outlets across the country a full month before the music was available to radio. A dance was created, and a national dance contest was begun.

The marketing ploy worked. The summer of 1992 saw the nation singing and dancing to "Achy Breaky Heart." Country music dance clubs popped up overnight, and the entire nation was suddenly dancing to country music.

Yet Billy Ray's "overnight success" involved years of hard work. Born August 25, 1961, in Flatwoods, Kentucky, Cyrus is the son of Kentucky state representative Ron Cyrus and his wife, Ruth Ann. The couple divorced when he was a child, which, according to the singer, caused a wound so deep that he was seldom seen to smile.

For Cyrus, making music was not his first career choice. As his muscular build shows, he is a natural athlete and had planned to be a professional baseball player. But after attending a Neil Diamond concert when he was 20, Cyrus changed his plans. The day after the concert, he bought a guitar, formed the band Sly Dog, and wrote down some goals. He dreamed of being successful in the music business and mapped out the path he would take.

The first milestone was to play in a club within ten months. Sly Dog landed a spot at the Sand Bar in Ironton, Ohio. It was a good training ground: Here Cyrus combined the sounds of Willie Nelson and Lynyrd

Cyrus's two albums have produced several number-one hits. Some Gave All *was a best-seller in 1992.*

Skynyrd to fashion his own style. Things went smoothly until a fire in 1984 destroyed the band's equipment. Discouraged by the run of bad luck, Cyrus headed to the West Coast. There he started a new band and sold cars to support his music career.

Two years later, Cyrus returned to his old Kentucky home and his musical roots. He married his first wife, Cindy, in 1986 and moved to Ironton. He spent the next five years working at the Ragtime Lounge in Huntington, West Virginia. On his days off, he sometimes made the six-hour drive to Nashville to pitch his wares.

Eventually he met *Grand Ole Opry* star Del Reeves, who led Cyrus to his present manager, Jack McFadden. McFadden took Cyrus under his wing and introduced him to Mercury Records Senior Vice-President Harold Shedd, who teamed Cyrus with veteran producers Joe Scaife and Jim Cotton.

Cyrus's first album, *Some Gave All*, has the undeniable Billy Ray stamp. Cyrus brought in his own band, Sly Dog, to record with him (a rarity for a new artist), and he wrote or cowrote six of the ten cuts. Working with an unknown artist, an unknown band, an unknown songwriter, and an untested marketing plan, Mercury Records took a gamble and released "Achy Breaky Heart" as Cyrus's first single.

Some Gave All became the first debut album to enter the pop charts at number one. (It was number one on the country charts as well.) It was one of the biggest-selling albums of 1992, edging out the albums of such rock and pop stars as Michael Jackson, Bruce Springsteen, Metallica, and Guns N' Roses. It produced five hit singles and garnered five Grammy nominations.

The album, with its Dixie-fried rock 'n' roll, also garnered more than its share of controversy. Pumped full with as many rock-tinged songs as the country industry could stand, *Some Gave All* knocked the neotraditionalists right out of the spotlight. The entertainment press could not get enough of Billy Ray Cyrus, whether it was about his personal appearance (only Dolly Parton receives more physique-oriented comments than Billy Ray) or the popularity of "Achy Breaky Heart."

Other country performers grumbled about the newfound importance of sex appeal in contemporary country music, but singer Travis Tritt went a step further and criticized Cyrus personally. He attacked "Achy Breaky Heart" for "not making much of a statement"

Billy Ray stretches the boundaries of country music with his rock 'n' roll sound and provocative image.

and accused the young singer of turning country music into an "ass-wigglin' " contest. Despite such criticisms, Billy Ray converted many new listeners to country music with his hybrid sound, particularly among younger audiences who might never have considered country-western as a viable alternative to rock 'n' roll.

Another key to Billy Ray's appeal is his immense popularity with female audiences, not only because of his enormous sex appeal but also because of the lyrics of his songs. His songs speak to the women in his audiences, telling them about how he has been betrayed, heartbroken, and jilted by the women in his life. Yet he loves them anyway. The overt romanticism of his songs offers women a male perspective that is neither threatening nor boastful.

The years of concentration on his music at the expense of his marriage took their toll. Billy Ray's personal life began to take on the characteristics of his songs. Billy Ray and Cindy divorced during the recording of *Some Gave All*. After she declared he had gotten "way too cocky" and tossed his belongings on the lawn, he wrote his hit "Where'm I Gonna Live" and gave her half the songwriting credit.

His rock-sounding second album, *It Won't Be the Last*, was released in May 1993, and sold nearly two million copies by September. The title song was written the night Cyrus's divorce from Cindy became final; he thought it was the first time she had broken his heart, but it wouldn't be the last. Late in 1993, Cyrus married his present wife, Letitia Finley.

Other songs from *It Won't Be the Last* include an Elvis Presley-style ballad called "When I'm Gone," which was penned by Don Von Tress, the man who wrote "Achy Breaky Heart." Cyrus gave Von Tress the idea for "When I'm Gone," and the two share a writing credit for the song. Cyrus did not intend to emulate Elvis so closely, but the use of the Jordanaires to sing backup vocals

Shown here with parents Ron and Joan Cyrus, Billy Ray was born and raised in Flatwoods, Kentucky.

added to the Elvis-like sound. Other notable tunes include "Ain't Your Dog No More" and "Right Face Wrong Time." Like *Some Gave All*, the collection of songs on *It Won't Be the Last* are only a stone's throw from rock 'n' roll.

Despite the overwhelming success that Mercury Records had with the Achy Breaky line dance in terms of promoting Billy Ray's first album, they wisely chose not to release a dance to accompany *It Won't Be the Last*.

Billy Ray Cyrus credits vision and goal setting for his current position at the top. "I charted my course, and I stayed focused on where I was. That's how I got to here."

BILLY RAY CYRUS

BORN: August 25, 1961, in Flatwoods, Kentucky

FIRST HIT: "Achy Breaky Heart" (1992)

OTHER NOTABLE HITS: "Talk Some" (1993); "When I'm Gone" (1993); "Where'm I Gonna Live" (1992); "She's Not Cryin' Anymore" (1992)

BEST ALBUMS: *It Won't Be the Last* (1993); *Some Gave All* (1992)

AWARDS INCLUDE: Country Music Association Single of the Year (1992)

PERSONAL: Cyrus is the son of Kentucky State Representative Ron Cyrus.

BILLY · DEAN

With his handsome, movie-star good looks, Billy Dean seems to belong on the big screen as much as he does on the radio. For a while, in fact, Dean did make a living as an actor, appearing in commercials for McDonald's, Chevrolet, and Valvoline Motor Oil. He even had a supporting role in the highly acclaimed but short-lived ABC-TV series *Elvis.* For Dean, acting was just a way to pay the bills. Music has always been his first love.

Dean grew up in Quincy, Florida, and began his musical career singing in his father's band. A mechanic by trade, the elder Dean taught his son to play guitar and encouraged him to develop his musical talent. Dean cites his late father as a major musical influence, along with more recognizable names such as Merle Haggard, Jim Reeves, Marty Robbins, and Dean Martin.

Dean attended East Central Junior College in Decatur, Mississippi, on a basketball scholarship. After a brief move to Las Vegas, he returned home in 1982, crossed the state line to Georgia, and entered the regional Wrangler Country Star Search talent contest in Bainbridge. After winning the state final, he advanced to the national contest, held at the Grand Ole Opry building in Nashville. Although he didn't win the national prize, he was named one of the top-ten finalists. More importantly, he decided to extend his visit to Music City into a more permanent venture.

Inspired by Merle Haggard and Marty Robbins, Dean got his start by entering national talent contests.

To support himself, Dean formed a band and started to tour, opening shows for such big-name acts as Mel Tillis, Gary Morris, Ronnie Milsap, and Steve Wariner. He began to concentrate on songwriting as well, enjoying a fair degree of success when Milsap, Randy Travis, the Oak Ridge Boys, Les Taylor, the Bama Band, and Shelly West recorded his songs. Eventually his songwriting and singing caught the ear of publisher/producer Jimmy Gilmer. It was songwriter Verlon Thompson, a friend of Dean's, who introduced some of Billy's tunes to Gilmer. Recognizing Dean's abilities, Gilmer quickly signed him to a songwriting contract in 1988. A record deal with Capitol Nashville/SBK soon followed.

On "Only Here for a Little While," Dean's first single from his 1991 debut album *Young Man*, the ambitious performer demonstrated a boyish appeal combined with a solid country sound. Despite the glut of albums released from handsome country hunks that year, Dean's follow-up single, "Somewhere in My Broken Heart," proved to be a breakthrough for the talented singer/songwriter. The song, which he cowrote with award-winning songwriter Richard Leigh, revealed the more emotional side of Billy Dean. Not only did the tune hit the top of the country charts, but it also received airplay on adult contemporary radio stations, was named Song of the Year by the Academy of Country Music, and earned a Grammy nomination.

Dean followed his impressive first album with *Billy Dean*, which again showcased his sensitive, personal side on such tunes as "Small Favors" and "You Don't Count the Cost." To avoid being "typecast" as a singer of heartbreaking romantic ballads, Dean also included a couple of harder-edged tunes on the album. "Hammer Down" tells the tale of a rogue who always seems to be in the right place at the wrong time; "(I Miss) Billy the Kid," about recapturing the innocence of a little boy's childhood, is clearly autobiographical. Perhaps because of the popularity of "Billy the Kid," Dean was chosen to write the theme song for the animated series *The Wild West C.O.W.–Boys of Moo Mesa*.

Dean's contemporary country sound continued on *Fire in the Dark*, released in 1993. Another mix of soulful ballads and rollicking, hard-driving tunes, the album emphasizes Dean's strengths—his clear country voice and skills as a songwriter. Dean proved his staying power with such hits as "That's What I Like About Love" and "Tryin' to Find a Fire in the Dark."

Dean and wife Cathy gave birth to a son, Eli, in 1993, which not only made an impact on his personal life but also on his songwriting. Following Eli's birth, Dean set aside time to write and record material for future albums. Among those songs is one about his newborn son called "He's Got My Hands."

No longer the new hunk on the block, Billy Dean has worked hard to distinguish his style and stage show from those of other young male artists. His songwriting skills and conventional but effective country voice ensure him a niche in the contemporary Nashville scene.

BILLY DEAN

REAL NAME: William (Billy) Harold Dean

BORN: April 2, 1962, in Quincy, Florida

MUSICAL INFLUENCES: his father, Billy Dean, Sr., Merle Haggard, James Taylor, Don Henley

FIRST HIT: "Only Here for a Little While" (1990)

OTHER NOTABLE HITS: "Tryin' to Hide a Fire in the Dark" (1993); "Only the Wind" (1992); "(I Miss) Billy the Kid" (1992); "If There Hadn't Been You" (1992); "Somewhere in My Broken Heart" (1991)

BEST ALBUMS: *Fire in the Dark* (1993); *Billy Dean* (1991)

AWARDS INCLUDE: Academy of Country Music (ACM) Top New Male Vocalist (1991); ACM Song of the Year (1991)

· DIAMOND · RIO ·

When "Meet in the Middle" hit the top of the country charts, Diamond Rio stepped into country music history. Never before had a country vocal group claimed the number-one position on the national charts with a debut single. The band's first album, *Diamond Rio* (1991), yielded five top-five hits and was eventually certified platinum.

Diamond Rio is a new country band with traditional roots. The group's initial release, "Meet in the Middle," topped the charts in 1991.

Six world-class musicians comprise the group Diamond Rio. Each brings a different influence to the band, which accounts for its contemporary country sound. Lead singer Marty Roe seemed destined from childhood for a career in country music. He was named after legendary singer/songwriter Marty Robbins; he learned his first song, Merle Haggard's "The Fugitive," at the tender age of three; and he began his professional career at age 12. While enrolled in David Limpscomb University in Nashville, Roe added to his musical experience by touring with a group called Windsong. In 1984, he joined the Tennessee River Boys, which eventually evolved into Diamond Rio.

Lead guitarist Jimmy Olander's talent for music was evident in childhood as well. He was teaching banjo by the time he was 12. Olander performed with such nontraditional country performers as Rodney Crowell, Duane Eddy, and the Nitty Gritty Dirt Band before hooking up with Diamond Rio. A renowned guitarist, Olander is known for combining technical virtuosity with state-of-the-art instrumentation.

The remaining band members are as talented as they are diverse. Gene Johnson adds mandolin magic to the band's unique sound. Also a top-notch fiddler and acoustic guitar player, Johnson previously played both live and in the studio with J.D. Crowe and the New South and David Bromberg. Dan Truman, a classically trained pianist, is a former member of the Brigham Young University Young Ambassadors. As a member of that prestigious group, he toured the world, performing for distinguished audiences, including former Indian prime minister Indira Gandhi. Bass player and vocalist Dana Williams is the nephew of bluegrass performers Bobby and Sonny Osborne.

Williams began playing bluegrass music for a living at the age of 12. Finally, drummer Brian Prout brings a rock influence to Diamond Rio. A native of New York, he moved to Nashville while still a member of the band called Heartbreak Mountain, which also spawned Shenandoah's Marty Raybon.

Tim DuBois, an executive at Arista, signed Diamond Rio to a recording contract after seeing the group open a show for George Jones. Still known as the Tennessee River Boys at the time, the band took the name Diamond Rio from a trucking company in Harrisburg, Pennsylvania, because it sounded contemporary. The band later visited the Diamond Rio facilities and received a mud flap as a souvenir.

Diamond Rio followed up its impressive debut album with *Close to the Edge* in 1992. For this second album, the group attempted to distill the best elements from its first effort and expand on those. The result is a collection of songs based in country tradition but delivered in the group's exuberant style, complete with tight harmonies and instrumental virtuosity. One of the biggest hits from the album, "This Romeo Ain't Got Julie Yet," revealed the group's weakness for puns but became a favorite with concert audiences, while "Oh Me, Oh My" showed off the band's sophisticated arrangements.

Diamond Rio has managed to combine its eclectic influences—ranging from bluegrass to rock to jazz—with a solid country foundation to become a riveting and highly successful band.

DIAMOND RIO

REAL NAMES: Marty Roe, Dana Williams, Brian Prout, Dan Truman, Gene Johnson, Jimmy Olander

FIRST HIT: "Meet in the Middle" (1991)

OTHER NOTABLE HITS: "In a Week or Two" (1992); "Nothing in This World" (1992); "I Was Made to Be with You" (1992); "This Romeo Ain't Got Julie Yet" (1992); "Mama Don't Forget to Pray for Me" (1992); "Mirror, Mirror" (1991); "Norma Jean Riley" (1991); "Nowhere Bound" (1991)

BEST ALBUMS: *Close to the Edge* (1992); *Diamond Rio* (1991)

AWARDS INCLUDE: Country Music Association Vocal Group of the Year (1993, 1992); Academy of Country Music Top Vocal Group (1992, 1991)

JOE · DIFFIE

Still relatively new on the list of up-and-coming male vocalists, Joe Diffie distinguished himself as a talented singer/songwriter only a couple of years ago. Since then he has mesmerized fans and critics alike with his powerful mountain-tenor vocals.

With three critically acclaimed albums under his belt—*A Thousand Winding Roads, Regular Joe,* and *Honky-Tonk Attitude*—plus a string of number-one singles and award nods, Diffie has rapidly become a country figure who caters to a large audience.

Although his hit songs, including "Home," "Is It Cold in Here," "If You Want Me To," "If the Devil Danced (In Empty Pockets)," and "Honky-Tonk Attitude," are fairly traditional, Diffie prefers not to be pigeonholed. He is neither the typical hat act, the pop-country performer, nor the on-edge artist.

Diffie's music and talent are perhaps best described with the titles of his three albums. His song material often takes the listener down roads and through situa-

Though many of his songs sound traditional, Joe Diffie cannot be described as a typical country artist.

tions that aren't always straight and narrow—"I'm not always Joe Brokenheart," he said of himself. "I like those songs that are, well, kind of rebellious in their own way, like 'I Can Walk the Line If It Ain't Too Straight.'"

Having experienced several life-changing triumphs and trials himself, Diffie's certainly the "regular Joe" type. But his emotion-packed music and sparkling personality can also create an atmosphere that's as rowdy, rip-roaring, and fun-loving as a crowded honky-tonk on a Saturday night.

His list of musical influences ranges from George Jones and Buck Owens to Merle Haggard. The legendary Tammy Wynette once remarked, "He's all my favorite country singers . . . rolled into one."

It was on New Year's Eve of 1990 that Diffie played his first big concert as a major recording artist—working with George Strait and Steve Wariner. From that point on, Diffie was unstoppable. Today, he can enjoy the distinct pleasure of helping newcomers who are opening for him.

Before Diffie landed a recording contract, he did what many aspiring country music artists do—he took on jobs in the Nashville area that would help him get a foot in the door. Diffie ultimately became one of Music City's top demo singers. His extraordinary talent and music business know-how finally got him where he wanted to be—in the studio recording the songs for his first album.

The singer's hits came almost instantly and prompted him to set

JOE DIFFIE

BORN: December 28, 1958, in Duncan, Oklahoma

MUSICAL INFLUENCES: George Jones, Buck Owens, Merle Haggard

FIRST HIT: "Home" (1991)

OTHER NOTABLE HITS: "Prop Me Up Against the Juke Box (When I Die)" (1994); "Honky-Tonk Attitude" (1993); "Is It Cold in Here" (1992); "Ships That Don't Come In" (1992); "If You Want Me To" (1991); "If the Devil Danced (In Empty Pockets)" (1991)

BEST ALBUMS: *Honky-Tonk Attitude* (1993); *A Thousand Winding Roads* (1990)

AWARDS INCLUDE: Country Music Association Vocal Event of the Year (with George Jones, et al., 1993)

ACHIEVEMENTS: Grand Old Opry member (1993)

PERSONAL: Arriving in Nashville in 1986, Diffie's next-door neighbor was Johnny Neal of the Allman Brothers Band, who helped Diffie secure a writing contract with a music company.

Diffie's hits include the hard-edged "Honky-Tonk Attitude" as well as the emotional ballad "Ships That Don't Come In."

the personal goal of improving his physical appearance. Diffie took an interest in getting rid of his lifelong weight problem. He went on a diet high in complex carbohydrates and low in fat and worked with a trainer, even while on the road. He eventually lost 30 pounds, went down four pant sizes, and proved to the world that he could not only sing like a winner but look like one as well.

Joe Diffie continues to take giant steps in both his music and his personal life, revealing a talent and drive that have just begun to assert themselves.

STEVE EARLE

Steve Earle is the restless heart of modern country music. He left his imprint on Nashville in 1986 with *Guitar Town*, an album that featured power-twang songs of the working class and drew critical comparisons with Bruce Springsteen and John Mellencamp. *Guitar Town* caused quite a stir in Nashville.

Steve Earle's high-energy music is often more rock than country. Earle hit the country charts in 1986 with his Guitar Town *album.*

Though it rode up the charts with relative ease, conservative industry officials felt it was too extreme for the country market. Fans accustomed to the work of such Nashville outsiders as Joe Ely and Jimmie Dale Gilmore, however, were impressed with the raw energy of Earle's sound. Unfortunately, Earle never lost his penchant for upsetting Nashville, which has affected the course of his career.

Earle was born January 17, 1955, in rural Texas. His father, an air-traffic controller, was often transferred around the San Antonio area. At age 14, Earle ran away from home to follow singer/songwriter Townes Van Zandt through Texas. Earle was on the road as a musician by age 16, married at 19, and in Nashville by 20, framing houses and digging swimming pools.

In 1981, after a second marriage, which took place at the Take 5 Bar in Nashville's Metro Airport (he has been married three times since), Earle left Nashville for what he described as "two tequila-drenched years" in Mexico.

He returned to Nashville in 1983 when he signed with CBS Records. After one album of neo-rockabilly tunes, Earle left the label. In 1986 he moved to MCA, garnering a seven-album deal. There, he followed up on the 1986 success of *Guitar Town* with 1988's *Exit 0*, in which the Dukes, Earle's roadhouse band, enjoyed a higher profile.

In 1989, Earle released *Copperhead Road*, a successful crossover album that incorporated the mandolin and other folk instruments and featured traditional Irish rockers the Pogues. Despite its hard-edged rock sound, *Copperhead Road* was rife with a rebellious hillbilly attitude. The story told in the title track, about a boot-legging family in the Deep South, seems torn from the pages of an Erskine Caldwell novel. By contrast, 1990's *The Hard Way* was a dark album that featured songs such as "Justice in Ontario," about abusive police, and "Billy Austin," about the death penalty.

Earle has always been more than happy to confound rock and country audiences. In the late 1980s he was an opening act for artists as diverse as the power-punk Replacements, country legend George Jones, and folk-rock icon Bob Dylan. He also played the Roxy and other Los Angeles rock clubs.

"There's a lot of technology now that can be used to make the message more powerful," Earle said in a 1986 interview. "But the main point is the song, and great country music's main point is always the song."

Earle's 1991 release, *Shut Up and Die Like an Aviator*, was a distorted live album recorded during a tour when rumors of the singer's failing health abounded. His career ran aground, and fans were forced to await further developments.

The year 1993 saw the release of a compilation album, *The Essential Steve Earle*, providing fans with a superb overview of Earle's MCA output. Featured on the album are such Earle hits as "Goodbye's All We've Got Left" and "Someday." The album was not strongly promoted, however, and Earle was still without a record deal. Later that year Earle scheduled four performances—at a Chicago area club— for the first time in three years. All four performances sold out in one day. Fans could only hope the long wait was finally over.

STEVE EARLE

BORN: January 17, 1955, near San Antonio, Texas

FIRST HIT: "Guitar Town" (1986)

OTHER NOTABLE HITS: "The Other Kind" (1990); "Nothing But a Child" (1989); "Copperhead Road" (1989); "The Rain Came Down" (1988); "Goodbye's All We've Got Left" (1987)

BEST ALBUMS: *Copperhead Road* (1988); *Guitar Town* (1986)

ACHIEVEMENTS: Number-one country album, *Guitar Town*, in 1986

PERSONAL: Earle has written short stories, collected motorcycles, framed houses, dug swimming pools, and co-owned a dirt-track race car, among other ventures. He is five-times divorced.

VINCE · GILL

For many years, Vince Gill was one of the best-kept secrets in Nashville. The stardom predicted for this highly respected singer/musician always seemed just beyond his grasp. Then in 1990, he released a tune called "When I Call Your

Vince Gill's talents include singing, songwriting, and instrumental work.

Name." The song went to the top of the charts and Gill became a country music star.

The only child of an Oklahoma City appellate judge, Gill credits his father, who played banjo and guitar, for piquing his interest in music. One of the first instruments young Vince played was his dad's banjo. An aspiring musician from an early age, Gill joined a local bluegrass band, Mountain Smoke, while still attending high school.

Word quickly spread about the budding young musician with the high, lonesome voice. Coincidentally, just as his musical reputation was formulating, Gill—an avid, accomplished golfer—was seriously considering a career in professional golf. The PGA was beckoning when Gill received an invitation to join a band called the Bluegrass Alliance, whose membership included bluegrass luminaries Sam Bush and Dan Crary. Loading his possessions into a van, Gill chose to follow his musical instincts and move to bluegrass country—Louisville, Kentucky.

Throughout the late 1970s, Gill paid his dues with a number of diverse bands and musical groups. In 1975, he joined Ricky Skaggs in a band called Boone Creek. The group struggled along with an innovative bluegrass style that featured steel guitar and drums. When Byron Berline invited Gill to join his group, Sundance, on the West Coast, the accomplished picker loaded up his van once more and headed to Los Angeles. The job with Sundance turned into a steady gig that lasted over two years before Gill changed bands once again. In 1978, the popular country-rock group Pure Prairie League held auditions for a new lead singer. Gill accompanied

Gill has recorded two duets with Reba McEntire, "Oklahoma Swing" and "The Heart Won't Lie."

a friend to the audition strictly out of curiosity. Mountain Smoke had opened for Pure Prairie League years before, and he wanted to see if the band members remembered him. Not only did they remember him, they offered him the job as lead singer. Gill's vocals, guitar playing, and songwriting guided Pure Prairie League to two top-ten hits, "Let Me Love You Tonight" and "Still Right Here in My Heart." Five of Gill's original compositions were included on the group's 1980 album, *Can't Hold Back.*

After Pure Prairie League's record sales began to slump and Gill's wife, Janis (who later founded Sweethearts of the Rodeo with sister Kristine Arnold), became pregnant. Gill left the group to join the Cherry Bombs, a band started by singer/songwriter Rodney Crowell.

Through his friendship with the members of Cherry Bombs, Gill landed his solo deal. Tony Brown, former keyboard player in the band, worked for RCA Records. Recognizing Gill's guitar mastery and distinctive voice, Brown signed him to the label. Shortly after moving to Nashville in 1984, Gill recorded his six-song mini-album, *Turn Me Loose.* The success of the title track and "Victim of Life's Circumstances" brought him his first taste of national acclaim as a solo artist.

Gill's second album, *The Things That Matter,* yielded two top-ten hits, "If It Weren't for Him" (a duet with Rosanne Cash) and "Oklahoma Borderline." Gill garnered more critical acclaim for *The Way Back Home,* his final album for RCA. One tune from that collection, "Everybody's Sweetheart," caught the attention of the Nashville music industry and set gossipy tongues wagging. Rumors circulated that Gill was jealous of his wife's successful career. He did write the tongue-in-cheek song about Janis, but as he explained to detractors, it was all in fun. Gill had, after all, helped Sweethearts of the Rodeo secure its record deal by taking the demo tapes to CBS Records.

Despite producing a steady string of hits, Gill failed to catch the attention of a broad range of fans, and RCA dropped him from its roster. Fortunately for Gill, Tony Brown, the man responsible for his RCA deal, had moved over to MCA Records. Still convinced that Gill could be a star, Brown signed him to MCA and became his producer.

With a new label and new producer, Gill found the freedom he needed

Janis Oliver

Janis Oliver, married to Vince Gill since 1979, is a performer in her own right. Janis is one of the two Sweethearts of the Rodeo, along with sister Kristine Arnold. Janis and Kristine grew up in suburban Los Angeles listening to the Byrds, eventually drawing on the group's highly influential 1968 album when it came time to choose a name for themselves. The Sweethearts's 1986 self-titled debut album produced five hit singles and attracted both country and rock audiences. *Buffalo Zone*, the pair's second album, was also well received. However, their third album, *Sisters*, apparently did not meet with CBS approval; it has since become an unreleased collector's item. Sweethearts of the Rodeo recently released a fourth album on the Sugar Hill label entitled *Rodeo Waltz*. This collection of songs accentuates a softer, more

bluegrass or folk side to the sisters' singing. As many fans know, Vince Gill's "I Still Believe in You" (1992) was written for Janis during the difficult time when Sweethearts was experiencing a career slump.

to utilize the full range of his musical talents on *When I Call Your Name*, Gill's first MCA album. It contained tunes ranging from dance hall swing to contemporary pop to rodeo songs. The first single, "Never Alone," which Gill wrote with Rosanne Cash, hit the top 20. The follow-up, "Oklahoma Swing," was an up-tempo, foot-tapping duet with Reba McEntire.

The popularity of "Oklahoma Swing" laid the groundwork for the overwhelming success of the album's title track. With Patty Loveless providing haunting harmony vocals, "When I Call Your Name" earned Gill his first number-one hit and a Grammy. In the fall of 1990, Gill gladly accepted the Country Music Assocation's Single of the Year award for "When I Call Your Name," starting a chain reaction of accolades and recognition.

Having proven his versatility with a wide range of songs on *When I Call Your Name*, Gill settled into a more clearly defined country style for his next album, *Pocket Full of Gold*, which was certified gold just five months after its release. The title tune, "Look at Us," and "Liza Jane" became instant hits.

Despite the popularity of these two albums, nothing prepared Gill for the enormous success of *I Still Believe in You*, released in late 1992. The album emphasized Gill's talents as a songwriter. He had set aside the first half of 1992 to compose material for the album, with the goal of touching on as many emotions as possible. The hard work yielded a finely crafted hit album that was not as resolutely traditional-sounding as *Pocket Full of Gold*.

The title song from *I Still Believe in You* was written by Gill with longtime friend John Jarvis. Though Gill is not a songwriter who tends to reveal the ups and downs of his personal life in his songs, he did write this love song with Janis in mind. The album features other ballads, including "No Future in the Past," as well as the upbeat "One More Last Chance" and the R&B-inspired "Nothin' Like a Woman."

Gill's professional good fortune stemming from the success of *I Still Believe in You* was marred by the death of his brother, Bob, and also by the passing of Conway Twitty. Gill had sung harmony on Twitty's albums for four years, and the death of the country legend marked the loss of a friend and mentor. Though Gill's 1994 album, *When Love Finds You*, does not directly refer to these tragedies, its concern for making the correct choices in life seems contemplative or reflective in tone. The powerful ballad "Whenever You Come Around" deals with communicating one's desires before it is too late, a theme relevant to Gill's life considering his personal losses.

Still an avid golfer, Gill, Janis, and their daughter, Jennifer, live in their dream house next to a golf course. Gill once joked that if he doesn't make it in music, he could still join the PGA.

VINCE GILL

BORN: April 12, 1957, in Norman, Oklahoma

FIRST HIT: "Victim of Life's Circumstances" (1984)

OTHER NOTABLE HITS: "Take Your Memory with You" (1992); "Liza Jane" (1991); "Pocket Full of Gold" (1991); "Look at Us" (1991); "Never Alone" (1990); "When I Call Your Name" (1989); "Turn Me Loose" (1984)

BEST ALBUMS: *I Still Believe in You* (1992); *Pocket Full of Gold* (1991); *When I Call Your Name* (1989); *The Way Back Home* (1987)

AWARDS INCLUDE: Grammy, Best Country Vocal Collaboration (1991); Grammy, Best Country Male Vocal Performance (1990); Academy of Country Music (ACM) Top Male Vocalist (1993, 1992); ACM Top New Male Vocalist (1984); Country Music Association (CMA) Entertainer of the Year (1993); CMA Male Vocalist of the Year (1993, 1992, 1991); CMA Vocal Event of the Year (with George Jones, et al., 1993; with Mark O'Connor & the New Nashville Cats, 1991)

ACHIEVEMENTS: Grand Ole Opry member (1991)

MERLE · HAGGARD

nyone who divides country music into camps of old and new is missing a critical point, one that Merle Haggard has hung his cowboy hat on for his entire career. A first-rate singer in the classic country style, Haggard has always had a commitment to preserving country music's traditional roots. Yet his greatest challenge has involved redefining that tradition.

Merle Haggard is a classic country singer who has risen to legendary status in the music industry.

Haggard's efforts to balance tradition and innovation have paid off. He has had over 40 number-one country hits, which is more than Hank Williams, Sr., and Johnny Cash combined. Haggard's 1973 confessional ballad "Today I Started Loving You Again" has been covered by some 400 artists. He has received 43 award nominations from the Country Music Association—more than any other male country entertainer. And, he has released over 65 albums.

Much of the material for Haggard's music came from his gritty past. In 1934, Haggard's parents spun out of the Dust Bowl in Oklahoma to settle in a Hoover camp in Oildale, California, near Bakersfield. The family was living in a converted boxcar when Merle was born on April 6, 1937.

Haggard's father got a job as a carpenter for the Santa Fe Railroad, a job that left a lasting impression on young Merle. To this day, Haggard's tour bus carries the Santa Fe Railroad logo. Haggard inherited his musical ability from his father, who played the fiddle—a pastime disapproved of by Mrs. Haggard, a devout Christian.

The death of Haggard's father undoubtedly contributed to Merle's rebellious youth. Merle started hopping short-line trains to run away from home, roaming all over the Southwest. About this time, he first heard the liberating yodel of Jimmie Rodgers.

"When I heard those Jimmie Rodgers songs, I felt it was something I had to do—hop some freights, and unconsciously go to prison, too," Haggard once said in a newspaper interview. "It's almost like there was a certain education I had to come by and certain things to get under my belt."

Haggard committed a number of petty crimes as a

Haggard's honky-tonk style has made him one of country's most influential artists.

teen. In 1957, Haggard landed in San Quentin Prison. Working in the prison textile mill, he began to repattern his life. Upon his release in 1960, Haggard returned to Bakersfield and began playing the country music he had heard and learned in prison.

Bakersfield was an active country music center at that time. Buck Owens was living and working there, as were other lesser-known but talented musicians. Here, Haggard met Fuzzy Owens, the man who is still his manager. Recording in a converted garage, they produced Haggard's first single, "Singing My Heart Out," for the Tally label in 1963. It sold 200 copies and received some local airplay. Later that same year, Haggard had his first hit with "Sing Me a Sad Song."

Hard Time

Haggard's father died in 1946, when Merle was just nine years old. Haggard's mother, Flossie, went to work as a bookkeeper to help support the family. This left young Merle on his own. By age 14, Merle had started running with a wild crowd. He was arrested a number of times, held in juvenile reformatories, and eventually wound up in prison at age 20, convicted of armed robbery. San Quentin turned out to be a turning point in Merle's life. It was there that he saw Johnny Cash perform, and it was there, too, that he spent time in solitary confinement and talked with inmates on death row. Haggard realized that he faced a clear choice—to continue in a life of crime or to make a new start. Shortly after his twenty-first birthday, which he spent in solitary confinement, Haggard started performing on the weekly *Warden's Show*. By the time Haggard was paroled from jail in 1960, he had two goals: to go straight and to work at a career in the music business.

Merle Haggard has had more than 40 number-one country hits and has been nominated by the CMA more than any other male artist.

In 1965, Haggard married Bonnie Owens, Buck Owens's former wife. This was Haggard's second marriage; his first wife was Leona Hobbs, with whom he had four children. Haggard also began a long and fruitful association with Capitol Records that same year. His first number-one hit, "I'm a Lonesome Fugitive," was released in 1966. This song ushered in a series of Haggard tunes about life in prison and as a fugitive. His 1968 song

"Mama Tried" was a reminiscence about his own mis-spent adolescence. When Haggard's prison record was made public, the authenticity of his songs became part of his mystique. By 1968, Haggard had established himself as a country music superstar.

From the first time Haggard walked on a stage, his style has been impossible to define. He has always played a kaleidoscope of pop, swing, blues, and what Haggard terms "country jazz." His innovative nine-piece band, the Strangers, developed new sounds as well. Recording on their own, the Strangers have won top honors as a touring band.

Haggard's songwriting topics gradually broadened to include social commentary. His 1969 song "Okie from Muskogee" defended small-town virtues against the vices of the turned-on generation. It became a theme song for the conservative Silent Majority and reputedly was a hit with then-President Richard Nixon, though Haggard claimed he wrote the song tongue-in-cheek. Haggard's tunes also chronicled middle-class economic woes. During the 1974 recession, he recorded "If We Make It Through December," which became a pop hit. The plight of the American farmer inspired Haggard's 1985 "Amber Waves of Grain."

In 1977, Haggard left Capitol to record for MCA. Although he had some hits while he was with MCA, he left the label for Epic in 1981. The following year Haggard teamed up with country music legend George Jones for *A Taste of Yesterday's Wine.* Haggard also recorded with outlaw Willie Nelson. The title song from their 1983 album, *Pancho and Lefty,* became a number-one hit. Epic's handling of the publicity for "Me and Crippled Soldiers" prompted Haggard to leave the label and sign with Curb Records in 1990. His first Curb album was *Blue Jungle. Merle Haggard 1994,* which included the autobiographical "Troubador" and "In My Next Life," confirmed his talents as country's premier songwriter.

Haggard's personal life remained turbulent through the years. Haggard divorced Bonnie Owens in 1978 and married Leona Williams, a backup singer with the Strangers. The couple separated in 1983. Later, Haggard married Debbie Parret, a marriage that also ended in divorce. Haggard is now married to Theresa Ann Lane; they have two children.

As the 1990s witnessed the explosion of country music and the rise of many young, talented performers, artists of Haggard's generation found it difficult to get radio airplay and industry attention. The business and marketing ends of country music seemed more interested in high-spirited, rock-influenced singers with pretty faces. Despite these obstacles, Merle Haggard remains a major inspiration to many young performers, from the tradition-based honky-tonk stylings of Clint Black to the gritty, rock-tinged sounds of Travis Tritt.

MERLE HAGGARD

BORN: April 6, 1937, in Bakersfield, California

FIRST HIT: "Sing Me a Sad Song" (1963)

OTHER NOTABLE HITS: "Big City" (1982); "Are the Good Times Really Over" (1981); "The Fightin' Side of Me (1970); "Okie from Muskogee" (1969); "Mama Tried" (1968); "I'm a Lonesome Fugitive" (1966); "All My Friends Are Gonna Be Strangers" (1965)

BEST ALBUMS: *A Friend in California* (1986); *Big City* (1981); *A Working Man Can't Get Nowhere Today* (1976); *The Fightin' Side of Me* (1970); *Okie from Muskogee* (1970); *Branded Man* (1968)

AWARDS INCLUDE: Grammy, Best Country Male Vocal Performance (1984); Country Music Association (CMA) Vocal Duo of the Year (with Willie Nelson, 1983); CMA Entertainer of the Year (1970); CMA Male Vocalist of the Year (1970); Academy of Country Music (ACM) Top Male Vocalist (1981, 1974, 1972, 1970, 1969, 1966); ACM Entertainer of the Year (1970); ACM Top Vocal Duet (with Bonnie Owens, et al., 1968; with Bonnie Owens, 1967, 1966, 1965); ACM Top New Male Vocalist (1965)

· FAITH · HILL

It's fitting that new country songstress Faith Hill hails from Star, Mississippi. With her Warner Bros. debut album, *Take Me As I Am*, soaring up the charts and two top-ten hits under her belt, including a record-breaking number-one sensation, the Mississippi native is giving the name Star a double identity.

Faith Hill's debut single, "Wild One," hit number one and earned her a place on the country scene.

Hill, the youngest of three children, grew up singing in church. She had formed her own band by age 17. "Singing just always made me happy," Hill told *Music*

City News. "It was just what I did. Some people played baseball and I sang."

Although the small-town opportunities were enough for a while, the singer soon realized she had to reach for a bigger star. When Hill turned 19, she left home and moved to Nashville.

Hill knew nothing of Music City except what she saw on television and heard on the radio. She had also followed the careers of some of her favorite performers, including Reba McEntire and Emmylou Harris.

As is true for most aspiring artists, stardom came neither easily nor quickly for the now 26-year-old. Naturally, she looked for a position in the music industry to better launch her career, but her musical aspirations kept getting in the way. Companies on Music Row wanted to hire someone who would devote themselves to the job, not someone whose real goal was to be a singer.

When Hill applied for a receptionist position at Gary Morris's publishing company, she specifically told the interviewer she was not a singer. Hill ultimately landed the job and worked for the company for over a year, learning as much as possible about the business side of country music.

An important breakthrough came when a local songwriter over-

FAITH HILL

BORN: September 26, 1967, in Star, Mississippi

MUSICAL INFLUENCES: Reba McEntire, Emmylou Harris, Patsy Cline, Amy Grant

FIRST HIT: "Wild One" (1993)

OTHER NOTABLE HITS: "Piece of My Heart" (1993); "Go the Distance" (1993)

BEST ALBUM: *Take Me As I Am* (1993)

AWARDS INCLUDE: Academy of Country Music Top New Female Vocalist (1993)

PERSONAL: Hill says her first paying job was for her mom, who, when Hill was still a child, used to pay her 25 cents to sing for houseguests or at small family reunions, and upped it to 50 cents for big family reunions.

Hill's talent was officially recognized in 1993, when she won the ACM's Top New Female Vocalist award.

heard Hill singing along with the radio at work and asked her to do a demo tape. Upon hearing the completed tape, Gary Morris was impressed too. The song Hill sang was "It Scares Me."

Afterward, the music industry seemed less scary. Hill eventually landed a spot singing backup for one of her favorite songwriters, Gary Burr, at Nashville's famed Bluebird Cafe. Shortly after, the singer signed with Warner Bros.

Hill's first single, the wildly successful "Wild One," made music history. The song held the number-one slot on the *Billboard* Country Chart for three consecutive weeks—a feat not accomplished by a newcomer's debut single since Jeannie C. Riley's "Harper Valley P.T.A." 25 years before. Hill's rapid success also garnered her widespread media attention. Her follow-up release—a remake of the Janis Joplin classic "Piece of My Heart"—traveled the same successful route.

Despite her move away from home, the turmoils of divorce, and some lean days in Music City, people are now taking Hill as she is— one of country music's newest stars.

ALAN · JACKSON

With his genuine honky-tonk vocals, songwriting gifts, and blond good looks, Alan Jackson seems like the quintessential country music star. He was born and raised in the small town of Newnan, Georgia, the youngest of five children born to a mechanic. Though financially strapped, Jackson's parents managed to instill a sense of self-worth and a strong set of values in their only son.

Alan Jackson quickly established himself in 1988 with the release of his debut album, Here in the Real World.

An auto enthusiast since he could walk, Jackson bought his first car at age 15—a 1955 Thunderbird, which he and his father rebuilt. Jackson's father worked for the Ford Motor Company and fostered his son's lifelong passion for motor vehicles. The Thunderbird was the only automobile Alan held onto for any length of time, selling it only when he was in his early 20s so he could make a down payment on a house.

As a teenager, Alan began performing duets with one of his buddies. The pair eventually put together a band and played on weekends. Jackson never considered a career in music at that time, because in Newnan—as in many small towns—it was expected that he'd do what everybody else did: He'd go to school, get married, and have a few children. A music career did not seem a realistic possibility.

At 17, the singer discovered another consuming passion: his beautiful blonde wife, Denise, whom he met in Newnan. Three years later, the couple married. They lived in Newnan for several years while Jackson tried to earn a living. After a series of jobs that included everything from building houses to waiting tables to driving a fork lift, Jackson decided to try his hand at a career in music, though he had no idea where to go or who to see. Jackson turned for inspiration to a friend who learned to fly small planes in the hope of becoming a jet pilot. Four or five years later, that friend had succeeded and was flying for a major airline. His friend's success triggered Jackson's aspirations to pursue his goal as well.

It was through Denise's occupation as a flight attendant that Jackson got his first real break in the music business. On a layover in Atlanta's airport, Denise spotted Glen Campbell and his band relaxing between flights. She walked up to the star and said, "Excuse

A traditional country singer, Jackson's heroes include George Jones, Merle Haggard, and Hank Williams.

me, my husband's about to move to Nashville to be a singer and songwriter. What does he need to do?" Campbell gave her a business card inscribed with his Nashville publishing company.

A contract was the eventual result, though it didn't happen overnight. After moving to Music City in 1985,

He then met Marty Gamblin, who managed Campbell's publishing company, Seventh Sun Music, and landed a writing deal with Seventh Sun. With a $100-a-week draw as a staff songwriter, Jackson was able to quit the mailroom job and put together his own band. Booked by Campbell's organization, Jackson and the band played honky-tonks all across the country, five sets a night, five nights a week. Despite the hectic schedule and the receptive audiences, Jackson failed to stir any interest with the record companies.

That changed when Jackson hooked up with a new manager, an Australian named Barry Coburn, who guided him to Arista Records. Arista had just opened a country division in Nashville headed by Tim DuBois, former manager and producer of Restless Heart, and a man known for his knack for discovering new talent. DuBois

Jackson's wife Denise (right) helped him land a songwriting contract in Nashville.

Jackson got a job at The Nashville Network mailroom and began playing gigs at local hotels in the evenings—all the while trying to make industry contacts. He became friends with Randy Travis when Travis was working as a singer and short-order cook at the Nashville Palace. Jackson recalls stopping by to congratulate Travis when his first records were taking off, wondering at the time if the same thing would happen to him.

Jackson's third album included "Chattahoochie," which remained on the charts for over a year.

Jackson has proven himself to be a talented songwriter and performer.

was looking for a new name to help launch the Nashville division, and he found his man in Alan Jackson. DuBois signed Jackson to the label in September 1989, and Jackson become the first artist to sign with the Arista country division.

Though Jackson's first single, "Blue Blooded Woman," enjoyed only modest success, his second, "Here in the Real World," blew the doors open, becoming the Georgia native's

first number-one hit. Jackson's first album, *Here in the Real World,* sold more than a million copies. He penned nine of the songs on this debut album, proving that the countless hours he spent polishing his songwriting skills at Seventh Sun paid off. Released in 1990, the album's success pushed Jackson into the limelight with several other young country singers, including Garth Brooks and Clint Black. The resulting media hype about "hunks in hats" detracted from the talents of these performers by lumping them together and tagging them as country heartthrobs. Actually, the styles of these performers are quite diverse, with Jackson's style clearly the one based most in traditional, mountain-flavored country music.

Jackson has earned multiple awards, including the ACM's Album of the Year in 1991 and 1993.

Success has not seemed to change Alan Jackson. He remains focused on his family and has a modest, down-to-earth manner.

Jackson's second album, *Don't Rock the Jukebox*, helped distinguish him from other so-called "hat acts" by showcasing his pure country voice and firmly establishing him as a solid traditionalist. Several songs explored his musical roots and honored his influences. "Just Playin' Possom" featured an aural cameo by George Jones, who also made a guest appearance in the "Don't Rock the Jukebox" video. "Walkin' the Floor Over Me" was both a reference to the country standard by Ernest Tubb as well as a twist on it. In "Midnight in Montgomery," Jackson offered a soulful meditation about how the spirit of Hank Williams looms large in every country singer's career. The video for the latter perfectly captured the haunting lyrics and was named Video of the Year at the Country Music Association and TNN Music City News award shows. *Don't Rock the Jukebox*, which was eventually certified double platinum, propelled Jackson to country music stardom.

Jackson's third effort, the critically acclaimed *A Lot About Livin' (And a Little 'Bout Love)*, outdistanced its predecessors by reaching triple-platinum status. The album, which spawned five singles, including "She's Got the Rhythm (And I Got the Blues)" and "Chat-

tahoochee," was released in 1992 but remained on the charts for well over a year. "Chattahoochee" became the biggest hit, garnering several awards from various country music organizations.

Now a certified country music superstar, Jackson has enjoyed personal as well as professional highlights in recent times. Happily married for many years, Alan and Denise have two daughters. Jackson's career highs include being inducted into the Grand Ole Opry in 1991 and performing for President George Bush. With friend and fellow country star Randy Travis, he cowrote "A Better Class of Losers," "Forever Together," and "She's Got the Rhythm (And I Got the Blues)," pointing to the potential for a powerful and creative partnership.

Noted for his live stage show, Jackson has one of country music's most state-of-the-art stage setups. His "A Lot About Livin' " quarter-million-dollar production included two video walls projecting footage of the singer and his band, the Strayhorns, with special segments of his music videos.

Despite the high-tech stage show, the awards, and the acclaim, Jackson demonstrates time and again a refreshingly humble and down-to-earth attitude. And if all the fame and prosperity were snatched from him, he believes he'd just carry on: "I'd earn a living somehow, I guess. The main thing is just to have my family. . . . I'm sure we could survive because, in a lot of ways, I miss the simple life."

ALAN JACKSON

BORN: October 17, 1958, in Newnan, Georgia

MUSICAL INFLUENCES: George Jones, Merle Haggard, Hank Williams

FIRST HIT: "Blue Blooded Woman" (1989)

OTHER NOTABLE HITS: "Chattahoochee" (1993); "Midnight in Montgomery" (1992); "Dallas" (1991); "Don't Rock the Jukebox" (1991); "Chasin' That Neon Rainbow" (1990); "Here in the Real World" (1989)

BEST ALBUMS: *A Lot About Livin' (And a Little 'Bout Love)* (1992); *Don't Rock the Jukebox* (1991); *Here in the Real World* (1990)

AWARDS INCLUDE: Country Music Association (CMA) Single of the Year (1993); CMA Music Video of the Year (1993, 1992); CMA Vocal Event of the Year (with George Jones, et al., 1993); CMA Triple Play Award (1992, 1991, 1990); Academy of Country Music (ACM) Single of the Year (1993, 1991); ACM Album of the Year (1993, 1991); ACM Top New Male Vocalist (1990)

ACHIEVEMENTS: Grand Ole Opry member (1991)

·WAYLON· ·JENNINGS·

During the 1970s, restlessness invaded the country music scene. On one side of Nashville, Waylon Jennings, Willie Nelson, and Kris Kristofferson were experimenting with a hybrid of country and rock that would lead to the outlaw movement. On the other side of town, producer Billy Sherrill's

Waylon Jennings and Willie Nelson helped change country music with their outlaw movement.

lush, suburban string arrangements in such period hits as Charlie Rich's "Behind Closed Doors" were helping country cross over to pop.

Jennings dipped his toe in the outlaw pool as early as 1973, when he recorded *Honky-Tonk Heroes,* an album of Billy Joe Shaver covers. Shaver was a spirited Texas songwriter whose iconoclastic themes were perfect for Jennings's deep and surly vocals.

The album served as a turning point not only for Jennings but also for Nashville music in general. Some of the songs on *Honky-Tonk Heroes* used no more than three instruments, which was a major departure from what was going on in Nashville at the time. Even *Rolling Stone* magazine took notice. The publication, then an alternative rock 'n' roll magazine, gave *Honky-Tonk Heroes* high marks.

Waylon Jennings was born on June 15, 1937, in Littlefield, Texas, into a musical family. His father, William Albert Jennings, was a sharecropper and a truck driver who also played guitar and harmonica in a local band. But it was Jennings's mother who taught him his first guitar chords. By the age of 12, Jennings had begun appearing as a disc jockey on a local radio station.

Jennings left school in the 10th grade (he earned his General Educational Development certificate

Early in his career, Jennings toured with Buddy Holly as his bass player.

Honky-Tonk Heroes, *Jennings's third album, was released in 1973. The singer won the CMA's Male Vocalist of the Year in 1975.*

in 1989). The Jennings family moved to Lubbock, Texas, where in 1955 Jennings met Buddy Holly. Holly hired Jennings in 1958 as a bass guitar player and produced Jennings's first single, "Jole Blon." "Buddy was the first guy to have any faith in me as a singer," Jennings once stated. "He was a rhythm guitar picker and that's basically what I am. He taught me that you can take country songs and put different rhythms to them."

Holly died on February 3, 1959, in a plane crash near Mason City, Iowa, along with J.P. "The Big Bopper" Richardson and Ritchie Valens. Jennings was supposed to have been on the plane, too. His survival is a part of rock 'n' roll legend—he gave up his seat at the last minute to his boss, Richardson.

It took Jennings a long time to recover from the shock, but by 1964 he was headlining in Phoenix, Arizona. In 1965, he was signed to Los Angeles-based A&M Records by trumpet player Herb Alpert, who was trying to push Jennings in a pop direction. "He loved my singing," Jennings quipped. "Only problem was, he was hearin' me and thinkin' of Al Martino, while I was hearin' Flatt & Scruggs."

Chet Atkins offered Jennings an RCA contract, which the singer signed later that year. His first album, *Folk Country,* was one of thirty he would do for the label. In 1969, he and a vocal group called the Kim-

In 1985, Jennings, Willie Nelson, Johnny Cash, and Kris Kristofferson recorded the Highwayman *album.*

berleys recorded a left-field version of songwriter Jimmy Webb's "MacArthur Park." This earned Jennings the first of his two Grammys for best group vocal performance (Jennings won his second in 1978 for his duet with Willie Nelson, "Mammas, Don't Let Your Babies Grow Up To Be Cowboys").

Real stardom eluded Jennings until the 1970s, when he took control of the style of his recordings. He insisted on recording with his own band, the Waylors—unheard

Jennings recorded Wanted: the Outlaws *with wife Jessi Colter (left), Willie Nelson, and Tompall Glaser.*

Waylon Jennings's hard-edged outlaw sound changed the course of country music in the 1970s.

of in Nashville, where sessions musicians were most often used. Other notable albums followed: He recorded *Good-Hearted Woman* in 1972 and *Honky-Tonk Heroes* in 1973. In 1975, Jennings was rewarded for his hard work when he was named Male Vocalist of the Year by the Country Music Association.

Then in 1976, Jennings got together with Jessi Colter (his wife), Willie Nelson, and Tompall Glaser to record the landmark album *Wanted: The Outlaws*. This album's massive popularity turned Nashville upside down. It was the first Nashville-recorded album ever to go platinum, it was named the CMA Album of the Year, and it became a top-ten pop album. "Good-Hearted Woman," a Jennings-Nelson duet from the album, earned the CMA Vocal Duo of the Year and Single of the Year awards.

Waylon Jennings was now a superstar. He rejoined Willie Nelson to record *Waylon & Willie*, another platinum album and a major hit on both the country and pop charts. His 1979 *Greatest Hits* album sold more than four million copies. In 1986, Jennings teamed up with Nelson, Johnny Cash, and Kris Kristofferson to produce the best-selling *Highwayman*.

Jennings left RCA in 1985, and then jumped from one major label to another. He actually recorded very little in the late 1980s, preferring to concentrate on performing.

In the summer of 1993, Jennings surprised fans and critics alike when he released a children's album called *Cowboys, Sisters, Rascals & Dirt*. Jennings wrote all the songs on the album from the perspective of a five-year-old boy. The inspiration for this unusual musical collection came from Waylon's devotion to his seven children, particularly his youngest son, Shooter. The album revealed a softer side to the gruff-looking outlaw, whose image as a hard-living rebel had been enhanced by a long-standing addiction to cocaine during the 1970s and 1980s—an addiction Jennings kicked without the aid of a treatment center.

Also in 1993, RCA contacted Jennings for help in putting together a boxed set of his earlier recordings, *Only Daddy That'll Walk the Line: The RCA Years*. Jennings was impressed with the musical integrity of the new management at RCA and agreed to come back and begin recording again.

Though Jennings's colorful outlaw persona stands out, it shouldn't overshadow the importance of his career to country music. With fellow outlaw Willie Nelson, Jennings fought against the conservative Nashville sounds and styles of the 1970s that depended on lush string arrangements and pop influences. In insisting on recording with his own band instead of relying on sessions musicians, he helped change the way things were done in Music City. And Waylon Jennings has clearly influenced those current performers, including Travis Tritt, who prefer "a little drive in their country."

WAYLON JENNINGS

BORN: June 15, 1937, in Littlefield, Texas

FIRST HIT: "Stop the World (And Let Me Off)" (1965)

OTHER NOTABLE HITS: "Highwayman" (with Johnny Cash, et al., 1985); "I've Always Been Crazy" (1978); "Luckenbach, Texas" (with Willie Nelson, 1977); "Good Hearted Woman" (with Willie Nelson, 1976); "Only Daddy That'll Walk the Line" (1968)

BEST ALBUMS: *Too Dumb for New York City, Too Ugly for L.A.* (1992); *Never Could Toe the Mark* (1984); *Music Man* (1980); *Ol' Waylon* (1977); *Wanted: The Outlaws* (with Willie Nelson, et al., 1976); *Honky-Tonk Heroes* (1973); *Good Hearted Woman* (1972)

AWARDS INCLUDE: Grammy, Best Country Vocal Performance by a Duo or Group (with Willie Nelson, 1978; with the Kimberleys, 1969); Academy of Country Music Single of the Year (with Willie Nelson, et al., 1985); Country Music Association (CMA) Album of the Year (with Willie Nelson, 1976); CMA Vocal Duo of the Year (with Willie Nelson, 1976); CMA Male Vocalist of the Year (1975)

·GEORGE· ·JONES·

Deep in the timbre of a George Jones song, you can hear the very soul of country music. The absolute purity of Jones's vocals assures that his style will never go out of fashion. Still in good voice even in his sixties, George Jones is one of country music's greatest male singers.

Jones's four Country Music Association Male Vocalist of the Year awards span two decades—he won in 1962 and 1963, when the award was still voted on by coun-

George Jones is one of the top names in country music, joining the ranks of Hank Williams and Ernest Tubb.

try disc jockeys, and in 1980 and 1981. He sings from the most cobwebbed corners of his heart. His textured voice communicates an unrelenting tension, his authoritative range running like a railroad train between honky-tonk and sorrow.

Jones's trademark is his playful country flutter. The alternating low moans and high wails lend an intensity to his singing that is very much evidenced in such classics as 1986's "Wine-Colored Roses."

George Glenn Jones was born on September 12, 1931, in rural Saratoga, Texas, in the "Big Thicket" region near Beaumont, Texas. He first learned to play the guitar from one of his Sunday school teachers. As Jones recalls, "I would go with Sister Annie and Brother Berle Stevens into this little town called Kuntz, Texas. Every Saturday afternoon, we'd sit inside the car with loudspeakers on the outside. Sister Annie would play guitar and I'd sing harmony with her or she'd sing harmony with me."

Jones's mother, Clara, was a very religious woman who played organ and piano in church. George Washington Jones, Jones's father, was a hard-living truck driver and pipe fitter. On the side, he played a little "square dancin' guitar," as Jones puts it. Clara was a Pentecostal who often shielded young George and his six brothers from the fallout of their father's drinking binges.

As a youngster, Jones listened to the *Grand Old Opry* on KRIC in Beaumont, Texas. Hank Williams, Sr., came to town in 1949 to play live on KRIC. Williams sang "Wedding Bells" with Eddie and Pearl, the husband-and-wife house band that featured an excitable 19-year-old George Jones on electric guitar. Jones was so nervous about

Jones recorded his first song, "Why Baby Why," in 1955. He later joined the Louisiana Hayride and then the Grand Ole Opry.

playing behind Williams that he never hit a note. "Hank sat and talked with us like he knew us his whole life," Jones remembers. "I worshiped him. His style was all in the feeling. He could sing anything and it would make you sad, but an up-tempo thing could make you happy."

And Jones's early recordings were happy. In 1953, the year Jones was discharged from the U.S. Marines, he signed with the Houston-based Starday label, for whom he recorded such hits as "Why Baby Why" and "Uh Uh No." But he followed up with raw rockabilly singles, such as "Rock It" and his own version of "Heart-

George Jones's versatile honky-tonk sometimes exhibits a hard-edged, rockabilly sound. Jones is also known for his country ballads.

break Hotel" (recorded under the pseudonym Thumper Jones to avoid upsetting traditional country fans). In fact, Jones's first number-one record, "White Lightnin' " (on Mercury Records), was written by rockabilly star J.P. "The Big Bopper" Richardson in 1959.

The Starday material was recorded in a living room. Egg crates were installed along the walls to help the sound and to keep out the noise of the trucks going by outside. But it was the rockabilly sound of those records that would later upset Jones the most. In retrospect, he felt so bad about playing rockabilly music that he once tried to buy up all the old Starday masters so people couldn't hear them. He felt he had betrayed his country roots.

After several years with Mercury, Jones signed a contract with United Artists Records, where he produced such top-ten hits as 1962's "She Thinks I Still Care" and the 1964 crossover hit "The Race Is On." In 1963, he released a duet with talented Melba Montgomery called "We Must Have Been Out of Our Minds." He recorded for Musicor Records between 1965 and 1971, releasing such hits as "Take Me" (1965), "Walk Through This World with Me" (1967), and "A Good Year for Roses" (1970).

George Jones's high-profile romance with Tammy Wynette began in 1967.

Their relationship can be chronicled in their song titles of the time, from George's hit "I'll Share My World with You" to Tammy's "Stand By Your Man."

In 1971, Jones switched to Wynette's label, Epic, where he started a decades-long relationship with producer Billy Sherrill. Jones and Wynette recorded a series of duets, including 1973's "Let's Build a World Together" and "We're Gonna Hold On." "Golden Ring" and "Near You" came out in 1976, the year after the couple divorced. Altogether, Jones and Wynette recorded some

George and Tammy

One of country music's most famous marriages is that of George Jones to Tammy Wynette. Jones and Wynette met in 1967 when both were playing the same package tour. Wynette was in a troubled marriage at the time, and she and Jones became romantically involved. The relationship caused a big stir—so much so that the two announced their marriage six months before the ceremony actually took place. When Jones released "I'll Share My World with You" in 1969, there was little doubt that he was singing it to Tammy Wynette. The record went to number two, bested on the charts only by Wynette's "Stand by Your Man." Jones and Wynette married in 1969, the same year they joined the Opry. The two were hailed as Mr. and Mrs. Country Music. Their union produced a daughter, Georgette. It also produced a number of hit singles (duets). The marriage grew stormy, however, when first Wynette and

then Jones began to enjoy greater success than the other, and as Jones's drinking bouts became worse. Wynette divorced Jones in 1975; she remarried the next year, just as the Jones/Wynette duets "Golden Ring" and "Near You" went to the top of the charts.

"I Don't Need Your Rockin' Chair," a joint effort from Jones and several other artists, was named the CMA's Vocal Event of the Year in 1993.

albums and more than a dozen hit singles together.

By this time, Jones's life was acquiring the characteristics of a country music song. Unfortunately, he had acquired his father's taste for alcohol. After missing 54 concerts—earning him the nickname of "No-Show Jones"—he filed for bankruptcy in 1979 and checked himself into a hos-

pital. He attempted to dry out again in 1982, but in 1983 he was arrested in Mississippi for cocaine possession and public intoxication. The next day he flipped his car and nearly killed himself. His weight had dropped from 160 to 105 pounds. Texas singer/songwriter Ray Wylie Hubbard tried to sing some sense into Jones by writing the song, "George, Put Down That Drink."

Though drinking was ruining his career, he managed some notable hits during this period. "He Stopped Loving Her Today" earned Jones the Country Music

Jones credits his wife, Nancy Sepulveda Jones, for helping him conquer alcoholism and cocaine addiction.

Association's Male Vocalist of the Year and Single of the Year awards for 1980 and 1981. He also recorded duets with a diverse range of artists. Duets with Linda Ronstadt, Emmylou Harris, Willie Nelson, Elvis Costello, and others were featured on the 1979 album *My Very Special Guests.* Jones recorded the popular "Yesterday's Wine" with Merle Haggard in 1982.

The terminally shy Jones credits much of his survival to his fourth wife, Nancy Sepulveda Jones. The Louisiana native met him in 1980 at a Jones concert in upstate New York. The couple married in 1983. Following some abortive attempts at reform, Jones did some solid thinking and finally weaned himself from the bottle. He has been sober since 1986. Today, George and Nancy Jones live in a modern mansion in Brentwood, a suburb of Nashville.

In 1991, Jones terminated his 20-year association with Epic and signed with MCA. His first disc, *And Along Came Jones,* proved Jones was as strong as ever. Released that year, it contained the hit "If You Couldn't Get the Picture, Maybe You Can Read the Writing on the Wall." He was elected to the Country Music Hall of Fame in 1992.

Jones shows no signs of slowing down after nearly four decades of singing. The appropriately titled "I Don't Need Your Rockin' Chair," a record and video Jones released in 1992, won the Country Music Association's Vocal Event of the Year award in 1993. The song and video featured the participation of many of country's latest stars, including Alan Jackson, Clint Black, Joe Diffe, Mark Chesnutt, Patty Loveless, Pam Tillis, and Travis Tritt, who were thrilled at the opportunity to contribute their talents to the work of a master. Though at one point his friends thought he'd never live to age 60, George Jones has survived to become a living legend and a guiding force for new country singers.

Jones's life experiences have influenced his music, his distinctive style has influenced other country artists.

GEORGE JONES

BORN: September 12, 1931, in Saratoga, Texas

FIRST HIT: "Why Baby Why" (1955)

OTHER NOTABLE HITS: "I Don't Need Your Rockin' Chair" (1992); "Wine-Colored Roses" (1986); "He Stopped Loving Her Today" (1980); "Bartender's Blues" (1978); "The Race Is On" (1964); "She Thinks I Still Care" (1962); "White Lightnin'" (1959)

BEST ALBUMS: *High-Tech Redneck* (1994); *And Along Came Jones* (1991); *One Woman Man* (1989); *Encore-George Jones & Tammy Wynette* (1981); *Still the Same Ole Me* (1981); *Burn the Honky-Tonk Down* (1970); *White Lightnin'* (1960)

AWARDS INCLUDE: Grammy, Best Country Male Vocal Performance (1980); Country Music Association (CMA) Vocal Event of the Year (1993); CMA Music Video of the Year (1986); CMA Male Vocalist of the Year (1981, 1980, 1963, 1962); Academy of Country Music Top Male Vocalist (1980)

ACHIEVEMENTS: Country Music Hall of Fame inductee (1992); Grand Ole Opry member (1969)

·WYNONNA · JUDD·

After ten years of singing and performing professionally, Wynonna Judd has stayed on top despite continual change in her personal life and career. She has matured from child to adult. She has shifted from a duo career with her mother, Naomi, to a successful solo career. Perhaps most

Wynonna Judd first performed with her mother, Naomi, as the Judds. When her mother retired, Wynonna ventured out on her own.

important, she has experienced the excitement of making a dream come true. Wynonna, who prefers to go by her first name as a solo artist, has soared from ground level to the sky.

Her solo career began with her debut project, *Wynonna*, in 1992. This collection of rock, blues, and gospel-flavored country tunes sold three million copies, yielded four number-one singles, and garnered rave reviews. Wynonna's follow-up album, *Tell Me Why*, also had healthy sales.

Before Wynonna's solo launch, Naomi Judd was forced to retire from the mother-daughter duo, the

Wynonna's solo efforts have won many new fans and earned her the ACM Top Female Vocalist award in 1993.

Generally known only as Wynonna, the singer performed with Clint Black in 1993, on their "Black & Wy" tour.

Judds, because of chronic hepatitis contracted during her earlier nursing career. This news not only dampened the spirits of millions of country fans, but also made Wynonna apprehensive. Although many had said that she could be successful on her own, doubts still lingered.

While Naomi and Wynonna Judd gained country music fame, sister Ashley (left) worked on a Hollywood acting career.

"I never in a million years thought I'd be on my own," said Wynonna. "It just wasn't in my makeup—because everything we did, we did together."

But the effort was a success. Wynonna made her first public appearance on network television at the American Music Awards, performing her album's first

The Judds

Now a solo performer in her own right, with top awards and hits to prove it, Wynonna first experienced success as part of the mother/daughter duo, the Judds. The Judds' big break came when Naomi gave one of the duo's demo tapes (made on a $30 tape recorder) to a record producer whose daughter was in Naomi's nursing care. This led to an audition for RCA, where the two sang the 1936 bluegrass ballad, "The Sweetest Gift." RCA immediately signed them and within a year they were scoring on the country music charts. The Judds' first single, "Had a Dream About You, Baby," broke into the top 20, while their follow-up, "Mama He's Crazy," hit number one. The Judds went on to sell more than ten million albums in an eight-year career, with every album going gold or better. The duo garnered country music's top awards, including the CMA's prestigious Vocal Group of the Year Award several years in a row, as well as a handful of Grammys. When

Naomi was diagnosed with untreatable chronic hepatitis in 1990, she announced her retirement. The Judds embarked on a year-long farewell tour that culminated in a wildly successful cable broadcast on December 4, 1991.

single, "She Is His Only Need." Copies of the single were sent to radio stations that night. By the end of the following day, solo artist Wynonna was already a radio sensation.

Before all the gold and platinum albums, number-one singles, and awards, life for Wynonna and her family wasn't quite so glamorous. Wynonna was born Christina Claire Ciminella in Ashland, Kentucky, but moved with her family to Hollywood because her father, Michael, had accepted a job in the area. Michael and Naomi were divorced while in California. After living on the West Coast for about seven years, the mother and two daughters—Wynonna and Ashley (now a successful actress)—returned to Kentucky and settled near the small town of Morrill.

By the time Wynonna was 12, her

Wynonna's self-titled debut album in 1992 established her position as a successful solo artist.

powerful vocal talent was beyond a doubt. She got her first guitar and began singing around the house with her mother and occasionally at a local church. During her senior year in high school, Wynonna was voted "Most Talented" in her class.

The family returned to the West Coast—this time living in Marin County, where Naomi attempted to complete her nursing degree. She hoped this would land her a good job and enable her and her daughters to move to the Nashville area. The three moved to Franklin, Tennessee, near Nashville, in 1979. Naomi worked as a nurse in Williamson County.

Even before Wynonna's high school graduation, the mother-and-daughter team had already begun finding its way around the Nashville music scene. One of their first public engagements required getting up at 3:30 A.M. to make early-morning appearances on *The Ralph Emery Show* on local TV. (Unable to remember their names, but recollecting that Naomi made her own lye soap, host Emery dubbed the pair the "Soap Sisters.") Eventually, Wynonna's strong voice and her mother's contributing harmony landed the two a series of auditions.

The period between the Judds' first number-one record and Wynonna's solo career was a time not only of growing success but of personal growth and maturity.

In Naomi Judd's biography, Love Can Build a Bridge, *Wynonna is painted as a natural-born rebel.*

It has been said that even after the Judds were first signed to RCA Records, Wynonna's sincerity and commitment to her career was not always what it could be. She was still young and thought life should be lived with carefree abandon. This laxity came into conflict with her mother's strong persistence. There were several spats, and once Naomi asked her daughter to move out. The departure from home was brief.

"I was 17 when we first met people on Music Row," Wynonna remembered. "I didn't know any better. I had the attention span of a flea. I knew I wanted to play my guitar and that was all. It wasn't until probably the last couple of years that I really started to understand the incredible miracle we got away with."

When she launched her solo career, she had the drive to give it her all. The responsibility of her first album started to build while the Judds were still on their "Love Can Build a Bridge" farewell tour. For the first time, Wynonna had to juggle the tour, select songs for her solo album, and deal with her mother's upcoming retirement from the musical stage. The experience made her a stronger person.

Wynonna's solo music struck an entirely different vein, revealing a strong rhythm-and-blues influence from her idol, Bonnie Raitt. Soon after its release, Wynonna saw her first album soar on the country charts, as well as *Billboard*'s Top 200. *Tell Me Why*, which features the hits "Tell Me

Wynonna simply cannot be matched in terms of vocal ferocity.

Why" and "Rock Bottom," has been equally successful. Wynonna refers to *Tell Me Why* as her "gypsy album" because of the diversity of the material. The songs range from the boogie beat of Mary Chapin Carpenter's "Girls with Guitars" to Naomi Judd's slow, bluesy "That Was Yesterday."

Wynonna's solo career came at a time when other female country performers were invading the industry. She has benefited from the success of a peer group that includes Carpenter, Kathy Mattea, and Trisha Yearwood just as they have benefited from her career.

WYNONNA JUDD

REAL NAME: Christina Claire Ciminella

BORN: May 30, 1964, in Ashland, Kentucky

MUSICAL INFLUENCES: old-time bluegrass performers Hazel and Alice, the Delmore Brothers, the Stanley Brothers, the Louvin Brothers, Bonnie Raitt

FIRST HIT: "She Is His Only Need" (1992)

OTHER NOTABLE HITS: "Tell Me Why" (1993); "Rock Bottom" (1993); "I Saw the Light" (1992); "No One Else on Earth" (1992); "My Strongest Weakness" (1992); "A Bad Goodbye" (with Clint Black, 1992)

BEST ALBUMS: *Tell Me Why* (1993); *Wynonna* (1992)

AWARDS INCLUDE: Academy of Country Music Top Female Vocalist (1993)

PERSONAL: Wynonna's sister is actress Ashley Judd.

·HAL · KETCHUM·

O ne of the best examples of country music's diversity in the 1990s is the enormous success of Hal Ketchum. Hailing from upstate New York, Ketchum describes his unique style as—aptly enough—"American music." *Past the Point of Rescue*, Ketchum's first album on the Curb Records label, was a standout effort, full of insightful and lyrically rich songs, many of which he wrote. The tune "Small Town Saturday Night" with its mesmerizing video blew open the doors of success for Ketchum. With that and other chart-toppers, including "I Know Where Love Lives," "Five O'Clock World," and the title track, his debut disc sold more than half a million copies.

Ketchum's second album on the same label, *Sure Love*, is imbued with the same poetry and eclecticism. His memorable "Some Place Far Away" views life through

Hal Ketchum's debut single, "Small Town Saturday Night," hit number one in 1991.

a child's eyes, and another song, "Daddy's Oldsmobile," again from a child's perspective, addresses the problem of homelessness. In keeping with Ketchum's penchant for honest, from-the-heart vocals, there's also "Trail of Tears," inspired by a series of meetings Ketchum had with Native Americans.

Ketchum grew up in Greenwich, New York, a tiny town located in the Adirondack Mountains near the Vermont border. Influenced by his banjo-playing father, the young Ketchum started his career in music by playing the drums. He was performing in a rhythm-and-blues trio by age 15. Though influenced by the traditional sounds of country stalwarts Merle Haggard and George Jones, Ketchum was swept away by such folk and rock artists as Van Morrison and Jonathan Edwards.

As an adult, Ketchum moved to Florida. He worked as a carpenter's helper and played drums part-time. In 1981, he relocated once more, this time to Texas, where the unique sounds of Southwestern-style country music caught his attention. He attended performances of Lyle Lovett and Townes Van Zandt and became enthralled with the local music scene. In Austin, Ketchum perfected his songwriting and gained enough confidence in his work to make trips to Nashville to test the musical waters.

In 1986, the singer recorded a collection of his own material for an independent album entitled *Threadbare Alibis*. Released by Line Records in Europe and by Watermelon Records in the States, the album helped pave the way for his subsequent fame.

After his first big publishing deal—with Nashville's Forerunner

Ketchum's unique sound has been influenced by traditional country and folk styles.

Music—was inked, Ketchum's personal life took a decided twist. The divorced father of two met Forerunner executive Terrell Tye and fell head over heels in love. They married in 1991.

The new business arrangement attracted the attention of Curb Records executive Dick Whitehouse. Whitehouse was duly impressed with Ketchum's folksy vocal style and songwriting prowess. A recording contract was soon signed.

With a gold-selling album under his belt, Ketchum showed no signs of jitters when he recorded *Sure Love*. With its invigorating title track and such additional hits as "Mama Knows the Highway," it was clear that, as an artist, Ketchum had arrived.

HAL KETCHUM

BORN: April 9, 1953, in Greenwich, New York

MUSICAL INFLUENCES: George Jones, Buck Owens, Merle Haggard, Van Morrison, Robert Johnson, Duke Ellington

FIRST HIT: "Small Town Saturday Night" (1991)

OTHER NOTABLE HITS: "Sure Love" (1992); "Hearts Are Gonna Roll" (1992); "Mama Knows the Highway" (1992); "Past the Point of Rescue" (1991); "I Know Where Love Lives" (1991); "Five O'Clock World" (1991)

BEST ALBUMS: *Sure Love* (1992); *Past the Point of Rescue* (1991)

ACHIEVEMENTS: Grand Ole Opry member (1994)

PERSONAL: Ketchum is married to Forerunner Music head Terrell Tye.

·ALISON· KRAUSS

Talented bluegrass performer Alison Krauss and her band, Union Station, show off their Grammy Awards.

Alison Krauss has moved the popularity of bluegrass music from the back burner up to full boil in just a few short years. This young singer and ace fiddler has racked up more accolades than many performers do in a lifetime. Inducted into the Grand Ole Opry in 1993, just shy of her 22nd birthday, she is the first bluegrass artist in 19 years to receive such an honor. "It's so great to see that the Opry feels that bluegrass music is still very important to what's going on," Krauss told *The Tennessean.*

Krauss's Opry induction falls on the heels of a string of awards, including a couple of Grammys, the International Bluegrass Music Association's Entertainer of the Year award, and several acclamations in the music video world. Her "I've Got That Old Feeling" video reached number one on Country Music Television and remained in heavy rotation on The Nashville Network—a rare feat for an independent artist who performs a regional style of music rather than conventional, Nashville-flavored country.

"It could've happened with any band," Alison told *Music City News* magazine. "We just had the first video out that introduced a lot of people to traditional bluegrass. I don't think it necessarily has a lot to do with me personally. It's the music that people are digging."

The music that Krauss is referring to is bluegrass, one of country's most easily recognizable styles. Developed in Kentucky, bluegrass music utilizes banjos, mandolins, guitars, and unamplified steel guitars (dobros). All the instruments are played acoustically, with the five-string banjo dominating. Alternating instrumental solos are a featured part of bluegrass as are two-, three-, and four-part harmony. The tempo is lightning quick compared to that of mainstream country. Traditional bluegrass does not deviate much from this formula while progressive bluegrass (called "newgrass") allows for electric instruments and other original touches.

Along with her band, Union Station, Alison recorded several successful albums, including *Too Late to Cry* and *Two Highways*,

when she was just a teenager. Her 1990 album, *I've Got That Old Feeling*, attempted to present a grown-up Krauss to country audiences. She left the traditional material behind to include such original tunes as "That Makes One of Us" and "Will You Be Leaving." She also subordinated her fiddle playing to exploit more of the group's sound. *Every Time You Say Goodbye* again blended traditional material with original songs, including Shawn Colvin's "I Don't Know Why" and Karla Bonoff's "Lose Again." In 1994, Krauss teamed up with one of bluegrass music's premier gospel groups to record *Alison Krauss and the Cox Family—I Know Who Holds Tomorrow*, a collection of new and traditional hymns.

When not touring, Krauss remains in constant demand for studio work. In the past couple of years she has sung and played on recordings by Vince Gill, Mark Chesnutt, Nanci Griffith, Alan Jackson, and Dolly Parton. Many critics have cited Parton as the performer Krauss most resembles vocally.

For Krauss, performing has been a way of life for many years. She began playing the fiddle at age five. Three years later she discovered bluegrass and started entering and winning fiddle championships. Krauss joined her first band when she was 12 years old. A couple of years later her talent and style amazed audiences at the Newport Folk Festival. She recorded her first album at 14, and was dubbed country's youngest rising star.

With Krauss's continued success all but assured, so too is the livelihood of bluegrass music for many years to come.

ALISON KRAUSS

BORN: July 23, 1971, in Champaign, Illinois

FIRST HIT: "I've Got That Old Feeling" (1991)

OTHER NOTABLE HITS: "Love Me Like a Rock" (1994); "Last Love Letter" (1992); "New Fool" (1992); "Lose Again" (1992);

BEST ALBUMS: *Alison Krauss and the Cox Family* (1994); *Two Highways* (1988); *Too Late to Cry* (1987); *Every Time You Say Goodbye* (1992); *I've Got That Old Feeling* (1991)

AWARDS INCLUDE: Grammy, Best Bluegrass Recording (1992, 1990); International Bluegrass Music Association (IBMA) Female Vocalist of the Year (1993, 1991, 1990); IBMA Album of the Year (1993, 1991); IBMA Entertainer of the Year (1991)

ACHIEVEMENTS: Grand Ole Opry member (1993); recorded her first album at age 14

·TRACY· ·LAWRENCE·

Tracy Lawrence may be one of the youngest performers in the business, but his gutsy vocals compare favorably with the great veteran voices. With his Southern-bred cowboy image and a glint of adventurousness in his eye, Lawrence is a tough one. He's proved it, professionally and personally.

Newcomer Tracy Lawrence is one of country music's youngest artists.

Being shot four times while trying to prevent a robbery in a Nashville hotel is now part of Lawrence's legend. He later bungee-jumped off a crane that towered

150 feet in the air. Today, he rides a Harley-Davidson—and unleashes a stage performance with enough power and passion to lift an entire coliseum of fans out of their seats.

Lawrence was born January 27, 1968, in Texarkana, Texas, one of six children. His father, a banker, moved the family to Foreman, Arkansas, when Tracy was four. As a teenager, he learned the guitar and started playing in local nightclubs. He spent two years at Southern Arkansas University, working on a degree in mass communications. Eventually he realized academia wasn't for him, so he left school and moved to Louisiana to join a band as its lead singer. The band fell apart when the bass player pulled out.

Alone, with no money and no contacts, Lawrence loaded his ancient car with a few possessions and drove to Nashville. He earned money by winning talent contests in local nightclubs. He began singing regularly on a Nashville radio show. His future managers heard him sing in a nightclub in Kentucky, which led to his contract with Atlantic Records in 1991.

Just after he finished recording the vocals for *Sticks & Stones*, he was seeing a woman friend back to her hotel when they were confronted by three men with guns. Trying to deflect a holdup, Lawrence took four bullets, one in his knee. Though his quick recovery astounded his doctors, at times he still performs in pain.

The shooting held up the release of the album until October 1991. But the wait has been worth it—in less than two years, *Sticks & Stones* has produced three number-one singles and has been certified gold. "Runnin' Behind," "Sticks and Stones," and "Today's Lonely Fool" all became number-one hits. Lawrence's follow-up album, *Alibis*, sold more than 500,000 copies in the first 17 days after its release—giving him the gold a second time around. With *Alibis*, Lawrence has finally come to realize how much he has grown as an artist.

"When I cut *Sticks & Stones*, I hadn't been performing very much in probably a year and a half," he said. "I was playing at Libby's in Kentucky, doing about three songs every Saturday night at the most. I just wasn't in near the shape that I was on the second album."

Much of the singer's strong performance with *Alibis* is due to the heavy touring schedule he's followed in the past two years—more than 250 performances in 1992. New artists usually build their tour dates gradually, but Lawrence kicked off in high gear, performing as much as possible. The singer has since learned that it's probably wiser to do better shows on fewer dates. He has toured with George Jones and George Strait, two of his musical heroes.

After a couple of years on the road and two albums under his belt, Lawrence is even tougher today—as a businessman as well as a performer. The reward for all this hard work was being named Top New Male Vocalist by the Academy of Country Music in 1993.

Being one of the youngest artists in country music, a field in which competitiveness can easily cause tension, Lawrence has refused to allow petty rivalries to get in his way. Experience has taught him that there's more camaraderie among artists than most people imagine.

TRACY LAWRENCE

BORN: January 27, 1968, in Texarkana, Texas

MUSICAL INFLUENCES: George Jones, Keith Whitley, Merle Haggard, George Strait

FIRST HIT: "Sticks and Stones" (1991)

OTHER NOTABLE HITS: "Alibis" (1992); "We Don't Love Here Anymore" (1992); "It Only Takes One Bar (To Make A Prison)" (1992); "Runnin' Behind" (1991); "Today's Lonely Fool" (1991)

BEST ALBUMS: *Alibis* (1992); *Sticks & Stones* (1991)

AWARDS INCLUDE: Academy of Country Music Top New Male Vocalist (1992)

PATTY LOVELESS

atty Loveless was born Patty Ramey in the coal country of Pikeville, Kentucky. One of eight children (seven siblings and a cousin), she and her family experienced the sadness and hardship of a rural working-class existence. The Ramey family was forced to move many times because of the scarcity

A cousin of Loretta Lynn, Patty Loveless has made a name for herself with a contemporary country sound.

of work. Relocating so often was particularly difficult for Patty, the second youngest.

By the time Patty was an adolescent, she began showing an interest in music. Her older sister, Dottie, had flirted with the music business when Patty was a child. Dottie had played a few dates with the Stanley Brothers, a well-known bluegrass group, and she had sung for the USO. Watching Dottie perform inspired Patty to want to be a singer too.

When Patty was 12, she began writing songs and singing at local shows around Louisville with her brother, Roger. In the summer of 1972, Roger and Patty drove to Nashville and pushed their way into the office of Porter Wagoner on Music Row. Wagoner was impressed with Patty's songwriting, though she was only 15 years old. He introduced the brother-sister act to his singing partner, Dolly Parton. Parton encouraged Patty and spent time with her whenever the teenager came to Nashville.

Patty and Roger got their first big break in 1974, when

Loveless's Honky-Tonk Angel *album proved to be her breakthrough.*

they landed a job opening for the Wilburn Brothers after the original opening act couldn't make it. The Wilburns were duly impressed with Patty's songwriting skills as well as her singing talents. They asked her to consider joining them on their syndicated television series and touring with them.

Roger moved to Nashville, and Patty joined him soon after she graduated from high school. The Wilburn Brothers attempted to get her a contract with MCA Records, but renowned producer Owen Bradley felt she was too young. After a short run on the road with the Wilburns, Patty was disappointed to learn that the brothers thought her too inexperienced as well.

At 19, she married the Wilburns'

Loveless's emotional songs are traditional country with rock 'n' roll and bluegrass influences.

drummer, Terry Lovelace. The couple moved to North Carolina, and Loveless stayed there for nine years. Patty was discouraged by her experiences in Nashville. She lost interest in writing songs and was content to defer to her husband's dream of playing rock 'n' roll.

The death of her father and a general unhappiness over the way her life was going led to some changes in Patty's life. By the early 1980s, her marriage was over, and she was ready to return to Nashville. Country music had changed while Loveless was away. Before

Patty Loveless showed an early interest in singing. At age 16, she began performing with the Wilburn Brothers.

she left, her old-fashioned, tradition-based style was out of step with the slick sounds coming from record companies in the late 1970s. By the mid-1980s, Music City was moving forward by looking back at the roots of country music. The change in attitude made the industry more receptive to her style.

Patty kept her husband's name but changed the spelling, and she started making contacts once again. Her brother, Roger Ramey, acted as her manager and landed a deal with MCA Records in 1986. Her debut album, *Patty Loveless*, was produced by the acclaimed Tony Brown and yielded two top-40 songs—"After All" and "Lonely Days, Lonely Nights." Her first top-ten hit was the title song from her second album, *If My Heart Had Windows*. The material on these albums showcased Loveless's pure country voice.

Producer Emory Gordy, Jr., worked with Brown on Loveless's first two albums. Gordy and Loveless fell in love, but they kept it secret (they were actually married in February 1989, though it was a full 18 months before it became public knowledge). Loveless says she insisted on secrecy because she wanted to get established on her own merits. With her third album, *Honky-Tonk Angel*, Loveless became a country music star. The album yielded five top-ten hits, including two number-one hits—"Chains" and "Timber, I'm Falling in Love." In 1988, she became a member of the Grand Ole Opry.

With her first major success, Loveless began to think seriously about how her career was being managed. After long consideration, she replaced her brother as manager with Larry Fitzgerald in 1991. The decision was a shock to her family, but Roger accepted his sister's choice and continued to support her in her career. Patty also felt that MCA was paying less attention to her than to its other female stars, Reba McEntire, Wynonna Judd, and Trisha Yearwood. In 1992, she asked to be released from her contract and signed with Epic Records. She and Gordy worked together on her final MCA album, *Up Against My Heart*, and her first for Epic, *Only What I Feel*.

In the middle of recording *Only What I Feel*, Loveless had some trouble with her voice. The problem was an aneurysm in her vocal cord. Loveless underwent emergency laser surgery and sat out the last three months of 1992. The recovery time was nerve-racking—she was unable to talk for four weeks, and she had to undergo voice therapy. Fortunately, the surgery was a success.

Only What I Feel was released in April 1993 and was a hit with both critics and fans. The powerful "How Can I Help You Say Goodbye," a poignant song for Loveless considering the loss of her father, became an enduring top-ten hit. The rest of the album demonstrated Patty's uncanny ability to select material that suits her voice and her personality. She responds to songs that she is able to relate to, and her powerful voice makes them seem so personal. "I've been there," she reveals. "I've been around so many people and heard so many heartbreaking stories that all I try to do is take those lyrics and give them edge."

PATTY LOVELESS

BORN: January 4, 1957, in Pikeville, Kentucky

MUSICAL INFLUENCE: Dolly Parton

FIRST HIT: "After All" (1987)

OTHER NOTABLE HITS: "How Can I Help You Say Goodbye" (1993); "Nothin' But the Wheel" (1993); "You Will" (1993); "Jealous Bone" (1992); "Hurt Me Bad (In a Real Good Way)" (1991); "Chains" (1990); "Don't Toss Us Away" (1989); "Timber, I'm Falling in Love" (1989); "If My Heart Had Windows" (1988)

BEST ALBUMS: *Only What I Feel* (1993); *Up Against My Heart* (1991); *Honky-Tonk Angel* (1988); *If My Heart Had Windows* (1988)

AWARDS INCLUDE: Country Music Association Vocal Event of the Year (with George Jones, et al., 1993)

ACHIEVEMENTS: Grand Ole Opry member (1988)

PERSONAL: Superstar Loretta Lynn is a distant cousin. Formerly married to Wilburn Brothers drummer Perry Lovelace, Loveless is now married to producer Emory Gordy, Jr.

LYLE LOVETT

yle Lovett likes to toy with conventions. He's a fourth generation Texan, but he's afraid of cows. He wears his hair tall, not short or long. He's touted as a country singer/ songwriter, and while he does play shuffles and waltzes, he's just as likely to play honking blues or swinging jazz or somber folk music.

Lovett uses his quirky views on life and love as his calling card. Though he hasn't achieved broad radio airplay, his albums have sold well thanks to positive reviews, widespread television exposure, and strong word-of-mouth among fans. His artistic standing was underlined when his second album, *Pontiac*, earned him a Grammy Award in 1989 for Best Country Vocal Performance by a Male. At the awards show, in typical Lovett fashion, he accidentally dropped the statue as he walked across the stage. As he grimaced and picked

Lyle Lovett's eclectic style represents the increasing diversity of country music.

up the pieces, the crowd howled with laughter at his self-deprecating charm and discomfort.

Lovett grew up in Klein, Texas, on the same plot of land that his great-great grandfather, town namesake Adam Klein, first settled. Today, Lovett lives in a home once owned by his late grandfather, which is part of the ranch where his parents, William and Bernell Lovett, reside and raise cattle.

Lovett began singing and writing songs while earning degrees in journalism and German at Texas A&M. He met singer/songwriter Nanci Griffith by interviewing her for the school paper. With her support, he started playing small nightclubs in Houston, Dallas, and Austin.

While performing in a folk festival in Luxembourg in 1983, Lovett hooked up with the J. David Sloan Band and followed them back to Arizona. Working with the Sloan band, Lovett recorded his first songs in a Scottsdale studio.

Lovett took his self-made tape to Nashville. The journey was encouraging enough for him to return to Arizona and record 14 more original songs. Esteemed songwriter Guy Clark, a new-found Lovett fan, passed the fellow Texan's new music to Tony Brown of MCA Records. Brown added a few instrumental parts to ten of Lovett's previously recorded songs and released them in 1986 as the critically acclaimed *Lyle Lovett*.

This first album revealed a singer/songwriter with a refined, assured vision and a witty way with words. Lovett sang about shaky love affairs, sturdy old porches, and hilari-

ous weddings with sharp insight and a distinctively personal point of view. With the song "An Acceptable Level of Ecstasy (The Wedding Song)," this debut disc also hinted at his ability to write swinging blues vamps. He expanded upon this talent in *Pontiac*, released in 1988, and then fully displayed his ability to blend jazz, blues, and country on his third album, *Lyle Lovett and His Large Band*, released in 1989. The album showcased his 11-piece, racially mixed touring band on most of the 12 songs, which were all composed and arranged by Lovett.

Country's Outsider

Lyle Lovett is a good example of the new breed of performers who blend traditional country sounds with other musical styles. At least as popular with rock fans as country fans, Lovett has managed to carve out an eclectic style that unites folk, gospel, swing, jazz, and r&b into a seamless mixture that could only be his own. The self-effacing Lovett admits he was surprised at his commercial success in Nashville. Like contemporaries Steve Earle, k.d. lang, and Nanci Griffith, Lovett has always been aware that he never quite fit the typical image of the country-western star. A native of Texas, Lovett came up through the Southwestern music ranks, playing clubs in Houston, Dallas, and Austin, and recording his first songs in Scottsdale, Arizona. Lovett hit Nashville in the 1980s, when country music was in a state of flux and in need of a new identity. He believes

that has a lot to do with how he was able to break through in the first place. For his fourth album, *Joshua Judges Ruth* (1992), Lovett switched to his label's pop side, feeling that as his music evolved, it appealed more to a wider, mainstream audience than to a straight country audience. Having prospered in Nashville, Lovett was ready to build on that experience and strike out in a new direction.

Lovett's music sometimes reveals his dry but hilarious sense of humor.

The early 1990s found Lovett busy with a variety of musical—and nonmusical—ventures. He cut tracks for the *Deadicated* album of Grateful Dead tunes ("Friend of the Devil") and the film *Switch*. He also toured extensively and produced an album for singer/songwriter Walter Hyatt.

Lovett even found time to try his hand at acting, appearing in the Robert Altman film *The Player*. Lovett described his role as that of a "mysterious character who kills bugs." The singer's unique looks and offbeat demeanor made him a natural for the group of stock players that frequently appear in Altman's films. Altman specializes in episodic films with large casts of character actors who often improvise dialogue and work out the details of their own scenes. After *The Player*, Lovett had a small but poignant role in *Short Cuts*. He also appeared in Altman's ode to the fashion industry, *Pret-a-Porter*.

Lovett's fourth album, *Joshua Judges Ruth*, was released in March 1992—to critical and popular acclaim. The first to be marketed through MCA's Los Angeles (as opposed to Nashville) division, it points to a mainstream breakthrough for Lovett. Nonetheless, none of the tunes would be out of place on one of Lovett's earlier albums. In fact, the modest Lovett maintains he's really not doing anything new on the album.

"It's not reflective of a musical evolution so much as just revealing a little bit more of the kinds of things I've been interested in all along."

Joshua Judges Ruth, which Lovett has jokingly described as "conversations with God about death, food, and women," features such well-known cuts as "Church," "I've Been to Memphis," "North Dakota," and "She's Leaving Me Because She Really Wants To." The album is indicative of Lyle Lovett's signature style because gospel-flavored tall tales mingle with swing tunes, cowboy songs, and traditional country ballads. A number of guest performances are featured, including those by Emmylou Harris, Leo Kottke, Rickie Lee Jones, and Was (Not Was) vocalists Sweet Pea Atkinson and Sir Harry Bowens. *Joshua Judges Ruth* is also notable for reuniting many of Lovett's Large Band members.

Like fellow Southwestern beatniks Guy Clark and Townes Van Zandt, Lovett's highly literate songwriting is the key to his art. Of his music in general, Lovett maintains, "If there's anything that makes my stuff worth listening to, it's just a point of view. The tradition that I would want my songs to fit into is the singer/songwriter tradition, like Newman and Prine, and Tom Waits and James Taylor and Jackson Browne—those guys were a real inspiration to me."

Although the self-effacing Lovett wouldn't admit it, his own eclectic style, unique vocal interpretations, and unsparing lyrics are an inspiration to other performers who aren't afraid to sing it like they want to.

LYLE LOVETT

BORN: November 1, 1957, in Klein, Texas

MUSICAL INFLUENCES: Guy Clark, Townes Van Zandt, Jerry Jeff Walker, Randy Newman, Tom Waits

FIRST HIT: "Farther Down the Line" (1986)

OTHER NOTABLE HITS: "Church" (1992); "She's Leaving Me Because She Really Wants To" (1992); "I Married Her Just Because She Looks Like You" (1989); "Here I Am" (1989); "She's No Lady" (1988); "Cowboy Man" (1987); "God Will" (1987); "Give Me Back My Heart" (1987)

BEST ALBUMS: *Joshua Judges Ruth* (1992); *Lyle Lovett and His Large Band* (1989); *Lyle Lovett* (1986)

AWARDS INCLUDE: Grammy, Best Country Male Vocal Performance (1989)

PERSONAL: Lovett married movie actress Julia Roberts in 1993.

LORETTA · LYNN ·

Loretta Lynn has won more awards from the Country Music Association and the Academy of Country Music than any other female performer. Her resourceful upbringing in the coal country of Kentucky and her rise to the top of the music industry has become a country music legend.

Lynn was born Loretta Webb on April 14, 1935, in Butcher Hollow, Kentucky, to a struggling coal miner

Loretta Lynn has achieved legendary status among fans and in the country music industry.

and his wife. The second of eight children, Lynn grew up in a log cabin in the backhills. Her only real link to the outside world was a radio tuned to the *Grand Ole Opry* on Saturday nights.

When Webb was 13, she met 19-year-old O.V. Lynn

(or "Mooney," as he was known to friends—a nickname derived from "Moonshine") at a town dance. The two started dating and within a month had obtained her father's permission to marry. Within a year, Mooney lost his job at a local coal company and hitchhiked to Washington with Loretta's brother, Jay Lee Webb, in search of work. Loretta stayed home, pregnant with their first child. She was 14.

Lynn eventually joined Mooney in Washington. She helped pay the rent by cooking for 30 farmhands at a

The movie, Coal Miner's Daughter, *based on Lynn's autogiography, was released in 1979.*

Loretta Lynn's life and her music have inspired many who struggle against oppression and poverty.

nearby ranch. By the time she was 18, Lynn had four of her six children; she became a grandmother at 32.

For Loretta's eighteenth birthday, Mooney bought her a Sears guitar, which she taught herself to play. With Mooney's encouragement, Lynn sat in with a local band one Saturday night. She did so well that she was asked to become a regular member of the Saturday night review. By the late 1950s, Lynn had formed her own band, with Jay Lee Webb on guitar, and had begun traveling around the Northwest. Mooney assumed a greater role in her career, becoming her manager.

Lynn's first record was "Honky-Tonk Girl," a tune inspired by a woman Lynn saw drinking and crying in a Washington tavern. Mooney mailed out 3,000 copies of the song to radio stations across the country, where it received some airplay. Favorable response gave Lynn the confidence to head for Nashville, where "Honky-Tonk Girl" became a small hit. In the fall of 1961, Lynn signed with Decca Records and joined the Grand Ole Opry.

Lynn had a difficult time establishing a musical identity. Her hard country tonality sounded very much like Kitty Wells, whom Lynn had emulated as a child. Producer Owen Bradley, instrumental in developing Patsy Cline's career, produced Lynn's first Decca hit, "Success." The ballad features the steel and twin fiddles that had been deemed inappropriate for the pop stylings of Cline.

Named the CMA's Entertainer of the Year in 1972, Lynn was the first female to receive such an honor.

Unfortunately Lynn tried to mimic Cline's quivering range, which compromised the caustic rural timbre that was

Crystal Gayle

Born Brenda Gail Webb in 1951, Crystal Gayle is Loretta Lynn's sister and the last of eight children born to the Webbs. At age 16 Gayle began touring with Loretta Lynn and Conway Twitty. It was Loretta who came up with the name "Crystal Gayle," after the Krystal hamburger chain. Gayle soon embarked on a solo career. Her first release on Decca Records, "I Cried (The Blue Right Out of My Eyes)" (1970),

cracked the country charts. Things moved slowly after this, however, and Crystal switched to UA Records. In 1975 her single "Wrong Road Again" and successful debut album, *Crystal Gayle*, put her back on the country charts. Other hits included "Somebody Loves You," "I'll Get Over You," and "You Never Miss a Real Good Thing." These years also saw the release of a best-selling third album, *Crystal*. In 1977, Gayle scored big with "I'd Do It All Over Again" and "Don't It Make My Brown Eyes Blue," her first major crossover single. Moving to the Columbia label in 1979, the number-one hits continued with "It's Like We Never Said Goodbye," "If You Ever Change Your Mind," and "Too Many Lovers." Gayle logged a chart-topper for new label, Elektra, in 1982 with "Till I Gain Control of You." Gayle also recorded a hit duet with Eddie Rabbitt called "You and I" and another called "Making Up for Lost Time" with Gary Morris. Gayle has won a number of major music awards, including a 1977 Grammy.

to define Lynn's later recordings.

Cline quickly befriended the newcomer in town, lending Lynn support and advice. But the friendship, just over a year old, was cut short when Cline died in a plane crash. Lynn writes poignantly in her 1976 autobiography, *Coal Miner's Daughter* (on which the 1979 film is based), of this devastating loss.

Lynn's independence resurfaced, however, and she began scoring hits with her own compositions. Her "Before I'm Over You" made the top ten on the country charts in 1963. Her follow-up hit was 1964's "Wine, Women and Song." In 1965, Lynn scored three top-ten singles—"Blue Kentucky Girl," "Happy Birthday," and "The Home You're Tearing Down."

An identity was finally being established. As social attitudes underwent rapid change in the mid-1960s, Lynn caught a cultural wave with such tough-talking compositions as "Don't Come Home A-Drinkin'" (1966), "Fist City" (1968), and "Your Squaw Is on the Warpath" (1968). More than a couple of these tunes were inspired by Mooney, who counted Cline's second husband, Charlie Dick, among his drinking buddies.

Lynn's sassy self-declaration shaped her into an almost mythical figure. Country music fans responded to her music and her life, which pointed to a way out of oppression and poverty. Lynn forged ahead with the deeply autobiographical "Coal Miner's Daughter" and the

traditional shuffle "You're Looking at Country," both released in 1970. In 1972, she was awarded the coveted Country Music Association Entertainer of the Year Award, becoming its first female recipient. Three years later, in 1975, the Academy of Country Music paid her a similar tribute, naming her their Entertainer of the Year.

Lynn also continued a country tradition of male-female duets. Between 1964 and 1969 Lynn sang with Ernest Tubb, and although their vocals were unsettled, the country charm was irresistible. A better match for Lynn's penetrating vocals was the softer style of Conway Twitty. The pair's most notable tunes were 1971's "After the Fire Is Gone," which won a Grammy, and 1978's "You're the Reason Our Kids Are Ugly," a novelty call-and-response tune.

Lynn's last statement of impact was 1975's "The Pill," a song endorsing birth control, which disc jockeys initially refused to play. Lynn stated, "If they'd had the pill when I was having babies, I'd be eatin' them like popcorn."

Although Lynn's recording career leveled off by 1980, she remained a staple on the touring circuit. The 1980s brought tragedy to Lynn as well as triumph. In 1984, she faced the death of her son, Jack Benny Lynn, who drowned while attempting to cross a river on horseback. Four years later, she was inducted into the Country Music Hall of Fame. The honor reminded the country music industry of Loretta Lynn's remarkable talent and career.

LORETTA LYNN

BORN: 1935, in Butcher Hollow, Kentucky

FIRST HIT: "Honky-Tonk Girl" (1960)

OTHER NOTABLE HITS: "The Pill" (1975); "Coal Miner's Daughter" (1970); "Don't Come Home A-Drinkin'" (1966); "The Home You're Tearing Down" (1965)

BEST ALBUMS: *Honky-Tonk Angels* (with Dolly Parton and Tammy Wynette, 1993); *Coal Miner's Daughter* (1971); *Don't Come Home A-Drinkin'* (1967); *Loretta Lynn/Country Music Hall of Fame* (1962)

AWARDS INCLUDE: Grammy, Best Country Vocal Performance by a Duo or Group (with Conway Twitty, 1971); Academy of Country Music (ACM) Artist of the Decade (1970-1979); ACM Top Vocal Duet (with Conway Twitty, 1976, 1975, 1974, 1971); ACM Entertainer of the Year (1975); ACM Top Female Vocalist (1975, 1974, 1973, 1971); Country Music Association (CMA) Vocal Duo of the Year (with Conway Twitty, 1975, 1974, 1973, 1972); CMA Female Vocalist of the Year (1973, 1972, 1967)

ACHIEVEMENTS: Country Music Hall of Fame inductee (1988); Grand Ole Opry member (1962)

KATHY · MATTEA ·

Fans of Kathy Mattea's vocals aren't surprised to find her 1994 single, "Walking Away a Winner," among *Billboard*'s top 20. If anything, the song's title aptly describes Mattea's approach to life—and the success she's earned after her long climb to the top.

The story of Mattea's rise starts in her tiny hometown of Cross Lanes, West Virginia. When a pal decid-

Contemporary country singer Kathy Mattea won a Grammy in 1991 for Best Country Vocal Performance.

ed to head to Nashville in 1978 to try his luck in country music, Mattea tied her mattress to the top of the car and tagged along. Her friend soon returned, but Mattea stuck it out.

For a while she worked an odd assortment of jobs and studied with a professional voice teacher. The vocal work paid off when she landed a position singing demos in 1982. A number of music executives got to hear her voice, and Mattea signed a recording contract with Poly-Gram on her 24th birthday.

Though Mattea was blessed with a warm country voice, her music reflected a bit of a folk influence. Folk and bluegrass music had held her interest when she attended West Virginia University. Unfortunately, Poly-Gram attempted to saddle their new singer with a sophisticated, almost sexy image, which did not suit Mattea's down-home back-porch personality. They also labeled and marketed her as a country-pop singer.

Her career waltzed forward in 1986 with her first top-ten hit, the striking "Love at the Five and Dime." Several more top-ten tunes followed, including "Walk the Way the Wind Blows," "You're the Power," and "Train of Memories." With the help of producer Allen Reynolds, Mattea pursued a direction that was closer to her musical interests. With each successive album, her music grew more sparse and acoustic, her songs more earthy, and her image more casual.

An important year for Mattea was 1988. She married songwriter Jon Vezner on St. Valentine's Day, had her first number-one hit, "Goin' Gone," and won awards for "18 Wheels and a Dozen Roses." The commercial and critical success of these tunes proved the commercial wisdom of Mattea and Reynolds in selecting material and forging a musical direction.

From there, the number-one hits continued. With renewed confidence and a new contract with Mercury Records, Mattea branched out. She recorded the unlikely hit, "Where've You Been," a poignant portrayal of her husband's grandparents. The song became the first country tune to cross over to the pop charts in three years. True to her easygoing musical eclecticism, Mattea's album *Time Passes By* incorporated the sounds of Celtic and Scottish music. The album featured Dougie MacLean, one of Scotland's premier folk artists. It also included three of her husband's songs.

In 1992, she dropped longtime producer Allen Reynolds to work with Brent Maheron on *Lonesome Standard Time.* Both *Lonesome Standard Time* and *Walking Away a Winner,* released in 1994, found Mattea moving away from her acoustic tracks toward a more fully arranged sound. During the production of *Lonesome Standard Time,* Mattea faced some vocal problems—she suffered from a leaking capillary on her vocal cord. The damage was less severe than originally thought, requiring a relatively short operation. Still, it was a frightening experience.

Kathy Mattea looks at her recovery time as a gift. Illness slowed her down, forcing her to concentrate on her music. It also opened her to other ways of thinking: "I learned that not everything is crucially important," she observed.

KATHY MATTEA

BORN: June 21, 1959, in Cross Lanes, West Virginia

FIRST HIT: "Street Talk" (1983)

OTHER NOTABLE HITS: "Walking Away a Winner" (1994); "Asking Us to Dance" (1991); "Time Passes By" (1991); "Where've You Been" (1989); "She Came from Fort Worth" (1989); "Eighteen Wheels and a Dozen Roses" (1988); "Goin' Gone" (1988); "Love at the Five and Dime" (1986)

BEST ALBUMS: *Good News* (1993); *Lonesome Standard Time* (1992); *Time Passes By* (1991); *Willow in the Wind* (1989)

AWARDS INCLUDE: Grammy, Best Country Female Vocal Performance (1990); Grammy, Best Country Song (1990); Country Music Association (CMA) Female Vocalist of the Year (1990, 1989); CMA Single of the Year (1988); Academy of Country Music (ACM) Top Female Vocalist (1989); ACM Song of the Year (1989, 1988); ACM Single of the Year (1988)

PERSONAL: Mattea is married to songwriter Jon Vezner.

·MARTINA· McBRIDE

"I've never done much else besides music. I've never even thought about doing anything else." So says talented young RCA Records songstress Martina McBride. Such humility belies the reputation she has earned—on the strength of her two albums, *The Time Has Come* and *The Way That I Am*—as one of country music's most focused artists.

Martina McBride's popular hits include "My Baby Loves Me" and "Independence Day."

A native of tiny Sharon, Kansas, (there were ten people in her graduating class) McBride began her career performing with her musical family, known as the Schiffters. She sang and also played keyboard. After high school, McBride began performing with various bands in her home state. It was while putting together a new band that she met her future husband, John McBride, owner of a sound company. After a two-year courtship, the couple wed and moved to Nashville in 1989 to pursue their respective careers—hers as a country music artist and his in the sound and lighting business.

While John looked for business opportunities, Martina pursued a record deal. She eventually gained the attention of RCA executives in a clever and somewhat unorthodox way. Bypassing the record company's strict policy against accepting unsolicited material, McBride put her demo tape in a purple envelope and marked it "Requested Material." The bold move resulted in a phone call from an RCA executive, which led to a contract.

Meanwhile, McBride took to the road selling T-shirts on the Garth Brooks 1991 tour—this in an effort to spend more time with husband John, who had been hired to oversee Brooks's sound production. Martina impressed Brooks with her determination and hard-work ethic. Upon the release of her debut album, *The Time Has Come*, Brooks promptly selected McBride as the opening act for his mammoth 1992 tour, ultimately exposing the

Martina McBride poses with her husband John.

fledgling singer to scores of potential new fans. McBride repeated the honors on Brooks's 1994 European tour.

For her sophomore album 1993's *The Way That I Am* (which the ambitious singer coproduced with Paul Worley), McBride shocked many by cutting off her signature brunette mane for a short, chic bob. Her new image firmly in place, McBride released the disc's first single, the catchy "My Baby Loves Me," with a sassy, defiant video that helped propel her to a new level of popularity. This song, along with such other cuts as "Life #9," "Independence Day," and "Goin' to Work," showed a grittier, more confident side to McBride than her debut album allowed.

With a handful of chart-topping hits, it's clear the time has indeed come for Martina McBride, who maintains a grateful, if slightly befuddled, attitude about her fame.

"I was prepared to give whatever it took," McBride summed up simply to *Music City News*. "There's no way in the world that I believed it would happen on my first try, and I'm real shocked that it happened as fast as it did. I feel real lucky."

MARTINA McBRIDE

BORN: July 29, in Sharon, Kansas

FIRST HIT: "The Time Has Come" (1992)

OTHER NOTABLE HITS: "My Baby Loves Me" (1993); "Independence Day" (1993); "Goin' to Work" (1993); "Life #9" (1993); "Cheap Whiskey" (1992); "That's Me" (1992)

BEST ALBUMS: *The Way That I Am* (1993); *The Time Has Come* (1992)

ACHIEVEMENTS: Coproduced her second album, *The Way That I Am*

·REBA· McENTIRE

One of the new breed of performers to shake up Nashville in the 1980s, Reba McEntire became the reigning queen of country music by focusing on a traditional sound, recording consistently high quality material, and remaining true to her roots. Along with George Strait and Ricky Skaggs, McEntire helped prove to Nashville that the strength and future of country music lay in its heritage.

McEntire was born in Chockie, Oklahoma, in 1954, the daughter of Jacqueline and Clark McEntire. Because

Influenced by country greats Loretta Lynn and Patsy Cline, McEntire's music is traditional country.

her father was a champion steer roper, Reba, brother Pake, and sisters Susie and Alice grew up traveling the rodeo circuit with their parents. During long stretches of highway, her mother taught the children how to sing harmony. By the time she was in high school, McEntire began to exhibit the influence of both parents. She competed in rodeo competitions as a first-class barrel racer

154

but also sang as part of the Singing McEntires, the vocal group she formed with Pake and Susie. They performed in clubs in southeast Oklahoma for as little as $13 each, sometimes singing until the early hours of the morning.

Reba entered Southeastern Oklahoma State University in Durant, Oklahoma, in 1974, intending to become an elementary school teacher. Reba's father supported her musical interest and encouraged her to sing the national anthem at the 1974 National Finals Rodeo. Singer Red Steagall, impressed by Reba's performance, helped her land a recording contract.

The feisty redhead debuted on Mercury/PolyGram Records in 1977 with the album *Reba McEntire*. One of her early singles, "I Don't Want To Be a One Night Stand," came out about the time she graduated from college. Newly married, she and husband Charlie Battles kicked off their honeymoon by visiting radio stations to promote the record, which was very similar to what Loretta Lynn and her husband did to promote Lynn's first single in 1960.

Slowly, her records entered the charts. "Three Sheets to the Wind," a duet with Jacky Ward (of "A Lover's Question" fame), reached the top 20 in July 1978. Her second album, *Out of a Dream*, spawned the successful singles "Sweet Dreams," "Runaway Heart," and another duet with Ward, "That Makes Two of Us." The determined singer finally hit the

Popular with both the country music industry and fans, Reba has hosted several awards shows.

top ten in 1980 with "(You Lift Me) Up to Heaven" and "I Can See Forever in Your Eyes," both from her *Feel the Fire* album. The following year, country fans were hearing more hit songs from the lady with the powerhouse voice, including "I Don't Think Love Ought To Be That Way" and "Today All Over Again." She soon delivered another top-ten hit, "I'm Not That Lonely Yet," the first single from her fifth album, *Unlimited*.

McEntire's modest success soon snowballed, and by January 1982 she had another chart-topping hit, "Can't Even Get the Blues." Producer Jerry Kennedy had planned to give the tune to Jacky Ward, but when McEntire heard it, she insisted that it was her song. Her instincts paid off because it became her first number-one record. She followed up with "You're the First Time I've Thought About Leaving," which became the second consecutive number-one hit for the determined Oklahoman.

Other female country singers began to follow through the doors she opened, but few had her vocal range. Though known for really belting out hard-country tunes, McEntire could also slide gracefully into a sweet ballad or attach an ache to her voice when singing about heartbreak. Reba's songs began to appeal to a broad audience because her strong, versatile voice allowed her to cross over from traditional country to more contemporary-sounding country music. In addition to her distinctive style and strong stage presence, she became known for addressing a female viewpoint in the content of her songs.

As more and more fans flocked to her concerts, the country music industry recognized her talents and contributions. In 1983, the Country Music Association nominated her for an award as Female Vocalist of the Year, as well as for the Horizon Award. Although she didn't take home any trophies that night, she was well on her way to becoming a household name.

Despite the success she had with Mercury/PolyGram, McEntire's association with that label ended after the release of the ironically titled "There Ain't No Future in This." McEntire changed to MCA Records in 1984 where producer Norro Wilson added fuel to McEntire's burning ambition to be a superstar. Her soulful, emotional vocal style emerged in full force with her first album for MCA, *Just a Little Love*. With "Every Second Someone Breaks a Heart," a song that edged closer to rock 'n' roll than she had ever gone before, McEntire showcased her versatility by pushing the boundaries of what constitutes "country." The song represented a calculated move to hold the attention of her younger fans and to build a larger following. That same year, Reba released *My Kind of Country*, which had a traditional, back-to-

basics-country sound and yielded such top-20 hit singles as "How Blue" and "He Broke Your Mem'ry Last Night."

By October 1984, with momentum rolling in her favor, Reba was named the Country Music Association's Female Vocalist of the Year. Indicating the degree to which McEntire influenced the course of country music during the 1980s, she won the honor four years in a row, from 1984 through 1987. McEntire is the only female performer in the history of the CMA Awards to hold that distinction.

In 1985, McEntire took the reins of her career firmly in hand and began coproducing her albums, starting

"It's Reba's Call"

Like so many of today's country performers, Reba McEntire has managed to carve out a highly successful career in the music business, while branching off into a number of other ventures. McEntire demonstrated a shrewd head for business with the establishment of her own publicity, management, and music-publishing companies. Acting has always been a second love for Reba. Her first feature film was the sci-fi thriller *Tremors*, costarring Kevin Bacon, Fred Ward, and Larry Gross. Reba played a gun-slinging madam in the NBC mini-series *The Gambler Returns: Luck of the Draw*, with Kenny Rogers. She also appeared in CBS's *The Man from Left Field*, at the request of Burt Reynolds, the film's star and director. In *North*, her second feature film, Reba fulfilled a dream by working with one of her favorite directors,

Rob Reiner. In all of her roles, Reba has received good notices, proving herself to be a convincing actress. Reba's autobiography, *Reba: My Story*, was published in 1994.

Reba's duet "Does He Love You" with backup singer Linda Davis (left), hit number one in 1993.

with *Have I Got a Deal for You*. Not only was it a successful career move that paid off for McEntire, but it was another indication of her clout. She also developed a more theatrical stage show, incorporating laser lighting effects, smoke machines, and numerous costume changes.

Her 1986 album *Whoever's in New England* began a new phase of accolades and acclaim. In October of that year, she was rewarded with CMA's coveted Entertainer of the Year award. In addition, her recording of "Whoever's in New England" garnered her a Grammy Award for Best Female Country Vocal Performance. Other awards included being named the Academy of Country Music's Top Female Vocalist from 1984 through 1989; she was honored as the Music City News Female Artist of the Year from 1985 through 1990; and she won the American Music Award for Favorite Female Country Vocalist from 1987 through 1989.

While she established new standards in country music, McEntire was unafraid to show the wide range of her style. Throughout her career, she demonstrated that she was not intimidated by legendary performances of classic songs. She enjoyed the challenge of taking a standard and making it her own, as with "Fancy," a former hit for Bobbie Gentry, and "The Night the Lights Went out in Georgia," a pop hit for TV actress Vicki Lawrence. She also recorded such familiar standards as Aretha Franklin's "Respect," the old torch song "Sunday Kind of Love," a stunning version of the Everly Brothers hit "Cathy's Clown," and an *a cappella* rendition of "Sweet Dreams." Much of Reba's material consists of story songs, which are very much like miniature plays. Often, the videos for these songs emphasize the song's plotline. Whether telling the tale of a tragic murder in "The Night the Lights Went Out in Georgia" or capturing the plight of a homemaker who goes back to school in "Is There Life Out There," McEntire has updated country music's longstanding penchant for storytelling through song.

McEntire's career flourished, but her marriage to Charlie Battles suffered. In 1987, after 11 years of marriage, she left their 250-acre cattle ranch near Stringtown, Oklahoma, moved to Nashville, and filed for divorce. McEntire's fans seemed to personalize the news of her divorce in a peculiar way, and she was suddenly deluged with letters denouncing the split. Reba answered as many letters as possible, telling fans it was her business, and they would have to trust her.

In early June 1989, McEntire surprised her fans

with an unexpected wedding to manager Narvel Blackstock. The two married in Lake Tahoe, Nevada, at a private ceremony attended by only a few family members. McEntire, a workaholic, was in the resort area for a series of performances at the Caesar's casino. Three days after the wedding, she was signing autographs at Fan Fair. Originally a steel-guitar player in McEntire's band, Blackstock formed Starstruck Entertainment with McEntire shortly after she left her former manager, Bill Carter, in 1987. The corporation handles song

Reba's powerful, versatile voice has made her a country superstar, but she has kept her down-to-earth attitude.

In her music videos and theatrical stage shows, Reba exhibits a flair for drama and showcases her acting ability.

publishing, booking, management, advertising, publicity, and promotion for McEntire and other Nashville stars. Reba's other business ventures include construction, jet service, and a horse farm. Although she once told a reporter that she never planned to have children, McEntire's newfound happiness with Blackstock changed her mind. She gave birth to their son, Shelby, in February of 1990.

Not content to dominate country music, McEntire has dabbled in acting, beginning with her music videos. Hollywood beckoned soon thereafter, and McEntire appeared in her first feature film, the science-fiction thriller *Tremors*. Her next role was as

Burgundy Jones, a gun-slinging madam in *The Gambler Returns: Luck of the Draw* with Kenny Rogers. She has appeared in *The Man from Left Field* and *North*, receiving favorable reviews for her acting ability.

Sadly, her good fortune was matched by terrible tragedy when her road manager and seven members of her band were killed in a plane crash en route to a concert in 1991. At the urging of Blackstock, she had skipped the flight, staying behind in San Diego to shake off a case of bronchitis. Always open with her emotions, McEntire shared her grief publicly and found solace in the support of her fans and her peers.

McEntire chose the songs for her next album, *For My Broken Heart*, to help her deal with the sorrow she suffered following the accident. McEntire channeled all of her sorrows into making the album a universal statement on heartbreak and sadness, and her fans responded overwhelmingly. *For My Broken Heart* was certified platinum just two months after it was released in October 1991. McEntire reflected, "For me, singing sad songs often has a way of healing a situation. It gets the hurt out in the open—into the light, out of the darkness. I hope this album heals all our broken hearts."

The year 1992 proved to be another award-winner for Reba. She

REBA McENTIRE

BORN: March 28, 1954, in Chockie, Oklahoma

MUSICAL INFLUENCES: Loretta Lynn, Patsy Cline, Dolly Parton

FIRST HIT: "(You Lift Me) Up to Heaven" (1980)

OTHER NOTABLE HITS: "Does He Love You" (with Linda Davis, 1993); "Take It Back" (1992); "Rumor Has It" (1991); "Is There Life Out There" (1991); "Fancy" (1990); "I Know How He Feels" (1988); "Whoever's in New England" (1986); "How Blue" (1985); "Can't Even Get the Blues" (1982)

BEST ALBUMS: *For My Broken Heart* (1991); *Reba* (1988); *Whoever's in New England* (1986); *My Kind of Country* (1984); *Feel the Fire* (1980)

AWARDS INCLUDE: Grammy, Best Country Female Vocal Performance (1986); Academy of Country Music Top Female Vocalist (1991, 1990, 1987, 1986, 1985, 1984); Country Music Association (CMA) Female Vocalist of the Year (1987, 1986, 1985, 1984); CMA Entertainer of the Year (1986)

ACHIEVEMENTS: Grand Ole Opry member (1986)

Reba married manager Narvel Blackstock in 1989; they have a son, Shelby.

won the Academy of Country Music's Top Female Vocalist as well as the Video of the Year for the number-one single "Is There Life out There." Her *It's Your Call* album scored such hit singles as "Take It Back" and "The Heart Won't Lie," a powerful duet with Vince Gill.

The release of *Greatest Hits Volume Two* included previously recorded singles and two new songs, "They Asked About You" and "Does He Love You." The latter, sung with Linda Davis, is an unsettling duet between the other woman and the wife. The song hit number one and helped Davis land a recording contract. McEntire followed with the release of *Read My Mind* in 1994 and the publication of an autobiography, *Reba: My Story*. Dedicated to her son, Shelby, the book shares the life experiences that have inspired and shaped her music.

Popular enough to be known by only her first name, Reba handles her career in a purposeful, professional manner. Named *Billboard* magazine's top-selling female country artist for the last nine years, Reba McEntire has become a country music institution.

◆ JOHN ◆ MICHAEL ◆ MONTGOMERY ◆

Although John Michael Montgomery had been performing regularly in the Lexington, Kentucky, area for years, national attention didn't come until the release of his first single. The song "Life's a Dance" sparked so much attention, with its catchy lyrics and melody, country listeners from

John Michael Montgomery's (left) love of country music came from his parents, both of whom were performers.

coast to coast were humming, snapping, or singing along.

It's no surprise that Montgomery has a passion for music—he inherited it from his parents. Montgomery's mother, who is now his fan club president, played the drums, and his father was a singer/guitar player. Montgomery has danced to the pulse of country music for most of his life—at five, he would often join his folks on stage in singing country classics.

His *Life's a Dance* debut album, released in 1992, went gold virtually overnight and is now certified platinum. Montgomery's impact on country music seemed to happen instantly, while the "Life's a Dance" tune gradually crawled up the charts. The song wasn't expected to become such a breakthrough for Montgomery. The strategy of his record company, Atlantic, was to present it as an introduction. Montgomery himself never expected the song to make the top ten. "We really sent that song out just to set up the next one," he revealed. "We figured it would just do well, push and open a few doors at least. We didn't expect it to dig out the Grand Canyon for us."

Montgomery's follow-up single, "I Love the Way You Love Me," gained even more attention. The heart-wrenching ballad secured Montgomery his first number-one record.

In an industry where it's not unusual for an aspiring artist to seek out a record company for a recording deal, the discovery of Montgomery was the result of tables turned. He had been playing regularly in Lexington and following the advice of his parents—never let your guard down on stage because the right people just might be in the audience. One night, executives

In 1993, Montgomery won the ACM's Top New Male Vocalist and Song of the Year for "I Love the Way You Love Me."

from Atlantic Records stopped by for his show. Montgomery impressed them with a dynamic performance. Soon afterward he signed a deal.

Montgomery turned the tables again when he was unhappy with the way his first album was turning out. He called the head of Atlantic's Nashville division to complain, and he got results in the form of a new producer.

His sophomore album, *Kickin' It Up*, was even more successful than his first. It reached number one not only on *Billboard's* country chart but the pop chart as well. Montgomery's continued success proves that the eager—and sometimes downright rowdy—young singer is no passing fad.

JOHN MICHAEL MONTGOMERY

BORN: January 20, 1964, in Danville, Kentucky

MUSICAL INFLUENCES: Merle Haggard, Lionel Ritchie, the Eagles, Lynyrd Skynyrd, his parents

FIRST HIT: "Life's a Dance" (1992)

OTHER NOTABLE HITS: "I Swear" (1994); "I Love the Way You Love Me" (1992)

BEST ALBUMS: *Kickin' It Up* (1994); *Life's a Dance* (1992)

AWARDS INCLUDE: Academy of Country Music (ACM) Top New Male Vocalist (1993); ACM Song of the Year (1993)

LORRIE · MORGAN

Lorrie Morgan's emotional vocals and provocative image have helped her secure a successful country music career.

L orrie Morgan's life has been plagued with the kind of twists of fate usually found in the lyrics of a country song. Most devastating of all was the death of her husband and fellow performer, Keith Whitley, in 1989. That he died from accidental alcohol poisoning while she was on tour made it that much harder to endure. Almost immediately after Whit- ley's death, Morgan had to go back on the road to support her two children, daughter Morgan and son Jessie Keith.

After she returned to the road, her life seemed to get back on track. Love came back into her life: While on tour with Clint Black in 1990, she fell in love with the singer's bus driver, Brad Thomas. The two were married in October 1991.

But trouble quickly surfaced again. Three weeks after the wedding, Morgan underwent an operation to remove an ovarian cyst. Two days later, the doctor

Daughter of Grand Ole Opry member George Morgan, Lorrie joined the Opry in 1984.

Lorrie Morgan and Marty Stuart (left) both began performing at a young age. Morgan debuted at age 13.

informed her that she needed a total hysterectomy. A couple of months after the operation, Morgan had to file Chapter 11 bankruptcy. By the end of 1992, she had completed her reorganization and paid her creditors in full.

Though she bounced back financially and emotionally, all these problems hurt her marriage. By spring of 1993, Morgan had filed for divorce from Thomas.

"A lot of people read these things and say, 'Oh my God, tragedy after tragedy.' All of a sudden you've got this title on you that you are a walking disaster area," she revealed in an interview. "There are a lot of good things in my life, too, and I wish they [the media] would capture some of that."

The daughter of *Grand Ole Opry* star George ("Candy Kisses") Morgan, Loretta Lynn Morgan was born on June 27, 1959. She made her debut on the *Opry* when she was 13 years old and received a standing ovation. Based on this experience, particularly the thrill of being appreciated by an audience, Morgan knew she wanted to be a performer. "My little 13-year-old knees were absolutely knocking," recalled Morgan, "but I saw Dad standing there just bawling, and these people gave me a standing ovation. I thought this is what I'm doing the rest of my life. I thought it was going to be that easy. Little did I know."

Lorrie discovered it was not easy to make her own way. She struggled in Nashville as a writer for Acuff-Rose, even working as their receptionist. She worked countless demo sessions during her lunch hours and after work.

Morgan's awards include CMA Vocal Event of the Year for a duet recorded with Keith Whitley before he died.

Keith Whitley

Despite a number of personal and professional successes, the past several years have not been easy for Lorrie Morgan. Most difficult to accept was the death of her husband, performer Keith Whitley, in 1989. A highly respected singer and songwriter, Whitley (born in Kentucky, in 1955) started

performing at age eight and, with best friend Ricky Skaggs, formed his first band at age 13. The two later played with Ralph Stanley's legendary Clinch Mountain Boys bluegrass band; Whitley was just 15 years old at the time. Whitley left the Ralph Stanley band to join bluegrass-newgrass combo J.D. Crowe & the New South, then embarked on a solo career. Making his way to Nashville, Whitley married Lorrie in 1986. In 1988, Whitley enjoyed long overdue success when his "When You Say Nothing at All" hit the top of the charts. His third album, *Don't Close Your Eyes*, saw Whitley at the top of his form with such cuts as Lefty Frizzell's "I Never Go Around Mirrors" and "Flying Colors." Tragically, most of Whitley's accolades came after his premature death from accidental alcohol poisoning.

For a while, she sang backup vocals for George Jones. Finally, as a result of her demo work, she was signed to Hickory Records, which was owned by Acuff-Rose. She released a couple of singles and was nominated as Top New Female Artist by the Academy of Country Music. Despite the recognition, her career did not take off as expected. She continued to try to establish herself by performing on the road, often with inadequate backup bands. She also landed a spot as a regular on the then-fledgling TNN Show, *Nashville Now*.

When she finally landed a deal at RCA, she released her first album, *You Can Leave the Light On*, in 1989. Five top-20 hits resulted from this sparkling debut album—"Dear Me," "Five Minutes," "Trainwreck of Emotion," "He Talks to Me," and "Out of Your Shoes," which went to the top of the charts. Her second album, *Something in*

Red, followed in 1991 and featured "We Both Walk" and "A Picture of Me (Without You)." Both albums have since gone platinum.

In 1990, Lorrie released the poignant duet, "'Til a Tear Becomes a Rose," which she had recorded with her husband Keith Whitley before he died. The single was named Vocal Event of the Year by the Country Music Association. She was also nominated as country's best female vocalist by both the Country Music Association and the Academy of Country Music.

Something in Red had given Morgan's country-pop style a sultry edge, which she continued to exploit with her next album, *Watch Me*. Lorrie had switched to the BNA label for this 1992 album, which yielded the hit singles "Watch Me" and "What Part of No." Lorrie's white blonde hair and provocative good looks enhanced her reputation as country music's hottest torch singer. Despite this image, Morgan's 1994 album, *War Paint*, featured a poignant ballad about Keith Whitley called "If You Came Back from Heaven." "Heaven" clearly reveals Morgan's range as a singer.

In addition to singing, Morgan has tried her hand at acting. She snared the lead role in the TNN movie *Proud Heart*, which cast her as a single working mother who struggles to succeed in a man's world.

Another new venture for Morgan is songwriting. After playing a few of her compositions for Kris Kristofferson, she was encouraged by his praise to take the demos of her songs off the shelf and start pitching them.

Morgan's contemporary country style has crossover potential.

LORRIE MORGAN

REAL NAME: Loretta Lynn Morgan

BORN: June 27, 1959, in Nashville, Tennessee

MUSICAL INFLUENCE: Johnny Mathis

FIRST HIT: "Trainwreck of Emotion" (1989)

OTHER NOTABLE HITS: "If You Came Back from Heaven" (1994); "Something in Red" (1992); "Except for Monday" (1991); "We Both Walk" (1991); "A Picture of Me (Without You)" (1991); "'Til a Tear Becomes a Rose" (with Keith Whitley, 1990); "Dear Me" (1989); "Out of Your Shoes" (1989); "Five Minutes" (1989)

BEST ALBUMS: *Watch Me* (1992); *Something in Red* (1991); *Leave the Light On* (1989)

AWARDS INCLUDE: Country Music Association Vocal Event of the Year (with Keith Whitley, 1990)

ACHIEVEMENTS: Grand Ole Opry member (1984)

PERSONAL: Morgan is the daughter of country singer George Morgan.

· WILLIE · NELSON ·

Willie Nelson remains as much an outlaw in the 1990s as he was 20 years ago because he makes Nashville bend for him rather than forcing his distinctive style into a traditional country sound. Nelson's deeply interpretive singing style gives him this flexibility. With a voice as smooth as scotch,

Five-time Grammy winner Willie Nelson has introduced country music to millions of new listeners.

and the savvy to consistently surround himself with musicians who carry the bite of a jagged ice cube, Nelson has enjoyed a long musical career.

Born on April 30, 1933, in Abbott, Texas, Nelson was very young when his parents divorced. He and his older sister, Bobbie, were raised by their grandparents.

As a youth, Nelson's ears were tuned into all kinds of music. He heard late-night jazz from a New Orleans radio station and piano boogie woogie from Freddie Slack. One of Nelson's earliest and most lasting influences was Frank Sinatra.

In 1943, Nelson landed his first professional job, as an acoustic guitarist with the Bohemian Polka Band in nearby Fort Worth. By the time he reached high school, Nelson had joined the Texans, a loose country aggregation fronted by his brother-in-law.

After graduating from high school in 1951, Nelson enlisted in the Air Force. A chronic back injury resulted in a medical discharge in less than a year. He rejoined the Texans and in 1952 married Martha Mathews, a 16-year-old Cherokee Indian.

Nelson had thought of becoming a preacher—in the early 1950s, he had taught Sunday school at a Baptist church in Fort Worth. But, in pursuit of a career in agriculture, he moved to Waco, Texas, and enrolled in Baylor University. To pay for his college education, he toiled at sev-

Early in his country music career, Willie Nelson was a bass player with Ray Price's band.

eral odd jobs, including selling vacuum cleaners and Bibles door to door.

After two years, Nelson dropped out of college and became a disc jockey in San Antonio. This job led to other radio gigs in California, Texas, and Vancouver, British Columbia. In the fall of 1956, while working at KVAN radio in Vancouver, Nelson decided to cut a record of his own. It was an original composition called "No Place For Me," with a Leon Payne tune, "Lumberjack," on the flip side. He had 500 copies of the single pressed and sold them over the radio at a dollar apiece. Today "No Place For Me" is regarded as Nelson's rarest recording.

Nelson returned to Texas in 1957 and settled in Pasadena, where he continued to pursue songwriting while working as a disc jockey. During this time he penned "Family Bible" and one of country music's biggest hits, "Night Life." Nelson, however, felt he was going nowhere fast in Texas, and in 1960 he took off for Nashville in a beat-up 1946 Buick.

Nelson had planned to be a songwriter, but after hanging around Tootsie's Orchid Lounge in downtown Nashville, he was hired in 1961 as a bass guitarist in Ray Price's band, the Chero-

Willie Nelson, who helps organize the Farm Aid benefit each year, is popular with both pop and country audiences.

kee Cowboys. Offstage, Nelson's songwriting career began to blossom. In 1961, he wrote "Crazy" for Patsy Cline, "Funny How Time Slips Away" for Billy Walker, and "Hello Walls" for Faron Young. Liberty Records signed him to the label in 1962.

By 1964, Nelson had become a regular on the *Grand Ole Opry*. Despite becoming increasingly disenchanted with the lush strings and emotive backing choirs that defined the Nashville Sound, Nelson achieved moderate success as a performer during the 1960s. After a December 1970 fire gutted his home in Ridgetop, Tennessee, Nelson returned to Texas, settling in Austin.

Nelson's commercial breakthrough came in 1972, when he signed with Atlantic Records. In February 1973, Nelson holed up for five days in a New York City studio and recorded a mass of material. From these sessions, the album *Shotgun Willie* was born. A seminal work in Nelson's career, the album was the first to showcase his unique vocal interpretations. His band included his sister Bobbie as pianist, Doug Sahm of the Sir Douglas Quintet, Larry Gatlin, and western swing fiddle player J.R. Chatwell. The soulful Memphis Horns, best known for their work with Stax Records, appeared on a couple of cuts. Nelson has often stated that the Atlantic period was the turning point in his career.

When Atlantic dissolved its country division in 1974, Nelson move to Columbia, where he had complete control. His debut album at Columbia, 1975's *Red-Headed Stranger*, was a smash. The album spawned Nelson's first pop hit, "Blue Eyes Cryin' in the Rain."

Nelson followed up the success of *Red-Headed Stranger* with 1976's *Wanted: The Outlaws*, on which he collaborated with Waylon Jennings, Jessi Colter, and Tompall Glaser. The album featured reissued material from Nelson's earlier years, but the instrumentation went against the commercial Nashville Sound. *Wanted* hit number one on the country charts, crossed over into

Outlaw

The release of *Wanted: The Outlaws*, a 1976 collaboration among Willie Nelson, Waylon Jennings, Jessi Colter, and Tompall Glaser (of Tompall and the Glaser Brothers), proved significant in many ways. The album, which contained the hit duet "Good-Hearted Woman" with Waylon Jennings, was the first certified platinum album in country music history. It spawned the "outlaw movement," a reworking of down-and-dirty honky-tonk music rooted in the pure sounds of Jimmie Rodgers, Ernest Tubb, Hank Williams, and Lefty Frizzell. The outlaws' album and their subsequent national tour attracted a crossover rock audience, inspiring massive new interest in country music. For Willie personally, the album was significant as the first of many recordings that featured Nelson in collaboration with other artists. These included *Waylon*

& Willie (1978); *One for the Road* (1979, with Leon Russell); *San Antonio Rose* (1980, with Ray Price); *Poncho and Lefty* (1982, with Merle Haggard); and *Highwayman* (1986, with Johnny Cash, Waylon Jennings, and Kris Kristofferson). By the early 1980s, Nelson had come to be known as the "king" of country duets.

Despite a busy schedule, Nelson still finds time for his wife, Anne Marie, and son Luke.

ring roles when he appeared opposite Dyan Cannon in *Honeysuckle Rose*, a film about a country singer's lifestyle on the road. Musical outlaw Willie got to play a real outlaw in the western *Barbarosa*, about a free-spirited gunslinger on the lam. Nelson's flirtation with Hollywood was brief, but it exposed him to even larger audiences.

the top ten on the pop charts, and was the first country album ever to go platinum. The Country Music Association voted it Album of the Year, and "Good-Hearted Woman," a Jennings-Nelson duo from the album, was named Vocal Duo of the Year and Single of the Year. The album's massive popularity set the conservative Nashville establishment on its ears, and Nelson's "outlaw" image was forever embedded in country music culture.

But Nelson turned an about-face on the red-bandanna outlaw image in 1978, releasing the resplendent *Stardust*, a collection of pop standards that has sold four million copies. The financial and popular success of *Stardust* led him to record a second collection of pop standards in 1981, *Somewhere Over the Rainbow*.

With his long hair, rugged physical appearance, and outlaw persona, Nelson seemed a natural for the movies. Hollywood came calling in the late 1970s, and Nelson costarred with Robert Redford in the 1979 film *The Electric Horseman*. In 1980, he graduated to star-

Nelson united with Johnny Cash, Waylon Jennings, and Kris Kristofferson (left) to record Highwayman.

To show his gratitude and support for the people of Austin, his adopted hometown, Nelson started his famous annual Fourth of July celebrations featuring country musicians outside the Nashville mainstream. In the 1980s, he devoted much of his free time to heading the Farm Aid movement, which raises money for American farmers.

Nelson has frequently recorded with other singers. He and Waylon Jennings reunited in 1978 to record *Waylon & Willie*, another platinum album and a major hit on both the country and pop charts. Nelson, Jennings, Johnny Cash, and Kris Kristofferson got together in 1986 to record *Highwayman*.

In late 1990, the Internal Revenue Service seized Nelson's property to ensure payment of $16.7 million in back taxes. Two of Nelson's ranch homes and many personal items were auctioned off to raise money. He recorded a mail-order album, *Who'll Buy My Memories*, to pay off the debt. It contained demos of 25 songs whose rights were seized by the IRS. But in 1993, after an investigation, the IRS reduced his debt to $5.4 million.

"There's nothing precious in life except loved ones," Nelson, who has been married four times and fathered several children, once stated. "All of these things I've lost are just things." Nelson's comment became an eerie prophecy: On Christmas Day, 1991, his son, Billy, committed suicide at the age of 33. But Nelson's storied life has been about bending, never breaking. Despite adversity, he continued to write songs and make music. His recent albums still showcase his eccentric vocal style, whether he is reworking familiar tunes in new arrangements or introducing new songs.

In 1993, he released the eclectic *Across the Borderline*, which included vocal contributions by Bonnie Raitt, Bob Dylan, and Sinead O'Connor. Nelson hearkened back to *Stardust* and *Somewhere Over the Rainbow* in 1994, when he put together *Moonlight Becomes You*, another album of pop and country standards.

Nelson's long career has left him at the pinnacle of success. As an innovator in country-western music, Willie Nelson helped push country away from the lush choruses and overly orchestrated arrangements that dominated Nashville in the mid-1970s. His Austin-inspired honky-tonk style and spare, minimalist instrumentations represented an alternative to the Nashville Sound—an alternative that later became a major movement. Despite his respect for pop singers and his own experimentations with pop music, he personifies progressive country music. Not the least of his contributions has been introducing new listeners, attracted by his crossover hits, to country music.

WILLIE NELSON

BORN: April 30, 1933, in Abbott, Texas

MUSICAL INFLUENCE: Frank Sinatra

FIRST HIT: "Willingly" (with Shirley Collie, 1962)

OTHER NOTABLE HITS: "Always on My Mind" (1982); "On the Road Again" (1980); "Mammas, Don't Let Your Babies Grow Up To Be Cowboys" (with Waylon Jennings, 1978); "Blue Eyes Cryin' in the Rain" (1975)

BEST ALBUMS: *Nite Life* (1989); *Always on My Mind* (1982); *Stardust* (1978); *Waylon & Willie* (1978); *Wanted: The Outlaws* (with Waylon Jennings, et al., 1976); *Red-Headed Stranger* (1975)

AWARDS INCLUDE: Grammy, Best Country Male Vocal Performance (1982, 1978, 1975); Grammy, Best Country Song (1980); Grammy, Best Country Vocal Performance by a Duo or Group (with Waylon Jennings, 1978); Country Music Association Vocal Duo of the Year (with Julio Iglesias, 1984; with Merle Haggard, 1983; with Waylon Jennings, 1976); Academy of Country Music (ACM) Pioneer Award (1991); ACM Entertainer of the Year (1979); National Academy of Popular Music Lifetime Achievement Award (1983)

ACHIEVEMENTS: Country Music Hall of Fame inductee (1993); Grand Ole Opry member (1964)

·K.T. · OSLIN·

Singer K.T. Oslin's rise to the top of the country charts was especially gratifying because it came at a time in life when many performers begin to fade from view. For Oslin, who was in her mid-40s when she found success as a country entertainer, it meant a whole new beginning.

Born in Crossitt, Arkansas, Kay Toinette Oslin grew up in Mobile, Alabama, and Houston, Texas. As a teen,

K.T. Oslin's contemporary country music offers listeners a female viewpoint.

she discovered rock 'n' roll and the Texas folk music scene. One of her earliest professional experiences was singing in a folk trio with songwriter Guy Clark.

A drama major in college, Oslin returned to her theatrical training when she landed a part in the chorus of the national touring company of *Hello Dolly!* with Carol Channing. She went on to join the Broadway company of the show, starring Betty Grable, and appeared in several other Broadway musicals—including *West Side Story* and *Promises, Promises*—before switching to more lucrative work as a studio backup vocalist and jingle singer.

Some time later, Oslin decided to try her hand at songwriting, an interest she had developed while doing college concerts in the southeastern United States in the early 1970s. She penned her first tune with a friend in the jingle business, titling it "Cornell Crawford"—a name inspired by something she had seen scrawled on a ladies room wall while on a concert tour. As Oslin fondly recalls, "I'm sitting there reading this sentence that said, 'I ain't never gonna love nobody but Cornell Crawford.' It literally made me throw back my head and laugh."

By 1981, Oslin's songwriting had attracted the attention of Elektra Records. However, Oslin's first two single releases, "Clean Your Own Tables" and "Younger Man," quickly faded into obscurity. Radio programmers thought Oslin's material was too feminist and feared it might offend their male listeners. Although Elektra dropped her from the label, Oslin wasn't ready to give up.

Oslin received the CMA Song of the Year award for "80's Ladies," becoming the first female songwriter to earn this distinction.

Other singers began cutting her tunes, giving Oslin the confidence to continue. Gail Davies had some chart success with "Round the Clock Lovin'," and she selected "Where Is a Woman to Go" (also recorded by Dottie West) as the title cut for her 1985 album.

Oslin persevered, borrowing $7,000 from her Aunt Reba, a stockbroker, to stage her own showcase in Nashville. In the audience the night of her performance was Harold Shedd, who was then producing Alabama's albums. Shedd was impressed with what he heard. He recorded three tunes with Oslin in the studio and played them for Joe Galante, then head of RCA's Nashville office. Galante, struck by the quality of the lyrics and the conviction in Oslin's voice, quickly called to offer her a record deal. Three months later, Oslin's debut single for the label, "Wall of Tears," hit the charts, where it had a respectable run, peaking at number 40.

Making the most of her drama background, Oslin portrays the Bride of Frankenstein for her "Come Next Monday" video.

With her second single, "80's Ladies," Oslin further secured her niche in country music as a performer offering contemporary tunes and a cosmopolitan image. By the time she bought a house in Nashville in June of 1987, the "80's Ladies" video had reached number one on Country Music Television. Two months later, Olsin's *80's Ladies* album debuted at number 15 on the *Billboard* country album charts.

That December, Oslin scored her first number-one hit with "Do Ya." The following year found Oslin flush with honors, including a Grammy—the music industry's highest accolade—and two awards from the Academy of

With her clever songs and strong vocal ability, Oslin has become popular as a songwriter and performer.

Country Music. Oslin added a gold record to her credit when *80's Ladies* was certified, becoming the first female country artist since Anne Murray (for *Snowbird* in 1973) to have a debut gold album.

Between awards and accolades, Oslin—called "the Diva" by some Nashville insiders—recorded "Face to Face," a chart-topping duet with Alabama's Randy Owen. By October of 1988, Oslin was riding the crest of her initial wave of success. The Country Music Association named her Female Vocalist of the Year and awarded "80's Ladies" Song of the Year—the first time a female songwriter earned this honor.

RCA released Oslin's second album, *This Woman*, in August of 1988. This highly successful follow-up garnered the singer two more Grammys—for performing and writing "Hold Me," the album's chart-topping hit. Oslin also picked up Best Female Vocalist honors from the Academy of Country Music and the Country Music Association. As 1989 came to a close, both *80's Ladies* and *This Woman* had gone platinum.

Oslin took a break from touring to concentrate on writing songs for her third disc, *Love in a Small Town*, released in November 1990. Leaner and more spare than her other albums, *Love in a Small Town* offered up earthy, slice-of-life vignettes about common folk, providing a perfect showcase for Oslin's enviable songwriting talents. The first single, "Come Next Monday," (accompanied by a video featuring Oslin as the Bride of Frankenstein) became an instant hit.

Oslin and Randy Travis (right) have both received Grammys for their contributions to country music.

In 1993, Oslin released a collection of her greatest hits entitled *Songs from an Aging Sex Bomb*, which served as a summary of her country career up to that point. A modest success, the album reflected the work of a mature singer who has found her niche.

Oslin once admitted that, as a child, she disliked country music because of its predominantly male point of view. With her sophisticated wit and uncompromising maturity, she has helped bring a much-needed female perspective to country music.

K.T. OSLIN

REAL NAME: Kay Toinette Oslin

BORN: May 15, 1942, in Crossitt, Arkansas

MUSICAL INFLUENCES: Hank Williams, Hank Snow, the Carter Family

FIRST HIT: "80's Ladies" (1987)

OTHER NOTABLE HITS: "Mary and Willie" (1991); "Come Next Monday" (1990); "Hey Bobby" (1989); "Hold Me" (1988); "I'll Always Come Back" (1988); "Do Ya" (1987)

BEST ALBUMS: *Love in a Small Town* (1990); *This Woman* (1988); *80's Ladies* (1987)

AWARDS INCLUDE: Grammy, Best Country Female Vocal Performance (1988, 1987); Grammy, Best Country Song (1988); Country Music Association (CMA) Female Vocalist of the Year (1988); CMA Song of the Year (1988); Academy of Country Music (ACM) Top Female Vocalist (1988); ACM Album of the Year (1988); ACM Top New Female Vocalist (1987)

· LEE · ROY · PARNELL ·

This tall, red-haired Texan with the fiery guitar has made his mark by infusing the hallowed sounds of traditional country music with his own rip-roaring, high-voltage style. Parnell caught listeners' attention with "Oughta Be a Law" and "Mexican Money" from his self-titled debut disc, but

Parnell merges musical styles such as blues and western swing to produce his unique country sound.

his breakthrough proved to be his second album, *Love Without Mercy*. Parnell's third and most successful album, *On the Road*, has yielded such favorites as

"Holding My Own" and the title track, making the charismatic singer/guitarist a familiar presence on the radio airwaves.

Born into a country-music-loving household, Parnell developed an early taste for a wide assortment of musical styles—blues, rock, western swing, and, of course, country. Hitting the road as a full-time musician after graduating from high school, Parnell spent the next dozen years paying his musical dues. He took up residence briefly in New York City, moved to Florida, then returned to Austin in the mid-1970s. Finally, in 1987, Parnell decided to go for broke and relocate to Nashville to try his luck as a country singer and songwriter.

By the time Parnell reached Nashville, he realized he had become caught in a downward spiral of excessive drinking and late-night carousing. Now a recovering alcoholic, Parnell has been open and remarkably candid about his battle with the bottle and its near destruction of his life.

After regaining his sobriety, Parnell was confronted with the devastating loss of both his parents and his beloved grandmother—all within a five-week period. Parnell credits his spiritual renewal with helping him to deal with his grief.

Emerging from some of the darkest days of his life, Parnell began to see good things coming his way. The singer met a beautiful, dark-haired woman named Kim who was working at his publishing company, and he found himself completely entranced. Twice divorced, with two small children, Parnell wasn't looking for an involvement. His initial reluctance soon behind him, the couple was married in a few short weeks by her father, a Baptist minister.

Signing with the newly formed Nashville division of Arista Records, Lee Roy set the country music industry abuzz with his 1990 debut album. Parnell's first collection of songs reflected a wide range of influences, from the blues to Texas swing. His interest in the latter is not surprising considering western-swing master Bob Wills was a family friend. The album, which emphasized horns but did include a bit of Parnell's slide-guitar playing, was perhaps too eclectic. The album made a respectable showing on the charts, but it was not the commercial success that Arista had hoped it would become.

Arista president and prominent producer Tim DuBois helped Parnell reign in his musical influences to forge a style that was more distinctive. The results were heard on Lee Roy's second album, *Love Without Mercy*, which brought his slide-guitar playing to the forefront and commercialized his blues-tinged, soulful voice. By *On the Road*, Parnell was sure enough of his sound and style to write six of the songs on the album. From "Straight Shooter" to "Country Down to My Soul," the album reflects Parnell's more mainstream direction.

With his newly refined style and stronger musical focus, Lee Roy Parnell shows every sign of enjoying a long and highly successful career.

LEE ROY PARNELL

BORN: December 21, 1956, in Abilene, Texas

MUSICAL INFLUENCES: Bob Wills, Allman Brothers, Jimmie Rodgers, Muddy Waters, Jimmie Vaughan, Merle Haggard

FIRST HIT: "Oughta Be a Law" (1990)

OTHER NOTABLE HITS: "I'm Holding My Own" (1993); "Country Down to My Soul" (1993); "On the Road" (1993); "Love Without Mercy" (1992); "Tender Moment" (1992); "What Kind of Fool (Do You Think I Am)" (1992); "Mexican Money" (1990)

BEST ALBUMS: *On the Road* (1993); *Love Without Mercy* (1992); *Lee Roy Parnell* (1990)

PERSONAL: One of Parnell's father's closest friends was the legendary Bob Wills; Parnell gave his first performance at the age of six, joining Wills on WBAP radio in Fort Worth, singing the classic "San Antonio Rose"; recalls Parnell, "He was the one who inspired me to listen to music in the beginning. I still listen to his music religiously."

DOLLY · PARTON ·

Dolly Parton has been part of the Nashville scene since 1967. She is a country music legend who has also found Hollywood fame.

Dolly Parton embodies country music largely because of her image as a down-home woman who never lost her country roots. In reality, Parton is something of an uplifting country-pop stylist rather than a pure country vocalist. In addition to her pop-music connections, Parton is also recognized as a veteran of television talk-shows and prime-time music specials, as well as numerous film roles.

Dolly has been affiliated with many facets of mainstream show business in recent years, and she has become a sophisticated entrepreneur. Dolly has her own star on Hollywood's famous Walk of Fame, a testament to her popularity and importance outside of country music.

It wasn't always that way. Parton comes from some of the most unpolished roots in contemporary country music. She was born January 19, 1946, in the impoverished mountain region of Locust Ridge, Sevier County, Tennessee. Her father could neither read nor write.

The fourth of a dozen children, the feisty Parton began singing as soon as she could talk. When she was eight, an uncle gave her a small Martin guitar, her first musical instrument. From that time on, Parton wanted to be a star. So starstruck was Dolly that she would sit on the back porch and sing to the butterflies using an old fruit cocktail can as a microphone. Parton has never forgotten her poor roots. Some of her best songs reflect the early days of her life, including "Tennessee Mountain Home," "Coat of Many Colors," and "Eagle When She Flies."

"That song ('Eagle When She Flies') is about an Appalachian mother with a kid on her hip and one in her belly and two hanging on her legs, stirrin' a pot of beans," Parton revealed in a 1991 interview. Such humble material has always been the perfect conduit for Parton's small soprano. Her voice knows when to glitter and when to glide, and became the perfect attribute for crossing over to pop.

Parton was the first member of her family to graduate from high school. The day after Parton graduated from Sevier County High School she headed to Nashville. In 1967, she met a shy asphalt-paving contractor named Carl Dean, whom she married. In an industry in which marriage is a dicey proposition, the Parton-

Parton often sings of her poor country roots. Her success, like Loretta Lynn's, is an inspiration to many.

Parton's talent as a songwriter and performer is often overshadowed by her provocative appearance and colorful image.

Dean marriage has survived for almost 30 years. Parton maintains that the marriage has lasted because Dean is not interested in show business. He prefers to live his own life and leave the spotlight to Dolly.

Before her marriage, Parton lived with Bill Owens, an uncle who was a part-time songwriter. In 1966, Parton and Owens penned "Put It Off Until Tomorrow," a top-ten country hit for Bill Phillips. The success with Phillips led Parton into her own deal with Monument Records. Her loquacious debut album, *Hello, I'm Dolly,* was released in 1967. One of her first Monument hits was 1967's "Dumb Blonde," one of the few songs that she has recorded that she has not written or cowritten. (She has published more than 3,000 songs.)

Dolly's combination of Smoky Mountain wit, golden gossamer wigs, an hourglass figure, and long false fingernails was beginning to simmer. Country star Porter Wagoner—hardly a wallflower himself with his rhinestone-studded suits and high-rise pompadour—helped develop her career for a while. Looking for someone to replace the affable singer Norma Jean on his famous television and road show, Wagoner turned to Parton.

They were an immediate success. By mixing Wagoner's tenor harmony and Parton's lead melody, they recorded such hit singles as "The Last Thing on My Mind," released in 1968, and "Always, Always," released the following year. The country music industry was delighted with the colorful pair, who attracted attention with their unique duets and their onstage chemistry. The Country Music Association voted them Vocal Group of the Year in 1968.

When time permitted, Parton recorded as a solo artist. In 1970, her ballad about a female mule skinner, "Mule Skinner Blues," became her first number-one song. Other tunes recorded during this period include such Parton classics as "Joshua" and "Jolene." Looking to stretch her wings, Parton left the Wagoner show in 1974. The initial split from Wagoner was amicable, and he continued to produce her records for three more years.

By 1976, Parton wanted to update her sound. She ended her long affiliation with Wagoner, who reacted bitterly and filed a lawsuit. While in litigation, Parton wrote one of her most widely known songs, "I Will Always Love You." The poignant ballad was actually written about the end of her friendship with Wagoner. Though never involved romantically, the termination of their professional relationship had been heartbreaking and grueling for Parton, and she captured those feelings in song. In 1992, a version of "I Will Always Love You" was recorded by pop star Whitney Houston as the theme song for the film *The Bodyguard.*

After ending her association with Wagoner, Parton signed with Gallin-Morey-Addis, a Los Angeles-based management company, to help expand her horizons. Wagoner wasn't the only Nashville figure to question Parton's move but she maintained, "I'm not leaving country, I'm taking it with me." And, Parton did take off.

Her 1977 album, *Here You Come Again* went platinum, garnering Parton her first Grammy. The follow-up album *Heartbreaker* went gold in 1978 as did 1979's *Great Balls of Fire*, in which Parton covered rock classics. Exploring different sounds and musical styles—from country to pop to rock and back again—defined Parton's output from the late 1970s to the mid-1980s. Though Dolly's voice never lost its country charm, she surrounded herself with lush, upbeat pop arrangements and contemporary rock musi-

cians. Her pop-flavored "Islands in the Stream" duet with Kenny Rogers was one of only two singles in the entire music field to go platinum in 1983.

Parton continued her flirtation with pop music throughout the 1980s with albums such as *Real Love* from 1985. Often, her albums included both country pop tunes and more traditional country songs. The 1980 album *9 to 5 and Other Odd Jobs* featured the pop-flavored title song from the film *9 to 5* plus a selec-

Dolly, Inc.

One of twelve children, Dolly Parton was born in 1946 in a one-room shack without electricity, a telephone, running water, or plumbing. Some 40 years later, conservative estimates put Parton's worth at $200 million and find her firmly in control of an empire that extends from Tennessee to Hollywood and Hawaii. Hard work and perseverance have helped Parton make many of her dreams come true. One of these was the opening of her Dollywood theme park in Pigeon Forge, Tennessee, in 1986. In addition to bringing jobs to the area, the amusement park funds an educational foundation based in Parton's birthplace of Sevier County, Tennessee. Dolly's lifelong love affair with makeup (as a child, she used to mix makeup out of crushed berries, burnt matches, and even Mercurochrome) found expression in her Beauty Confidence Collection, a cosmetics line introduced by Revlon. A real-life rags-to-riches story,

Dolly's empire includes a production company, real estate holdings, restaurants, and self-help books. Dolly is also a successful movie actress, having appeared in several films, including *9 to 5*, for which she earned an Oscar nomination, *Best Little Whorehouse in Texas*, *Steel Magnolias*, and *Straight Talk*.

Parton's acting career includes a starring role in Steel Magnolias. *Pictured (left to right) are Shirley MacLaine, Daryl Hannah, Sally Field, Parton, and Julia Roberts.*

tion of country tunes with work-related themes, including "Dark as a Dungeon" and "Working Girl." Several collections of Parton's best work were issued as well, including *The Best of Dolly Parton* in 1987 and *Dolly Parton's Greatest Hits* in 1988.

During the 1980s, Parton expanded her career to include projects in film and television. Her acting career began in 1980 with the high-profile comedy *9 to 5*, which starred such major-league stars as Jane Fonda and Lily Tomlin. Her venture in acting served as her

inspiration to lose a great deal of weight. Occasional movie roles followed throughout the decade, including a starring role in the 1992 comedy *Straight Talk* opposite one of her favorite actors, James Woods. Dolly realizes that her bubbly personality is best suited to comedies, and she is cautious about venturing into dramatic roles. "I'm never going to be a Meryl Streep," she maintains. "But then, she'll never be a Dolly Parton either!"

Dolly has also tried her luck on the small screen. In addition to the made-for-television film *Wild Texas Wind*, she was the host of her own television variety series in 1988, and she often cohosted the critically acclaimed country music program *Hot Country Stars* in the early 1990s.

In 1987, Parton moved from RCA to Columbia. The change in recording companies marked a move by Parton back into the country music fold. Her sound not only echoed with a richer country flavor than it had during the 1980s but her 1990s music also included the participation of country music's finest songwriters, producers, and artists. *White Limozeen*, released in 1989, was produced by Ricky Skaggs. The album included the sassy "Why'd You Come in Here Lookin' Like That" and "Yellow Roses," a classic country tale of heartbreak.

Parton followed *White Limozeen* with *Eagle When She Flies* in 1991 and *Slow Dancing with the Moon* in 1993. Once again, she relied on the participation of Nashville's best artists, producers, and songwriters to come up with some of her best work in years. Both albums feature the participation of country's biggest names. *Eagle* includes a duet with Ricky Van Shelton called "Rockin' Years" and another with Lorrie Morgan titled "Best Woman Wins."

The title cut from *Slow Dancing* was written for her by Nashville veteran Mac Davis, though Dolly herself wrote or cowrote eight of the dozen songs on the album. The high-profile hit from *Slow Dancing* was a role-reversal tune called "Romeo," which featured guest vocals from Mary Chapin Carpenter, Kathy Mattea, and Tanya Tucker. The song—about a male sex object who gets the once-over from the women—also includes the participation of country heartthrob Billy Ray Cyrus. Duet partners on other various cuts include John Hiatt, Billy Dean, and Collin Raye, with harmony vocals from Vince Gill and Rodney Crowell. Even legendary guitarist Chet Atkins picks along on "I'll Make Your Bed."

With her musical output in the 1990s, Parton has worked hard to regain her place in the country music industry. By including the talents and participation of the industry's best and brightest, she was able to return to Music City in peak form.

Though Dolly is the first to poke fun at her larger-than-life image, her physical appearance and country candor sometimes overshadow her many accomplishments and contributions to country music. Her talent as a songwriter, which surfaced again on *Eagle When She Flies* and *Slow Daning with the Moon*, and her unique voice qualify her as a major force and influence in country music.

DOLLY PARTON

BORN: January 19, 1946, in Locust Ridge, Tennessee

FIRST HIT: "Dumb Blonde" (1967)

OTHER NOTABLE HITS: "Romeo" (1993); "Islands in the Stream" (with Kenny Rogers, 1983); "9 to 5" (1980); "Here You Come Again" (1977); "Jolene" (1973); "Coat of Many Colors" (1971)

BEST ALBUMS: *White Limozeen* (1989); *Trio* (with Emmylou Harris and Linda Ronstadt, 1987); *9 to 5 and Other Odd Jobs* (1980); *Great Balls of Fire* (1979); *Heartbreaker* (1978); *Here You Come Again* (1977)

AWARDS INCLUDE: Grammy, Best Country Vocal Performance By a Duo or Group (with Linda Ronstadt and Emmylou Harris, 1987); Grammy, Best Country Female Vocal Performance (1981, 1978); Country Music Association (CMA) Entertainer of the Year (1978); CMA Female Vocalist of the Year (1976, 1975); Academy of Country Music (ACM) Top Vocal Duet (with Kenny Rogers, 1983); ACM Top Female Vocalist (1980); ACM Entertainer of the Year (1977)

ACHIEVEMENTS: Grand Ole Opry member (1969)

COLLIN · RAYE

Collin Raye has experienced the kind of success most performers only dream about. Yet he has remained the gracious country gentleman he always was. When his second album, *In This Life*, was certified gold, Raye presented gold albums to every songwriter who had contributed to the album.

Raye's albums showcase his talent for singing upbeat, honky-tonk tunes such as "That's My Story" and "I Want You Bad."

Born Collin Wray in DeQueen, Arkansas, Raye was raised in Texarkana in a musical family. At one time or another, his mother opened shows for such big-name performers as Elvis Presley, Johnny Cash, Jerry Lee Lewis, and Carl Perkins.

When Raye was 13, he and his brother Scott started their own band, the Wray Brothers. They moved to Oregon in the 1980s and played the Pacific Northwest for several years, where they won regional acclaim and released a few singles. Lucrative offers to perform at Reno casinos followed. The brothers landed a singles deal with Mercury/Nashville, but an executive shake-up left them out in the cold. Scott dropped out, leaving his brother to carry on solo.

Raye learned a lot about performing from his Reno days, experience he drew on when he began hunting for a new recording contract. In 1991, after performing a showcase for industry executives that was hailed by songwriter extraordinaire Harlan Howard as "the best I've seen since k.d. lang," he signed with Columbia Records and recorded his debut album *All I Can Be*. His albums, *In This Life* and *Extremes*, have spawned such hits as "That Was a River," "Somebody Else's Moon," "That's My Story," and "Little Rock."

Along the road to big-selling albums and sold-out concerts, Raye has seen his share of hard times. In 1980 Raye married former nightclub owner Connie Parker. She suffered severe complications while giving birth to their second child and slipped into a two-month coma. Son Jacob, now eight, was born with cerebral palsy and Connie underwent months of grueling physical rehabilitation. A devoted father to Jacob and daughter Brittany,

Raye's contributions include his breakthrough hit, "Love, Me," and the country ballad "Little Rock."

both of whom guest-starred in their father's "Love, Me" video, Raye often takes his children on the road with him and spends his dwindling off-time in Greenville, Texas, where the children live with their mother, who has made a full recovery. Divorced since 1987, Raye has never remarried, though the handsome singer has been linked with Tanya Tucker.

Collin Raye is best known for power ballads—"Love, Me" and "In This Life," among them—but he more than does justice to such romping tunes as "I Want You Bad" and his humorous ode to male misbehavior, "That's My Story." Careful to blend a rip-roaring, uptempo anthem with a heart-melting ballad, Collin Raye proves to be a versatile artist with great potential.

COLLIN RAYE

REAL NAME: Collin Wray

BORN: August 22, 1962, in DeQueen, Arkansas

MUSICAL INFLUENCES: Waylon Jennings, George Jones, the Eagles

FIRST HIT: "Love, Me" (1992)

OTHER NOTABLE HITS: "Little Rock" (1994); "That's My Story" (1993); "In This Life" (1992); "That Was a River" (1992); "Somebody Else's Moon" (1992); "All I Can Be" (1991)

BEST ALBUMS: *Extremes* (1994); *In This Life* (1992); *All I Can Be* (1991)

PERSONAL: Collin first took the stage at age 7, singing harmony for his mother, Susan Raye. During his live shows, it's become a tradition for Raye to douse the audience with a giant water machine gun.

·RICKY·VAN·SHELTON·

Some might find it hard to believe that Ricky Van Shelton was once a died-in-the-wool rock 'n' roll fan, who had no desire to be a country singer. That began to change one night when his brother Ronnie asked Shelton to grab his guitar and join him and his bluegrass band for a gig. Ricky wasn't at all inclined to go along until Ronnie told him that he could drive. It wasn't just any car that convinced the

Quiet and reserved offstage, Ricky Van Shelton saves his more expressive side for the suits he wears onstage.

14-year-old Ricky to take his brother up on the offer—it was Ronnie's 1964 Ford Fairlane 289.

Shelton soon realized that he wasn't going along just because he got to drive. He truly liked the music they were playing, and he began listening to classic country artists including Hank Williams and the Osborne Brothers. Over the next several years, Shelton performed country music for audiences wherever he could find them—at fish fries, local clubs, even in his friends' living rooms. To avoid confusion with another Ricky Shelton who lived in the area (they kept receiving each other's mail), he started using his middle name, Van. Not only did his mail start arriving on time but the name stuck and his friends started calling him Ricky Van.

Although Shelton had to work hard most of his life, he always found time to devote to his songwriting, a pastime he enjoyed even before

Shelton's music can be described as an updating of honky-tonk by way of rockabilly.

he discovered country music. Shelton worked up his first song, a slow rocker called "My Conscience Is Bothering Me," on the guitar when he was 13. Consumed by his music, the handsome Virginian's social life was limited. In fact, he once joked that his primary date was a guitar. Shelton did find time, however, to meet his future wife, Bettye. The two were married in 1980.

Shelton and Bettye moved to Nashville, so that Shel-

ton could pursue his dream. Through Bettye's efforts, one of Shelton's homemade demo tapes eventually made its way to Jerry Thompson, a columnist for Nashville's morning paper, *The Tennessean.* Thompson alerted Rick Blackburn, then head of CBS Records, who agreed to watch Shelton perform in June 1986. He and producer Steve Buckingham, who also attended, were impressed.

Shelton's career took off quickly. Within two weeks of this performance, he was in the studio recording his first album, *Wild-Eyed Dream*, with Buckingham producing. Buckingham and Shelton proved a magical combination, with the two selecting songs written by several of Nashville's most respected tunesmiths, including Harlan Howard, Roger Miller, Buck Owens, and Merle Haggard. The album's first single, "Crime of Passion," soared into the top ten. Its follow-up single, "Somebody Lied," became the first of many number-one records for Shelton. In June 1987, he was invited to appear on the *Grand Ole Opry* and was so enthusiastically applauded that he was called back for an encore—a rare occurrence on the Opry stage.

Singer, songwriter, author, and gourmet cook, Shelton is country music's Renaissance man.

Wild-Eyed Dream provided the perfect showcase for Shelton's talents, from his aching, dramatic treatment of the ballad "Life Turned Her That Way" to his rip-roaring command of such rocking tunes as "Ultimately Fine" and "Crazy Over You." The album went platinum and brought Shelton a slew of awards in 1988. He was named Top New Male Vocalist by the Acad-

As a teenager, Shelton peferred rock 'n' roll to country-western—a musical interest that has strongly influenced Ricky's contemporary country sound.

emy of Country Music, and he received the Country Music Association's prestigious Horizon Award. The soft-spoken singer also became a member of the Grand Ole Opry that year.

Shelton and producer Buckingham reteamed for *Loving Proof*. Once again, they relied on a combination of rockabilly-style tunes alongside ballads, which showcase Shelton's smooth baritone voice. Shelton's music, as honed by Buckingham in the studio, is a commercially solid sound that features a rock 'n' roll beat backed by heavy drumming but "countrified" through the use of fiddles and a taut-sounding steel guitar. Despite the flirtation with rock 'n' roll and rockabilly, Shelton likes to cover the songs of such country music legends as Ernest Tubb, Merle Haggard, and Patsy Cline. *Loving Proof* included an updated version of the Cline hit "He's Got You." Shelton's talents as a songwriter were revealed in his composition "The Picture."

Shelton's third effort, *RVS III*, continued the same mix of the old and the new, the honky-tonk music and the rockabilly, that characterized his earlier work. It also produced four top-five hits—"Statue of a Fool" (a number-one remake of the Jack Greene classic), "I've Cried My Last Tear for You," "I Meant Every Word He Said," and "Life's Little Ups & Downs."

Shelton followed up in 1991 with *Backroads*, another collection of tunes demonstrating his rich, powerful country voice. The album showed the talented singer/songwriter to be equally at home with a rocking backbeat or a soaring ballad—and ready to venture into new territory with his chart-topping duet, "Rockin' Years," with Dolly Parton.

As Shelton's career soared, he began to expand his interests and pursue new goals. In 1992, Shelton wrote and published *Tales from a Duck Named Quacker*, the first in a series of children's books. The series focuses on valuable moral lessons as the main character, Quacker, journeys through life. He penned a second book, *Quacker Meets Mrs. Moo*, the following year. Expanding his musical horizons, Shelton recorded and released an old-time gospel album called *Don't Overlook Salvation* in 1992.

Fans eagerly awaited the release in 1993 of *A Bridge I Didn't Burn*, Shelton's first studio album in over two years. After pursuing a rock-flavored style for most of his career, Shelton moved into the traditional country arena, with sounds reminiscent of early George Jones and Ray Price. The title track, "Heartache Deep in the Heart of Me," and "Roses After the Rain" echo the type of country music heard 30 years ago. Like the title of the album, Shelton did not burn all of his rockabilly bridges, because he did include a rollicking cover of the old Ray Sharpe hit "Linda Lu."

Combining a humble manner and rich Virginia drawl with a life-long dedication to country music, Shelton has become one of country's most popular entertainers.

RICKY VAN SHELTON

BORN: January 12, 1952, in Grit, Virginia

MUSICAL INFLUENCES: Merle Haggard, Hank Williams, the Osborne Brothers

FIRST HIT: "Wild-Eyed Dream" (1987)

OTHER NOTABLE HITS: "A Bridge I Didn't Burn" (1993); "Keep It Between the Lines" (1991); "I Am a Simple Man" (1991); "Rockin' Years" (with Dolly Parton, 1991); "Statue of a Fool" (1990); "Living Proof" (1990); "I'll Leave This World Loving You" (1988); "Life Turned Her That Way" (1988); "Somebody Lied" (1987); "Crime of Passion" (1987)

BEST ALBUMS: *RVS III* (1990); *Loving Proof* (1988); *Wild-Eyed Dream* (1987)

AWARDS INCLUDE: Country Music Association (CMA) Male Vocalist of the Year (1989); CMA Horizon Award (1988); Academy of Country Music Top New Male Vocalist (1987)

ACHIEVEMENTS: Grand Ole Opry member (1988); published author of two children's books

· RICKY · SKAGGS ·

R icky Skaggs served an impressive apprenticeship before he had the opportunity to record his own music for a major record company. He quickly proved he'd learned his lessons well. Between 1980 and 1986, Skaggs created 16 top-ten hits with a fresh sound that updated bluegrass and honky-

Ricky Skaggs broke the stranglehold pop music had on Nashville by making old-time bluegrass and acoustic music commercially successful.

tonk music with breathtaking musical arrangements and a modern rhythmic bounce. The former bluegrass prodigy's success steered country in a new direction and set the stage for the return to traditional sounds.

Skaggs was born July 18, 1954, in Cordell, Kentucky. By age five, he was taking mandolin lessons from his father and learning traditional mountain songs from his mother. When he was seven, the youngster performed on a TV show hosted by bluegrass stars Flatt & Scruggs. At age 15, Skaggs joined the band headed by one of his idols, Ralph Stanley. In 1972, at age 17, he recorded an album with childhood friend Keith Whitley, also a member of Stanley's band.

Skaggs spent the mid-1970s as a member of several highly acclaimed, progressive bluegrass bands, including the Country Gentlemen, J.D. Crowe and the New South, and his own Boone Creek. Emmylou Harris recruited him to join her Hot Band in the late 1970s, and Skaggs began recording solo albums for the independent Sugar Hill label.

These independent recordings set the stage for Skaggs's first Nashville album for Epic Records. *Waitin' for the Sun to Shine* took country music executives by surprise with its huge sales and earned Skaggs his first Country Music Association honors. In 1982, the CMA named the young singer Male Vocalist of the Year and winner of its Horizon Award for most significant career growth. That same year, Skaggs was inducted into the Grand Ole Opry.

Skaggs's next three albums— H*ighways & Heartaches, Don't*

Cheat in Our Hometown, and *Country Boy*—sold in equally impressive numbers. The albums spawned a number of hit singles—most notably Skaggs's cover of Bill Monroe's "Uncle Pen," which became the first bluegrass number by a solo artist ever to reach number one on *Billboard*'s country charts.

In 1985, Skaggs and his band went on tour, recording the highly acclaimed *Live in London* album, which featured a guest appearance by Elvis Costello. That year he earned country music's most prestigious annual honor when the CMA named him Entertainer of the Year. He won Grammys for Best Country Instrumental Performance in 1984 and 1986, and he shared the CMA's 1987 Vocal Duo of the Year award with his wife, Sharon White, for "Love Can't Ever Get Better Than This." While recording and coproducing 1989's *Kentucky Thunder*, Skaggs also produced Dolly Parton's country music comeback album, *White Limozeen*.

Skaggs's creative energies have continued unabated in the 1990s. With Vince Gill and Steve Wariner, he shared a Grammy in 1991 for best country vocal collaboration ("Restless"). His tenth album for Epic, *My Father's Son*, is vintage Ricky Skaggs—and a real family affair. Skaggs's young son appears in the video for the album's first single, "Life's Too Long (To Live Like This)," and Skaggs and his wife, Sharon, share lyrics on "Hold on Tight (Let It Go)." Said Skaggs, "This album is about priorities, and my family's the most important thing to me on earth."

RICKY SKAGGS

BORN: July 18, 1954, in Cordell, Kentucky

FIRST HIT: "You May See Me Walkin'" (1981)

OTHER NOTABLE HITS: "Life's Too Long (To Live Like This)" (1992); "Same Ol' Love" (1992); "Cajun' Moon" (1986); "Uncle Pen" (1985); "Don't Cheat in Our Hometown" (1984); "Highway 40 Blues" (1983); "Heartbroke" (1982); "Don't Get Above Your Raising" (1981)

BEST ALBUMS: *My Father's Son* (1991); *Family & Friends* (1985); *Country Boy* (1984); *Highways & Heartaches* (1982); *Waitin' for the Sun to Shine* (1981)

AWARDS INCLUDE: Grammy, Best Country Instrumental Performance (1986, 1984); Country Music Association (CMA) Vocal Event of the Year (with Mark O'Connor & the New Nashville Cats, 1991); CMA Vocal Duo of the Year (with Sharon White, 1987); CMA Entertainer of the Year (1985); CMA Instrumental Group of the Year (1985, 1984, 1983); CMA Male Vocalist of the Year (1982); CMA Horizon Award (1982)

ACHIEVEMENTS: Grand Ole Opry member (1982)

· DOUG · STONE ·

Doug Stone seemed to have everything going his way in the spring of 1992. He had racked up several hits on the charts, was building a solid base of admirers, and was opening shows for superstar Kenny Rogers. After years of scrambling, Stone had it all. What could go wrong?

Following a concert in Princeville, Oregon, he experienced chest pain that traveled down through his arm. The pain was so intense that he could hardly grip the

Doug Stone's emotional delivery has made him a premier country balladeer.

microphone. He was flown back to Nashville—and found that at age 35 he needed a quadruple bypass. Ironically, the song he had on the charts was entitled "Come In Out of the Pain."

Stone's relative youth was to his benefit, and within five weeks after surgery he was singing at Fan Fair, an annual festival in Nashville that draws crowds of as many as 25,000. By summer he was back touring, having shaken his three-pack-a-day cigarette habit and cut out the fried-food binges.

Born, June 19, 1956, in Atlanta, Stone claims Newnan, Georgia, as his hometown. (Newnan is the birthplace of country star Alan Jackson.) Stone learned the guitar and an appreciation of music from his mother, also a performer. From his father, a mechanic, Stone learned practical living skills that paid the bills. His parents divorced when Stone was 12, and he and his two older brothers went to live with their father. They figured their father could teach them a trade. In Stone's case, that trade was diesel mechanics.

The four lived in Newnan in a trailer that had no running water or indoor plumbing. Stone quit school at age 15; by the time he was 23 he was married and the father of two. By day he was a mechanic; by night he played music and worked in his homemade recording studio. The constant traveling and long hours away from home took a toll on his marriage, and Stone was soon divorced.

Stone worked not only as a diesel mechanic but also as a truck driver, a factory worker, and a construction laborer. He thinks his job history helps him relate to his fans, because he's had the same types of work experiences.

During an engagement at a VFW hall, Stone met comanager Phyllis Bennett. She offered him a deal contingent on her arranging a recording contract within a year. Bennett teamed Stone with producer Doug Johnson, and the singer found himself singing for the head of Epic Records. He got his contract, and Bennett is still his manager.

Stone's eponymous debut album, released in 1990, produced his first hit single, the forlorn "I'd Be Better Off (In a Pine Box)," which was nominated for a Grammy. That album eventually went platinum and produced four other hits. His second and third albums, *I Thought It Was You* and *From the Heart*, have been certified gold. Seven of Stone's singles have reached number one on the charts: "In a Different Light," "I Thought It Was You," "Too Busy Being in Love," "Fourteen Minutes Old," "A Jukebox with a Country Song," "Why Didn't I Think of That," and "Come In Out of the Pain." His fourth album, *More Love*, was released in late 1993 and featured the hit single "I Never Knew Love." *More Love* meant more to Doug than just his latest album, because he wrote or cowrote five of the ten songs, representing his biggest songwriting contribution to date. Of particular importance was the title track, which he penned with Gary Burr, because it was loosely based on the experiences of his mother.

Stone is at his best with heartbreaking ballads. His smooth, expressive voice brings a touch of romance to his music that has attracted a large following of female fans. Despite the sadness in his ballads, Stone is a witty man who naturally wears a smile.

Stone lives in a log house on a 51-acre plot near Nashville with his wife, Carie, and their two children. He prefers living in the country and thinks it's a great place to raise kids. The area reminds him of Georgia.

DOUG STONE

REAL NAME: Douglas Brooks

BORN: June 19, 1956, in Atlanta, Georgia

FIRST HIT: "I'd Be Better Off (In a Pine Box)" (1990)

OTHER NOTABLE HITS: "More Love" (1994); "Addicted to a Dollar" (1993); "I Never Knew Love" (1993); "A Jukebox with a Country Song" (1992); "Come In Out of the Pain" (1991); "I Thought It Was You" (1991); "In a Different Light" (1991); "These Lips Don't Know How to Say Goodbye" (1991); "Fourteen Minutes Old" (1990)

BEST ALBUMS: *From the Heart* (1992); *I Thought It Was You* (1991); *Doug Stone* (1990)

GEORGE · STRAIT

When George Strait first visited Nashville, he was told his music was behind the times. Looking back, it's clear the singer was actually a sign of the times—a bellwether who pointed the way to greater popularity and prosperity for country music.

In the early 1980s, the prevailing attitude among those running the country music industry was that Strait's blend of western swing, traditional honky-tonk, and romantic ballads was old-fashioned and out of style. At various times, he was told to throw away his cowboy hat, exchange his boots for leather loafers, and trade in his denim jeans for a pair of dress slacks. It was also suggested that he do away with the fiddles and steel guitars and bathe his mellow, deep-toned voice in the more con-

George Strait has been credited, along with Randy Travis, for returning country music to its roots—a movement now referred to as "neotraditionalism."

temporary sounds of strings and synthesizers.

By the end of the 1980s, however, Nashville was singing a different tune, and Strait now stands tallest among the handful of artists who changed the sound and the look of country music. Strait's new brand of traditional country music led country to new heights of success and helped convince Nashville music executives to give other young, traditional-sounding country artists an opportunity—a trend that has provided country music with its biggest sales boom in history. "I think there was always an audience out there craving traditional country music," Strait contends. "They just weren't getting it until recently. Then a few of us came along who were doing music with this kind of flavor, and country music has gotten bigger and better. If I had a small part in helping that happen, then, hell, I'm proud of it."

In the little over a decade that has passed since the release of *Strait Country*, the Texan's 1981 debut album, the singer has racked up over 25 number-one songs and seen each one of his albums go gold or platinum. Twice he has received country music's most prestigious annual honor, the Country Music Association's Entertainer of the Year award. And he is cited as a primary influence by nearly every successful Nashville newcomer.

Through it all, Strait's boots stayed firmly planted on the ground and his head never outgrew his trademark Resistol hat. He's still the soft-spoken, down-to-earth family man who finds too much off-stage attention uncomfortable and who remains dedicated to performing the kind of music that got him where he is today.

Strait was born May 18, 1952, the second of three children. His father was a junior high school math teacher and part-time rancher in Pearsall, Texas, a tiny settlement in the South Texas brush country located about 60 miles south of San Antonio. In his youth, Strait learned to ride horses and rope steers—an interest he still holds today. His first musical experience was singing

Texan George Strait has earned the right to wear his cowboy hat. He is a charter member of the Professional Rodeo Cowboys Association.

"Louie, Louie" and other rudimentary rock songs with a garage band made up of high school buddies. Shortly after graduation, Strait and his high school sweetheart eloped to Mexico. Now, more than 20 years later, he and

The strong, silent type, Strait showed off his natural charm and romantic nature in the film Pure Country.

wife Norma still reside in South Texas with their son, George, Jr., born in 1981.

Strait enrolled in the army in 1971 to help out with family finances. A year later, while serving as a clerk at the Schofield Barracks in Hawaii, he taught himself to play guitar by studying a Hank Williams songbook. Before long, the base commander recruited the young Texan to lead a country band. Strait's duties during his last year in the service consisted largely of performing country music on military bases.

Upon returning home, Strait enrolled in Southwest Texas State University in San Marcos. On campus, he pinned a note to a bulletin board advertising himself as a singer in search of a country band. He got a call from a group by the name of Ace in the Hole. With Strait as lead singer, the band began performing nightly in honky-tonks within a 200-mile radius of San Marcos.

In 1979, Strait received a bachelor's degree in agriculture and began managing the family ranch, which by that time had grown to include more than 1,000 head of cattle. He worked from sunup to sundown on the ranch, then quickly cleaned up and joined the other Ace in the Hole band members for their nightly gig. The band's popularity steadily grew, and Strait's voice became more confident and flexible with his regular performances of traditional Texas dance hall music—including a healthy dose of songs made famous by Bob Wills, Hank Thompson, Johnny Bush, Lefty Frizzell, Merle Haggard, and George Jones. Years later, Strait acknowledged a debt to the vocal phrasing of Haggard and Jones. He claimed he developed his style by singing their hits night after night and trying to mimic the way they brought out the emotion of the lyrics.

In the late 1970s, Strait recorded a few songs for D Records, a Houston-based company owned by Pappy Dailey, who had given George Jones his first break more than two decades before. Strait's first single, "Ace in the Hole," received enough attention to give him the confidence to travel to Nashville. He would make this trek three times without getting a response.

By 1979, Strait figured he had given his dream a shot, and it was time to be more practical. He applied for several jobs, nearly accepting a position with a firm in Uvalde, Texas, designing cattle facilities, but his wife persuaded him to give music one more year.

Among Strait's other supporters was Erv Woolsey, a former music industry executive who managed a San Marcos nightclub, the Prairie Rose, where the Ace in the Hole band often performed. In 1979, after Woolsey had returned to the music business as a promotion executive for MCA Records, he helped Strait arrange a Nashville recording session with producer Blake Mevis. The songs recorded during that session earned Strait a recording contract with MCA Records less than six months after he had turned down the job in Uvalde.

The first hit from Strait's debut album, *Strait Country*, was a stripped-down, dynamic Texas two-step titled "Unwound." It became the singer's first top-ten hit, confounding those who thought radio wouldn't accept such a raw, traditional country style. Even champions of the back-to-basics sound were skeptical about Strait's future.

More than a decade later, Strait was still going strong—and setting new standards. In 1987, the Texan's *Ocean Front Property* disc became the first in country music history to debut at number one on *Billboard's* country album chart. In 1988, Strait received a Grammy nomination for "All My Ex's Live in Texas." In 1990, Strait's "Love Without End, Amen" became the first song since 1977 to remain in the number-one position on the country charts for

five consecutive weeks. His "Famous Last Words of a Fool" was the next song to repeat that feat, staying at number one for five weeks in early 1991.

Amid the success, Strait also faced tragedy. His 13-year-old daughter, Jennifer, was killed in an auto accident in 1986. Strait withdrew from interviews for more than a year following the accident, and even now only reluctantly agrees to appear on television or talk to the press. Always private about his personal life, Strait has never allowed cameras into his San Antonio home or onto his ranch, where he raises horses and cattle.

Strait's most recent ventures have included a major role on the silver screen. He starred in *Pure Country* (1992)—a film written specifically for him—playing a successful country singer who feels he has lost touch with his musical and emotional roots. The film features eleven songs performed by Strait, and the album by the same name went platinum. Strait's disc *Easy Come Easy Go* (1993), his eighteenth for MCA, shows the singer to be very much at the top of his game. The album features Strait's signature blend of swinging honky-tonk and romantic ballads.

Of his music, Strait says: "I can't really see it changing very much. It's not that I set out to create a certain style or to change country music. It's just that I record the songs I like, and I do them in a way that feels right to me."

GEORGE STRAIT

BORN: May 18, 1952, in Pearsall, Texas

MUSICAL INFLUENCES: Merle Haggard, Bob Wills, Hank Williams, George Jones, Lefty Frizzell

FIRST HIT: "Unwound" (1981)

OTHER NOTABLE HITS: "Chill of an Early Fall" (1992); "Love Without End, Amen" (1990); "All My Ex's Live in Texas" (1987); "Ocean Front Property" (1987); "The Chair" (1985); "Does Fort Worth Ever Cross Your Mind" (1985); "Right or Wrong" (1984); "Amarillo By Morning" (1983)

BEST ALBUMS: *Chill of an Early Fall* (1991); *If You Ain't Lovin' (You Ain't Livin')* (1988); *#7* (1986); *Something Special* (1985); *Right or Wrong* (1984); *Does Fort Worth Ever Cross Your Mind* (1984); *Strait from the Heart* (1982); *Strait Country* (1981)

AWARDS INCLUDE: Country Music Association (CMA) Entertainer of the Year (1990, 1989); CMA Male Vocalist of the Year (1986, 1985); Academy of Country Music (ACM) Entertainer of the Year (1989); ACM Top Male Vocalist (1988, 1985, 1984)

· MARTY · STUART

Colorful and talented country music star Marty Stuart likes to say he earned his high school diploma as a mandolin player in Lester Flatt's band in the 1970s and his university degree as lead guitarist in Johnny Cash's band in the early 1980s. Stuart grew up Philadelphia, Mississippi, where his father was a factory supervisor, and his mother a bank teller.

A champion of progressive bluegrass music and a self-proclaimed hillbilly rocker, Marty Stuart does not easily fit the image of a country performer.

He was hired at age 12 to play mandolin with a gospel-bluegrass band, the Sullivan Family. A year later, he was recruited by the late, legendary Lester Flatt after the singer had split from longtime partner Earl Scruggs. Following Flatt's death in 1979, Stuart hooked up with another music legend, Johnny Cash, performing with him until 1985.

All along, Stuart knew he wanted to create his own music—when the time was right. He released two independent albums, *Marty: With a Little Help from His Friends* in 1978 and the acclaimed *Busy Bee Cafe* in 1982, on the Sugar Hill label. Four years later, he joined CBS Records and put out *Marty Stuart*, featuring the top-20 country hit, "Arlene." But CBS and Stuart disagreed about musical direction, and the young veteran went looking for other opportunities.

Stuart continued to write prolifically while working to establish his singing career. His songs were recorded by such diverse performers as Mark Collie, Emmylou Harris, Buck Owens, and Jann Browne.

In 1989, Stuart reemerged on MCA Records with *Hillbilly Rock*. The album put a fresh spin on indigenous American music by going back to the place where the roots of country and rock 'n' roll intertwine. "This is not a rockabilly album," Stuart said when *Hillbilly Rock* was released. "This is hillbilly music—with a *thump*." The album's radio hits included a version of Johnny Cash's "Cry, Cry, Cry," and Stuart's own "'Til I Found You" and "Hillbilly Rock," which became his signature song.

By this time, Stuart had developed a unique stage style built upon a 400-piece collection of vintage rhinestone jackets, hand-tooled cowboy boots, and other fancy stagewear. He updates the colorful western-style attire worn by such country legends as Hank Snow, Porter Wagoner, and Webb Pierce with faded Levis and black or bleach-white T-shirts.

Stuart's next album, *Tempted*, kept the momentum of *Hillbilly Rock* going. Also produced by Tony Brown and Richard Bennett, it showcased the singer/instrumentalist's talent for bluegrass and gospel while letting him expand on his country-rock style.

If *Hillbilly Rock* and *Tempted* laid the groundwork for Stuart's climb to the top, 1992's *This One's Gonna Hurt You*, clinched it. Two duets with friend Travis Tritt, the title cut and "The Whiskey Ain't Workin'," earned the pair several music awards and launched their successful "No Hats" tour. The album was Stuart's first to go gold.

Stuart's superb effort *Love and Luck*, coproduced with Tony Brown, occupied much of his time in 1992 and 1993. He spent a year writing and gathering songs for the album and actually postponed recording it for several months until he found the right music. The outcome is a highly personal album in which emotions run deep, particularly in the straight-from-the-heart ballad "That's What Love's About" and the title track. After Stuart finished the album, he put together a new band, the Rock and Roll Cowboys, to showcase his new music. With talent like Stuart's, he won't have to rely on luck to soar to new heights.

MARTY STUART

BORN: September 30, 1958, in Philadelphia, Misisisippi

MUSICAL INFLUENCES: Buck Owens, Merle Haggard, Johnny Cash

FIRST HIT: "Hillbilly Rock" (1990)

OTHER NOTABLE HITS: "The Whiskey Ain't Workin'" (with Travis Tritt, 1992); "Tempted" (1991); "Little Things" (1991); "'Til I Found You" (1991)

BEST ALBUMS: *Tempted* (1991); *Hillbilly Rock* (1990)

AWARDS INCLUDE: Grammy, Best Country Vocal Collaboration (with Travis Tritt, 1993); Country Music Association Vocal Event of the Year (with Travis Tritt, 1992)

ACHIEVEMENTS: Grand Ole Opry member (1992)

PERSONAL: Stuart is well known for his collection of Western suits designed by classic country stagewear designers Nudie and Manuel. Stuart and Johnny Cash's daughter, Cindy, were married for five years.

· PAM · TILLIS ·

Although Pam Tillis's career in music began several years ago, it wasn't until 1991 that she was recognized for her long list of talents, including her dynamic vocal ability. Her signature song "Don't Tell Me What To Do" got the ball rolling. Since then she has had a string of hit records, several

Though Pam Tillis is the daughter of renowned country crooner Mel Tillis, she insists on singing her own style of music and going her own way.

award nominations, and two certified gold albums— *Put Yourself in My Place* and *Homeward Looking Angel.*

Tillis's performance onstage is as energetic and captivating as her voice is torchy, forceful, and direct. Although it is her voice that has captured the attention of millions, Tillis is one of those extraordinary singers whose talents stretch far beyond singing.

Even before the world was hearing her voice ring out on radio and video, Tillis had already achieved success with her strong songwriting ability—a craft she continues to hone even while she's busy touring. Despite the hustle-bustle of touring, she finds time to collect her creative thoughts and put them on paper. In addition to writing much of her own material, Tillis has also penned songs for a number of artists, among them Chaka Khan, Highway 101, Juice Newton, Ricky Van Shelton, and the late Conway Twitty.

Tillis was introduced to country music by her father, renowned singer Mel Tillis. Pam tagged along with her father to the recording studio as well as to the Grand Ole Opry. At the Opry, she met such country queens as Dottie West and Tammy Wynette. These childhood

Pam Tillis's "Cleopatra, Queen of Denial" is an excellent example of country music's proclivity for puns.

experiences left a lasting impression on Tillis, who's fond of saying, "I've got one foot in old Nashville and one foot in new Nashville."

Her performance debut was with her father on the stage of the Ryman Auditorium in Nashville when she was only eight years old. While still a teenager, she began her country music career as a Stutterette, one of the backup vocalists in her father's band. But, as she has revealed in interviews, the singer found that sharing her father's stage was "like being a little plant in the shade of a big tree. I couldn't grow."

Being overshadowed by Mel Tillis aggravated what she considers a natural shyness. Tillis's low self-esteem only intensified following a terrible car accident at age 16. The accident broke many bones in her face, and her jaws were wired for seven weeks. Several grueling and stressful oper-

Tillis expresses herself not only in her music but also through her unique fashion sense.

ations followed over the course of the next few years.

Eventually Tillis focused on her dream once again and began singing at several writers' showcases in Nashville. Tillis also worked as a receptionist at her father's publishing company.

After high school graduation, she registered at the University of Ten-

---

Mel Tillis

An accomplished singer and songwriter, Mel Tillis, father of Pam Tillis, has been a major force in country music for over 35 years. Tillis's gift is the ability to blend country shuffle with classic pop melody. He has composed over 500 songs, including the Kenny Rogers

hit, "Ruby, Don't Take Your Love to Town," and Bobby Bare's top-ten hit, "Detroit City." Not shy about tackling tough topics in his songs, his "Ruby..." is the story of an impotent Vietnam vet begging his wife to stay with him. Known as a songwriter during his early Nashville years, Tillis's commercial break came with his gruff baritone rendition of the Harlan Howard classic, "Life Turned Her That Way." Hits continued throughout the 1960s and 1970s, including "These Lonely Hands of Mine," "Good Woman Blues," "Burning Memories," and "Southern Rains." Born on August 8, 1932, in Pahokee, Florida, Tillis turned a potential handicap—his stuttering—into an asset. He has used it as comic relief during concert performances; he entitled an early 1980s album *M-M-Mel Live*; and he even called his autobiography *Stutterin' Boy*.

nessee in Knoxville. But before classes began, Tillis joined her first band, pointing her in a rock 'n' roll direction. After playing up and down the Cumberland Strip in Knoxville, she decided school wasn't for her. In a move that surprised even Tillis, the young singer teamed up with a jazz pianist and formed a fusion band. The group then relocated to California. In the mid-1980s, Warner Bros. Records offered her a recording contract. The album that resulted, *Above and Beyond the Doll of Cutie*, was an eclectic collection of pop and rock songs. There was one lone country song on the album titled "It Ain't Easy Bein' Easy." Looking back, Tillis considers the tune a transitional work on an album by a singer "searching for herself."

Tillis eventually returned to Nashville and to country music. There, she became a much-sought-after sessions singer. In 1990, she landed a songwriting deal with Tree International, one of country music's largest publishing companies. While working in the studio on a demo of "Someone Else's Trouble Now" (recorded by Highway 101), she was offered a contract with Arista Records' Nashville division. There, Tillis's true style emerged because Arista allowed her to sing the way she wanted—no shadows, no coattails, just positively Pam.

Pam's debut single "Don't Tell Me What To Do" soared to the top of the country charts in 1991. Then *Put Yourself in My Place*, her debut country album, was certified gold the following year. Other hit songs on the album included "One of Those Things" and "Maybe It Was Memphis." Her second album,

Homeward Looking Angel, produced such hits as "Shake the Sugar Tree" and "Cleopatra, Queen of Denial." "Let That Pony Run," about a woman who builds a new life after her husband leaves her for a young waitress, reminded Pam of her mother, who survived the separation from Pam's father. Tillis's third album for Arista, *Sweetheart's Dance*, was released in 1993 and yielded the hit single "Spilled Perfume."

Tillis's marriage to songwriter/guitarist Bob DiPiero is a success story in itself. The two were at first in a business relationship only: Tillis and DiPiero had been cowriting together. One night, the two writers went out to dinner to celebrate DiPiero's number-one hit, "That Rock Won't Roll," by the country group Restless Heart. The first dinner outing led to a second, and so on. After a three-and-a-half-year courtship, DiPiero married Tillis on Valentine's Day in 1991.

The third member of the family is Ben, Tillis's son from her first marriage. Raising him may have slowed her rise to stardom, but Pam declares she would not have traded it for anything.

Tillis is the first to admit that the road to fame was not easy, but there's something to be said for experiencing the ups and downs of real life. This is a recurring theme in her songs—and is underscored by her powerful delivery. Perhaps that's why so many country music fans say Pam Tillis is one of their favorites.

"I like realism in the things I sing," she reflected. "I like songs you can sing very honestly, where you admit that love isn't always beautiful."

PAM TILLIS

BORN: July 24, 1957, in Plant City, Florida

FIRST HIT: "Don't Tell Me What To Do" (1991)

OTHER NOTABLE HITS: "Spilled Perfume" (1993); "Shake the Sugar Tree" (1992); "Let That Pony Run" (1992); "Cleopatra, Queen of Denial" (1992); "Maybe It Was Memphis" (1992); "Put Yourself In My Place" (1991); "One of Those Things" (1991)

BEST ALBUMS: *Homeward Looking Angel* (1992); *Put Yourself in My Place* (1991)

AWARDS INCLUDE: Country Music Association Vocal Event of the Year (with George Jones, et al., 1993)

PERSONAL: Tillis is the daughter of veteran country star Mel Tillis. She is married to songwriter and musical collaborator Bob DiPiero.

· AARON · TIPPIN ·

There isn't anything glitzy or commonplace about singer/ songwriter Aaron Tippin. With a traditional country sound reminiscent of Hank Williams, Sr., and a fondness for songs with blue-collar themes, Tippin has reaped praise for his exuberant yet penetrating brand of country music.

"Tippin's vocals are authentic country pushed to the extreme," observed *Billboard* magazine in a review of his first album, *You've Got to Stand for Something*.

"Aaron Tippin is a star. You read it here first," gushed critic Robert K. Oermann in his *Music Row* magazine review.

At one time a self-described "90-pound weakling," Tippin underwent a seven-year body-building regimen, adding 30 pounds of muscle to his physique. He main-

Aaron Tippin gained a reputation as a singer of powerful anthems, such as "You've Got to Stand for Something" and "Read Between the Lines."

tains a six-day-a-week workout program even when on the road.

Tippin has a natural affinity for straight-ahead country; his music bears no hint of the contemporary. Born on July 3, 1958, in the small town of Travelers Rest, South Carolina, he proudly sports a tattoo of a palmetto tree—the symbol found on the state flag—on his arm. The singer, who was raised on a farm, recalls that his first musical revelation occurred when one of his friends brought over a portable eight-track player.

"We didn't have any tapes to play in it, except his daddy's tape of Hank, Sr.'s greatest hits," Tippin recalled. "At first, we were making sport of it—whooping and hollering. But later, I took that tape home and couldn't stop playing it. I wore it out."

Williams continued to influence Tippin's music, and soon he was performing in and around his hometown in little pickup bluegrass and country bands. Tippin had originally planned a career in aviation—he is a licensed commercial multiengine pilot. The energy crisis of the late 1970s and a devastating divorce forced him to reevaluate his career choice. By that time, Tippin had already begun writing songs. One of his tunes came to the attention of Nashville publisher Charlie Monk, who urged the singer/songwriter to relocate to Music City. For the quick-witted Tippin, it made good sense. "For years, every time I flew over Nashville I'd always look down and sorta wonder what they're doing down there," he wryly observed. "Finally, I ran out of reasons not to come here and get in the pile."

Supporting himself by working the night shift at a mill in Russellville, Kentucky, Tippin honed his singing and writing skills by day in hopes of getting a publishing and recording contract. On weekends he'd drive home to South Carolina to visit his daughter, Charla.

Tippin, in time, landed a spot on the songwriting staff of the prestigious Acuff-Rose publishing firm. Tippin sang his own tunes on the demo tapes, and he soon began attracting attention with his undeniably nasal, but country-to-the-core vocal style. After appearing at a Nashville nightclub, Tippin landed the much-sought-after recording deal—with RCA Records.

Tippin scored several top-ten hits off his 1991 *You've Got to Stand for Something* debut album, including the title track and "The Sky's Got the Blues." The newcomer charmed the critics and listening public once again with his second disc, *Read Between the Lines*. On the strength of the memorable single, "There Ain't Nothing Wrong with the Radio," Tippin's second album was declared platinum.

In 1993, he released *Call of the Wild*, which secured his niche in the country music industry. The album's biggest hit single, "Working Man's Ph.D.," was a country anthem that reflected Tippin's blue-collar background. His working-class image combined with his hard-line, tradition-based singing style have garnered him a large following of country fans who are not enamored with rock-influenced country music or pyrotechnic stage shows. Tippin, who has toured with everyone from Reba McEntire to Billy Dean, still manages to put on a lively, no-holds-barred show.

AARON TIPPIN

REAL NAME: Aaron (Tip) Tippin

BORN: July 3, 1958, in Travelers Rest, South Carolina

MUSICAL INFLUENCES: Hank Williams, Jimmy Rodgers, Ernest Tubb, Hank Snow, Hank Thompson, Lefty Frizzell

FIRST HIT: "You've Got to Stand for Something" (1990)

OTHER NOTABLE HITS: "Trim Yourself to Fit the World" (1993); "I Wouldn't Have It Any Other Way" (1992); "She Made a Memory Out of Me" (1990); "The Sky's Got the Blues" (1990); "I Wonder How Far It Is Over You" (1990); "The Man That Came Between Us" (1990)

BEST ALBUMS: *Read Between the Lines* (1992); *You've Got to Stand for Something* (1991)

·RANDY· ·TRAVIS·

Minnie Pearl, country music's most famous humorist, once described Randy Travis as "a new vehicle with old wheels." She meant he sounded good, he looked good, and he was moving country music into the future by harnessing the musical styles of the past. It was a high

Randy Travis's first album, Storms of Life, *is credited with launching the new traditionalism.*

compliment from a colorful lady who had worked alongside the greatest country music singers of all time, and she underlined her feelings about Travis's talents by adding: "A voice like his only comes along once in a generation."

Travis turned the country music world around in 1986, the year he became the biggest overnight sensation in Nashville's long and illustrious history. *Storms of Life*, his debut album on Warner Bros. Records, ranks as the first debut album by a country music artist to sell more than a million copies within a year of its release.

Travis's success came at a time when country music sales were at an all-time low, having steadily decreased during the early 1980s. John Anderson, Ricky Skaggs, George Strait, and the Judds had already sent ripples of optimism through the industry by swimming against the flow of pop-influenced, cosmopolitan country music coming out of Nashville at that time. The meteoric success of Travis turned the tide completely, opening the gates for the flood of successful traditional artists that followed.

Like most "overnight" sensations, Travis spent several hard-working years paying his dues before getting his big break. The second of six children, Travis was born Randy Traywick on May 4, 1959, in the small North Carolina town of Marshville, located about 30 miles from Charlotte in an area known as the Piedmont Crescent. His father, Harold Traywick, bred horses, raised turkeys, and managed a small construction firm. His mother, Bobbie Traywick, worked in a fabric mill.

At age eight, Travis diligently set to work learning chords on an acoustic guitar. Two years later, he and his three brothers donned western suits, picked up their acoustic guitars, and began performing as a country harmony act known as the Traywick Brothers. Even then, say Randy's folks, the young man owned a voice that drew notice.

By the time he reached his teens, Travis had veered into trouble. He dropped out of school before finishing the ninth grade and got caught up in a life of fast cars, hard drinking, and recreational drug use. Several scrapes with the law culminated in an arrest at age 17 for breaking and entering—a felony carrying a possible jail sentence of five years. Some time before his scheduled court date, the troubled 17-year-old signed up for a talent contest at Country Music City USA, Charlotte's preeminent country music honky-tonk. There he met Lib Hatcher, the club's manager and part owner. Hatcher recalls dropping a load of papers she was carrying the first time she heard Travis's voice. She stopped what she was doing and listened. By the time Travis had finished singing, says Hatcher, she knew this skinny 17-year-old had the

Randy Travis married his longtime manager Lib Hatcher in 1991.

207

stuff to be a star. Travis went on to win the contest, Hatcher introduced herself afterward, and with his parents' consent, she appealed to the court to put him on probation and in her care. Travis moved in with Hatcher and her husband, and he took over as vocalist at Country Music City USA. Hatcher dedicated herself so completely to grooming the young roustabout that her marriage fell apart. Hatcher's husband left her and filed for divorce.

In 1978, singer Joe Stampley heard Travis sing and offered to help. He produced a handful of songs with Randy, two of which were released under the name of Randy Traywick on the independent label, Paula Records. He also took tapes of the songs back to Nashville and presented them to several record companies, but no one showed any interest.

Hatcher and her protégé weren't ready to give up. In 1980, Hatcher sold her nightclub and the two moved to Nashville, renting one floor of a three-story, yellow-brick building on 16th Avenue near Music Row, where most of the Nashville music industry is located. The ground floor of the building housed the offices of the trade magazine *Radio & Records*. In the early days, Travis swept

Travis learned to play the guitar at age eight, taking lessons from Kate Mangum in North Carolina.

and scrubbed the offices once a week for $30.

Hatcher talked her way into a job managing the Nashville Palace, a tourist-oriented music club and restaurant located in a strip of shops directly across from the entrance of the Opryland Hotel. Travis went to work with her there, mopping floors and flipping hamburgers. He also sang whenever he could, performing under his new stage name, Randy Ray. At first, he had to sneak in a few songs at the invitation of the nightly headliner; eventually he worked his way into a full-time slot, leading the band five nights a week, three sets a night.

Hatcher continued to work tirelessly to promote Randy's career. She organized shows at the club featuring performances by stars of the Grand Ole Opry, allowing Travis an opportunity to meet and mingle with several of Nashville's well-traveled veterans. Invitations went out to everyone and anyone involved in the recording industry encouraging them to visit the club, enjoy a free meal, and hear the featured singer. Through the early 1980s, every record company in Nashville turned down a chance to sign Randy Travis. Not once, but twice. That list included Warner

Bros. Records, with whom Travis would later sign.

However, Martha Sharp had yet to hear or see the Palace star. The top talent executive at Warners, she finally accepted an invitation from Hatcher in 1985. The singer was grilling steaks when Sharp arrived and asked to hear him sing. Hatcher hurried into the kitchen to relieve him of his duties so Travis could take the stage. The moment Sharp heard Travis sing, she knew she wanted to sign him to a record contract. She also knew she would have a hard time convincing her superiors to back a singer so obviously devoted to traditional country music. In the face of strong corporate doubt, she succeeded.

Sharp introduced Travis to Kyle Lehning, an accomplished engineer who had worked with Ronnie Milsap and was moving into record production. Lehning produced most of *Storms of Life* (two songs were produced by Keith Stegall). Before releasing the album, however, Warners wanted to test the reaction of radio listeners. The first single, "On the Other Hand," received a disappointing initial rating, climbing only to number 67 on the country charts. The next song, "1982," fared much better, introducing Travis to the top ten. Warners, in an unusual move, decided to give "On the Other Hand" another chance. This time the tune took Travis to number one, a position he would visit more than a dozen times in the next five years. *Storms of Life*, in addition to its record-setting sales pace, spent 12 weeks at

Travis dominated many of the award shows during the 1980s, winning more than 40 honors by 1990.

Randy Travis: A truer, more resonant country voice simply doesn't exist.

number one. It also helped Travis gain induction, in December 1986, into the the Grand Ole Opry—the youngest male singer ever to earn this distinction.

With his second album, *Always and Forever* (1987), Travis sealed his status as a country superstar. The album spawned four consecutive number-one songs—"Forever and Ever, Amen," "I Won't Need You Anymore," "Too Gone, Too Long," "I Told You So"—and spent an astounding ten months atop the country album charts.

Along the way, Travis set the mold for the new breed of male country star: clean-cut, square-jawed, and crisply attired—with a pleasing traditionalism about his wardrobe and manner. He's humble, polite, and respectful of the stars who preceded him. Travis is also a tee-totaler who monitors his diet and prefers a gym to a party. He sings with uncontrived sincerity, his lower register featuring a warmth and breadth that brings a mournfulness to all of his work.

Travis dominated many of the award shows in the late 1980s, winning more than 40 honors in his first four years, including two Grammys for Best Country Vocal Performance and several awards from the Country Music Association and the Academy of Country Music. His albums *Old 8 X 10, No Holdin' Back,* and *Heroes and Friends* extended his million-selling streak into the 1990s. In 1991, as if to

confirm his stardom and solidify his link to country music's past, Travis starred in an HBO cable-TV special with the legendary George Jones. And in May of that year, the young star married Lib Hatcher in a private ceremony in Maui, Hawaii. Also that year, the critically acclaimed *High Lonesome* was released. The album was a departure for Travis in that it featured five songs cowritten by Randy, three of them—"Together Forever," "Better Class of Losers," and "I'd Surrender All"—with Alan Jackson.

Travis continued to write and record his own compositions with his 1994 effort, *This Is Me.* The disc features "The Box," a tune Travis cowrote with Buck Moore, as well as songs by such notable writers as Larry Gatlin, Jerry Phillips, and Max T. Barnes. Another single from the album, "Before You Kill Us All," became one of country's hottest hits.

As the mid-1990s approached, Travis spent less time on the highway. Touring is the backbone of the country industry, and performers can climb to stardom or fall from grace depending on their success on the road. Travis's decision to scale down his touring schedule shocked some industry insiders, but Randy had developed another interest he wanted to pursue.

Spending less time on the road allowed Travis to devote more time to acting. A veteran of several films, including *Frank & Jesse,* in which he played outlaw Cole Younger, Travis plans to continue reading scripts and acting in the future.

RANDY TRAVIS

REAL NAME: Randy Traywick

BORN: May 4, 1959, in Marshville, North Carolina

MUSICAL INFLUENCES: Hank Williams, Merle Haggard, George Jones, Lefty Frizzell, Ernest Tubb

FIRST HIT: "1982" (1986)

OTHER NOTABLE HITS: "Better Class of Losers" (1992); "Heroes and Friends" (1991); "Too Gone, Too Long" (1988); "Forever and Ever, Amen" (1987); "On the Other Hand" (1986)

BEST ALBUMS: *High Lonesome* (1991); *Heroes and Friends* (1990); *Old 8 X 10* (1988); *Always and Forever* (1987); *Storms of Life* (1986)

AWARDS INCLUDE: Grammy, Best Country Male Vocal Performance (1989, 1988); Country Music Association (CMA) Male Vocalist of the Year (1988, 1987); CMA Horizon Award (1986); Academy of Country Music (ACM) Top Male Vocalist (1987, 1986); ACM Top New Male Vocalist (1985)

ACHIEVEMENTS: Grand Ole Opry member (1986)

·TRAVIS · TRITT·

Travis Tritt's reputation as the "bad boy" of country music probably stems from his habit of saying exactly what he thinks. The dust still hasn't settled from his 1992 remark about Billy Ray Cyrus's megahit "Achy Breaky Heart." Travis bluntly declared that the catchy tune with the memo-

Dressed in his trademark leather, Travis Tritt looks every bit the rebel he claims to be.

rable hook didn't make much of a statement and that country music wasn't a butt-wiggling contest. The controversy resurfaced in 1994 with further remarks about

Cyrus and his style of music, which Tritt thinks monopolizes the radio airwaves at the expense of such country legends as George Jones and Waylon Jennings. Tritt's views were strongly expressed in his 1994 hit "Outlaws Like Us."

But Tritt does have a less outrageous side. In his 1991 video *Anymore*, filmed at the Alvin C. York Veterans Hospital in Murfreesboro, Tennessee, Tritt plays a paralyzed veteran. The emotional video led him to serve as the national chairman of the Department of Veterans Affairs National Salute to Hospitalized Veterans.

From his stage act, it is difficult to tell that Tritt's musical career began in the church choir.

in the church choir and taught himself the guitar at the age of eight. He was writing songs when he was 14. But his parents and his first wife, whom he married after graduating from high school, realized a successful career in music was a long shot and discouraged him.

Tritt went to work for an air-conditioning supply company and was promoted into management, but he maintained a heavy schedule of club dates. His boss supported Tritt's desire for a career in music and encouraged him to spend his full energy on it. Tritt quit his day job in 1984. His marriage failed in 1985,

Not part of the neo-traditionalists who dominated country music in the early 1990s, Tritt has been more influenced by Hank Williams, Jr., than by Hank Williams. Though he claims the country outlaw movement of the 1970s as his main inspiration, Travis has done some out-and-out rocking in his music. He has even teamed up with such singing partners as Little Feat, members of Lynyrd Skynyrd, and the Eagles. His image is more reminiscent of the biker than the cowboy: He wears leather and boots, not cowboy hats.

Tritt's background is simple and down-home. Born and raised in Marietta, Georgia, near Atlanta, Tritt sang

and several months later he married for the second time. Unfortunately, his second wife's intense involvement in his career overshadowed their relationship, and they divorced in 1989.

Eventually Tritt met Danny Davenport, a local representative for Warner Bros. Records, and approached him about making a demo tape in Davenport's studio. In 1987, Davenport took the tape to Warner Bros., and they offered Tritt a contract. His debut album, *Country Club*, hit the streets in 1990.

From that point on, Tritt set foot on a rocket ride. *Country Club* went platinum in 1991, and Tritt won the

Country Music Association's Horizon Award that same year. His follow-up album, *It's All About to Change*, was certified gold within two months. It generated four number-one hits, including his trademark kiss-off song "Here's a Quarter (Call Someone Who Cares)." The song was penned the night Tritt signed his second set of divorce papers. He says he writes most of his songs from personal experience.

Part Hank Williams, Jr., part Southern rock, Travis Tritt represents outlaw country.

By 1992, Tritt's career was still climbing. He received two Grammy nominations (for Best Male Country Vocal Performance and Best Country Song for "Here's a Quarter"). His third album, *T-R-O-U-B-L-E*, was released in 1992 and eventually went platinum. Its title song is a cover of the 1975 Elvis Presley hit.

At the summer 1991 Fan Fair in Nashville, Tritt met "hillbilly rocker" Marty Stuart, and they became fast friends. In 1992, the two embarked on their well-received "No Hats" tour. The tour's title is a tongue-in-cheek reference to the fact that both Stuart and Tritt consider themselves apart from the neo-traditonalists who are usually decked out in cowboy hats. Stuart and Tritt's duet "The Whiskey Ain't Workin'" won a Grammy in 1993.

Tritt's music has been heard on the silver screen. His song "Bible Belt" was on the soundtrack for the Joe Pesci movie *My Cousin Vinny*, and his "Burning Love" cut was on the soundtrack for *Honeymoon in Vegas*. He not only wrote the title song for the 1994 film *The Cowboy Way*, he also appeared in a small role as a rodeo cowboy who is bested by the film's star, Woody Harrelson. Prior to that, he had a small role in the made-for-television western *Rio Diablo*, with Kenny Rogers and Naomi Judd.

In 1994, Tritt's career diversified as he and super-manager Ken Kragen took a decidedly aggressive approach. He released his fourth album, *Ten Feet Tall and Bulletproof*, which almost instantly

Tritt once joked that his social life consisted of spending time with his dog, Otis! Looks like things have improved.

reached the top 20 on the popular charts. He published his autobiography (at age 30!), also called *Ten Feet Tall and Bulletproof*. He became permanent host of the *Country Countdown* series on cable channel VH-1. Tritt helped reunite the legendary rock group the Eagles for the video of his remake of that band's "Take It Easy," and he recorded a duet with the soulful Patti LaBelle for the widely touted *Rhythm, Country & Blues* album, which musically explores the ties between country and rhythm and blues. Tritt's greater visibility and exposure represented his desire to reach the next plateau of his career.

Although his stage show is a rollicking one, Tritt still does an acoustic set during his performances—a kind of throwback to the old club days when he sang with only a guitar and a microphone. "There is something—call it power, call it ego, whatever you want—about walking on that stage, just you and your guitar," declared Tritt. "You are naked in front of them. They hear it all. I don't have anything to hide behind."

TRAVIS TRITT

REAL NAME: James Travis Tritt

BORN: February 9, 1963, in Marietta, Georgia

MUSICAL INFLUENCES: the Allman Brothers, the Marshall Tucker Band, Merle Haggard, George Jones

FIRST HIT: "Country Club" (1989)

OTHER NOTABLE HITS: "Foolish Pride" (1993); "Lord Have Mercy on the Workin' Man" (1992); "Can I Trust You with My Heart" (1992); "Here's a Quarter (Call Someone Who Cares)" (1991); "The Whiskey Ain't Workin'" (with Marty Stuart, 1991); "Put Some Drive in Your Country" (1990); "Help Me Hold On" (1990)

BEST ALBUMS: *T-R-O-U-B-L-E* (1992); *It's All About to Change* (1991); *Country Club* (1990)

AWARDS INCLUDE: Grammy, Best Country Vocal Collaboration (with Marty Stuart, 1993); Country Music Association (CMA) Vocal Event of the Year (with George Jones, et al., 1993; with Marty Stuart, 1992); CMA Horizon Award (1991)

ACHIEVEMENTS: Grand Ole Opry member (1992)

·TANYA · TUCKER·

T anya Tucker came roaring into country music like a Texas tornado with her first single, "Delta Dawn." Fans enjoyed her lusty vocals but were shocked to discover that the husky, sensual voice belonged to a 13-year-old. While industry insiders considered her overnight success at such an early age a head start on a promising career, Tucker would later remark that she felt she had started a little late. After

Tanya Tucker has been a country music star since she scored a hit with "Delta Dawn" at age 13.

all, she knew she wanted a career in music when she was just eight years old, and by nine, she and her family were already making plans and setting goals.

Born in Seminole, Texas, Tucker spent her early years in Wilcox, Arizona. Her parents, Juanita and Beau

While still a teenager, Tucker smashed the stereotype of the female country singer with her songs of sex and murder.

in 1967. There, Tanya and her father went to as many country concerts and local fairs as possible. They heard Mel Tillis, Leroy Van Dyke, Ernest Tubb, and many others, and Tanya began joining the stars on stage for an impromptu song. Later, Tucker's parents arranged for her to audition for the movie *Jeremiah Johnson*, which starred Robert Redford. She landed a small role in the 1972 film—a bit of trivia unknown to many of her fans.

After the family relocated to Henderson, Nevada (near Las Vegas), Beau Tucker financed a demo tape for his young daughter. The tape, which included her renditions of "For the Good Times" and "Put Your Hand in

Tucker and Glen Campbell were a duet both on and off the stage during the 1980s.

(who now serves as her manager), encouraged their young daughter to pursue her dream. In fact, Beau drove nine-year-old Tanya to Nashville from their home in Wilcox so she could get a first-hand look at the home of country music. The family moved to Phoenix, Arizona

Tucker's music is sometimes upbeat and sizzling, sometimes low-down and bluesy, but always spicy.

the Hand," eventually reached producer Billy Sherrill. Impressed by her vocal strength and maturity, Sherrill signed Tucker to Columbia Records.

The confident teenager had strong opinions about the type of material she wanted to record for her debut

Tucker's son, Beau, was born the night she was named the CMA's Female Vocalist of the Year.

album. Sherrill introduced her to a song he considered a surefire hit, "Happiest Girl in the Whole USA." Tucker turned it down without reservation. Although the tune eventually became a hit for its cowriter Donna Fargo, with its pop leanings and sugary lyrics, the song was not right for Tucker. She picked a winner on her own, "Delta Dawn," which became her first hit record.

Tucker quickly proved that her initial success was not just a product of youthful dumb luck. She followed up "Delta Dawn" with such hits as "Jamestown Ferry," "What's Your Mama's Name," "Blood Red and Goin' Down," and 1974's controversial "Would You Lay with Me (In a Field of Stone)." In so doing, Tucker established herself as a dynamic singer who used her powerhouse vocal style to convey dramatic stories about the harsh side of life.

After winning her battle with alcohol and cocaine addictions, Tucker revived her career and racked up the awards.

Tucker's life calmed down considerably after the birth of her two children, though she still maintains a demanding touring schedule.

In 1975, Tucker moved to the MCA label. That year, she scored her only pop hit with "Lizzie and the Rainman" and the country hit "San Antonio Stroll." By the time she reached her eighteenth birthday, the sultry teenager had become a sophisticated and successful performer with a string of top-ten albums: *Delta Dawn, What's Your Mama's Name, Would You Lay with Me (In a Field of Stone), Tanya Tucker,* and *Lovin' and Learnin'.* She had also racked up a number of other top-ten hits, including "You've Got Me to Hold On To" and "Here's Some Love."

In addition to becoming one of country music's hottest singers, Tucker gained a reputation as a hard-living free spirit. Canceling almost $1 million in concert dates in 1978,

Tucker has survived financial trouble, a string of rocky romances, and drug and alcohol addictions.

Tucker moved to Los Angeles and repackaged herself as a spandex-clad siren for her MCA *TNT* album, which pushed her style toward rock 'n' roll. Although the album, which featured the hit "Texas (When I Die)," was a best-seller, the move backfired. Her career slowly fizzled, and several well-publicized romances—including a high-profile affair with Glen Campbell—went bust. By 1982, having spent her last $7,500 on a friend's cancer treatment, Tucker was broke. Despite the personal hardships, Tucker enjoyed some musical success during this period. She recorded duets with Campbell before the two parted in 1981. Backtracking from her pop-rock image, she released two solid country singles, "Pecos Promenade" and "Can I See You Tonight," in 1980. Both became top-ten hits. She scored another hit with "I Feel Right" in 1982 after switching to Artista Records.

Following a three-year break from recording, Tucker signed with Liberty Records (then Capitol) in 1986. Her first Capitol album, *Girls Like Me*, marked a return to the distinctive, melodic vocals that had made her a star 14 years earlier. She ended her dry spell on the charts with "One Love at a Time," "I'll Come Back as Another Woman," and "Just Another Love." With her 1987 album, *Love Me Like You Used To*, Tucker reclaimed her position as one of country's leading ladies.

Although her career was back on track, the dynamic singer battled more personal problems in 1988, eventually checking into the Betty Ford Clinic for six weeks to overcome alcohol and cocaine addic-tions. Fiercely independent, Tucker made headlines the following year when she gave birth to her daughter, Presley Tanita (named after Elvis Presley), and announced that she intended to remain unmarried and raise Presley by herself. Along with the birth of her daughter, Tucker had two new albums to celebrate—the softer, uncluttered *Strong Enough to Bend*, produced by longtime friend and supporter Jerry Crutchfield, and a *Greatest Hits* album.

With her 1991 album, *What Do I Do with Me*, featuring the hit tune "Down to My Last Teardrop," Tucker scored her first platinum album and seemed firmly established as one of Music City's most dependable hitmakers. Tucker became a double winner on October 2, 1992, giving birth to a son, Beau Grayson, just hours before being named the CMA's 1991 Female Vocalist of the Year. The year 1992 also saw the release of the bluesy *Can't Run from Yourself*. With the award-winning single "Two Sparrows in a Hurricane," the album proved that the year's successes were no fluke. Tucker's next effort, *Soon* (1993), showcased her softer, more soulful side.

Not content to rest on her laurels, Tucker has produced a low-impact aerobics video—this in addition to raising two small children and maintaining a demanding touring and recording schedule. Tucker also enjoys competing in the National Cutting Horse Association's annual Futurity, in which she's won top honors. Clearly, Tanya Tucker has her work cut out for her—and that's just the way she likes it.

TANYA TUCKER

BORN: October 10, 1958, in Seminole, Texas

FIRST HIT: "Delta Dawn" (1972)

OTHER NOTABLE HITS: "Two Sparrows in a Hurricane" (1993); "Down to My Last Teardrop" (1991); "Strong Enough to Bend" (1988); "Love Me Like You Used To" (1987); "One Love at a Time" (1986); "Can I See You Tonight" (1981); "San Antonio Stroll" (1979); "Would You Lay with Me (In a Field of Stone)" (1974)

BEST ALBUMS: *Can't Run from Yourself* (1992); *What Do I Do with Me* (1991); *Tennessee Woman* (1990); *Strong Enough to Bend* (1988); *Love Me Like You Used To* (1987); *Girls Like Me* (1986); *TNT* (1978)

AWARDS INCLUDE: Country Music Association Female Vocalist of the Year (1991); Academy of Country Music (ACM) Video of the Year (1992); ACM Top New Female Vocalist (1972)

ACHIEVEMENTS: By age 15, had been nominated for a Grammy, had appeared on the cover of *Rolling Stone* magazine, and had a greatest hits package

·LARI·WHITE·

Within country music's new breed of performers, every artist possesses unique qualities that help him or her stand out from the crowd. New country songstress Lari White's originality seems to leap out and roar. The granddaughter of a flamboyant Baptist preacher, it's no won-

Before her success, Lari White worked as a sessions singer. She once sang in a Toyota commercial in Spanish.

der that Lari White approaches singing with high-energy spirit and conviction. With her first two singles, the gutsy "What a Woman Wants" and the soulful "Lead Me Not," from her debut album, White's outstanding performing qualities became evident.

The stunning results of her *Lead Me Not* disc, in addition to her songwriting abilities, built a strong foundation for the artist's sophomore project, titled *Wishes.* Lari describes the album as more focused and consolidated than her first effort and one that brings together all of her musical influences.

A Dunedin, Florida, native, White is the product of a home with diverse musical tastes. Her parents, both public school teachers, listened to all kinds of music. "We had classical records and atonal modern music, right next to Ray Charles and John Denver albums," White recalls. Lari (rhymes with "starry") spent her childhood singing—first in a trio with her parents when she was only four and later as a part of the White Family Singers, after her younger brother and sister joined the group. In high school, she performed in talent shows and played in a rock 'n' roll band, ultimately landing a full academic scholarship to the University of Miami, where she majored in music engineering and minored in voice. Lari spent her evenings singing in top-40 bands and her days in the studio doing backup vocals and jingles. During her last year in college, she also began writing songs.

By the time White arrived in Nashville in 1988 to participate in a talent contest—TNN's *You Can Be a Star*—she was hooked. "I simply fell in love with the town and the whole creative community," explained Lari. She wound up winning first prize in the contest, and the cash awards enabled her to focus all her energies on her music.

White won TNN's You Can Be A Star *contest in 1988.*

White eventually released a single on Capitol Records (now Liberty) that met with limited success, signed a publishing deal with Ronnie Milsap's publishing company, and ventured into acting— an activity that honed her performing and songwriting skills.

Her big break came when Rodney Crowell invited her to sing backup for him on his 1991 summer tour. A recording deal followed, with Crowell producing her first album. Less than three years later, White had a new album, *Wishes*, a nomination from the Academy of Country Music for Top New Female Vocalist, and a brand-new marriage to noted Nashville songwriter Chuck Cannon.

The country music scene expanded tremendously during the 1990s, becoming particularly partial to new female singers who represented a range of musical influences. White was able to smoothly glide into contemporary country through the doors opened by Rosanne Cash and Mary Chapin Carpenter.

LARI WHITE

BORN: May 13, 1965, in Dunedin, Florida

MUSICAL INFLUENCES: Ray Charles, Rodney Crowell, Rosanne Cash

FIRST HIT: "What a Woman Wants" (1993)

OTHER NOTABLE HITS: "That's My Baby" (1993); "Just Thinking" (1993)

BEST ALBUM: *Lead Me Not* (1993)

PERSONAL: White recently married Nashville songwriter Chuck Cannon.

HANK · WILLIAMS, JR. ·

Hank Williams, Jr., performed his first concert at the tender age of eight. He recorded his first song—and top-ten hit—at 14. He scored his first number-one country song at 16. But as suggested by the title and lyrics of that second hit, "Standin' in the Shadows (Of a Very Famous Man)," the

Hank, Jr., has come to terms with his famous father's legacy.

young man who had changed his name from Randall Hank Williams to Hank Williams, Jr., was quite aware that he was riding the coattails of his legendary father.

Hank, Sr., died from the effects of hard living in 1953, leaving behind a haunting legacy for his three-year-old son. Hank, Jr., spent the 1960s performing his father's songs, adhering to his mother's career direction, and indulging a growing appetite for drugs and alcohol.

In 1974, Williams decided to step out of his father's long shadow and stand on his own. Against the wishes of his mother, Audrey Williams, he moved from Nashville to Cullman, Alabama. He then initiated a divorce from his second wife, and he began an album that combined Southern rock, Delta blues, and rebel country.

Williams celebrated the completion of this new, ground-breaking collection of songs by going on a hunting and hiking trip in Montana. During an outing, he suffered massive head injuries when he slipped on a ledge and fell 500 feet down a jagged, rocky slope of Mount Ajax. He underwent several operations over the next eight months to reconstruct his face. Adding to the stress of his rehabilitation was the death of his mother three months after his fall.

While the singer recuperated, the landmark *Hank Williams, Jr. & Friends* album was released. A bold

An accomplished musician, Williams plays guitar, banjo, fiddle, piano, steel guitar, and drums.

departure for Williams, it featured contributions from country rock performers such as Charlie Daniels, Toy Caldwell of the Marshall Tucker Band, and Chuck Leavell of the Allman Brothers Band. The album's rock edges alienated Williams from the Nashville establishment and from his longtime record company, MGM Records. However, the album represented a personal breakthrough for Williams. It contained the confrontational ballad, "Living Proof," in which a drunkard taunts Hank, Jr., that he will never be as good as his father. Williams later adopted it as the title of his 1979 autobiography, which was then turned into a made-for-television movie starring Richard Thomas as the colorful singer.

Williams continued the country-rock mix that distinguished 1975's *Hank Williams, Jr. & Friends* with the release of *The New South* in 1977. The album, a pointed statement about his vision of what a new musical style should be,

By the late 1970s, Williams had developed his own style of Dixie-fried country rock.

established him as a full-fledged member of the "outlaw" movement within country music. Produced by Waylon Jennings, *The New South* was Williams's first disc after joining Curb Records, the new record company established by music industry mogul Mike Curb. This album began Hank, Jr.'s association with Curb/Warner Bros. that would last until 1992. At first, Williams's singles for the new label failed to make much impact on the *Billboard* charts. Williams made it back to the Country top 20 with "I Fought the Law" (1978). Williams closed the 1970s by setting personal sales records. He released the *Family Tradition* album in April 1979 and followed it with *Whiskey Bent and Hell Bound* in October of the same year. Both albums topped 500,000 in sales within a year. Thirty years after his birth on May 26, 1949, in Shreveport, Louisiana, Williams had succeeded in forging his own identity. Manager and close friend Merle Kilgore declared via song that he wasn't going to call Williams "Junior" anymore, which was his way of acknowledging Hank's new, unique style.

By 1982, Williams had attracted a fanatically loyal following. In concert, he regularly drew crowds of 10,000 or more fans, a rarity for a country music artist at that time. And he continued to pull in those numbers for the remainder of the decade.

In October 1982, the nine albums he had created in the previous five years ranked on *Billboard* magazine's Top Country Albums chart—a record-breaking accomplishment that still stands unequalled. (The albums were *One Night Stand, The New South, Family Tradition, Whiskey Bent and Hell Bound, Habits Old and New, Rowdy, The Pressure Is On, High Notes,* and *Hank Williams Jr.'s Greatest Hits.*) By the end of the 1980s, Williams' total sales topped the $25 million mark.

Despite his success, Williams was shunned by the country music awards organizations. He was viewed as an outsider even more than country outlaws Waylon Jennings and Willie Nelson. His open criticism of Nashville's recording and business practices had apparently hurt him within the tight-knit country community.

Family Tradition

In his 1966 hit, "Standing in the Shadows (Of a Very Famous Man)," Hank Williams, Jr., lets us know just how difficult it is to have such a famous performer for a father. Williams spent years rehashing his father's old hits, largely at the insistence of his mother, Audrey Williams. Hank was just three years old when his father died of a drug and alcohol overdose. By the time Hank was eight, he was touring with Audrey's Caravan of Stars show. He changed his name from Randall to Hank, Jr., and performed Hank, Sr.'s hits in Hank, Sr.'s style, as his mother requested. By the time he was 16, Hank, Jr., had recorded two hits; many more would follow. However, the more Hank, Jr., suppressed his own talents to showcase his famous father's, the unhappier he became, and the more he turned to drugs and alcohol to escape. Hank, Jr., finally rebelled in

1974, moving from Nashville to Alabama, linking up with his old buddy James R. Smith, and working on forging a new sound. The acclaimed *Hank Williams, Jr. & Friends,* featuring country rock musicians Charlie Daniels, Toy Caldwell, and Chuck Leavell, among others, marked the highly successful culmination of this effort.

Hank, Jr., attends the ceremony for the unveiling of the postage stamp honoring Hank, Sr.

Eventually, the country music industry began to come around. In 1985, Williams received a Video of the Year award from the Country Music Association for "All My Rowdy Friends Are Coming Over Tonight." When accepting the trophy, he quipped, "You know, I make a little audio, too."

Two years later, Williams began to gain the recognition that seemed so long overdue. The Academy of Country Music kicked off his big year by naming him Entertainer of the Year, and a few months later, the CMA granted him their version of that same honor. The CMA also gave the Video of the Year award to his video version of "My Name Is Bocephus." In 1988, he was again named Entertainer of the Year by both country music organizations, and *Born to Boogie* was designated Album of the Year by the CMA. In 1989, he received the CMA's Vocal Event of the Year Awards for his hit "There's a Tear in My Beer," a high-tech duet recording that combined Williams's voice with a long-lost but newly discovered audio track of Hank, Sr. He also won an award for the video rendition of the song, which used special effects to place the younger Williams into old film footage of the senior Williams in performance. In 1990, Hank, Jr., won his first Grammy Award, for the same father-son vocal duet.

Meanwhile, *Monday Night Football* on ABC-TV introduced Williams's music to the mainstream audience in a unique way. The tune "Born to Boogie" became the theme song for the popular sportscast. In 1991, he rewrote the song as "Monday Night Football Boogie" especially for the program.

Williams's introduction of a rock sound to country music had a pervasive influence. The success of the Kentucky Headhunters, Travis Tritt, Pirates of the Mississippi, and others in the late 1980s made this influence apparent. Williams championed the youthful new sound with his hit song "Young Country" in 1988, and he has served as an elder statesman of progressive country music to the newcomers.

The singer continues to be an avid outdoorsman, retreating for a period each year to a 300-acre spread in Montana to hunt big game and fish. He even moved his business office to Paris, Tennessee, which is located in an area suitable for outdoor recreation.

As the last decade of the twentieth century moves forward, Williams continues to make changes and grow as a performer. In 1990, he married his fourth wife, Mary Jane Thomas. The following year he terminated several long-standing business associations when he switched his concert bookings to the William Morris Agency and signed a multiyear recording contract with Curb/Capricorn Records. Under that label, he has released the albums *Maverick*, *The Hank Williams, Jr., Collection*, and *Out of Left Field*.

HANK WILLIAMS, JR.

BORN: May 26, 1949, in Shreveport, Louisiana

FIRST HIT: "Long Gone Lonesome Blues" (1964)

OTHER NOTABLE HITS: "Hotel Whiskey" (with Clint Black, 1992); "There's a Tear in My Beer" (with Hank Williams, Sr., 1990); "Born to Boogie" (1987); "All My Rowdy Friends (Have Settled Down)" (1981); "Whiskey Bent and Hell Bound" (1979); "Family Tradition" (1979)

BEST ALBUMS: *Wild Streak* (1988); *Born to Boogie* (1987); *Major Moves* (1984); *Rowdy* (1981); *The Pressure Is On* (1981); *Whiskey Bent and Hell Bound* (1979); *Family Tradition* (1979); *The New South* (1977); *Hank Williams Jr. & Friends* (1975)

AWARDS INCLUDE: Grammy, Best Country Vocal Collaboration (1990); Country Music Association (CMA) Vocal Event of the Year (with Hank Williams, Sr., 1989); CMA Entertainer of the Year (1988, 1987); CMA Video of the Year (with Hank Williams, Sr., 1989, 1987, 1985); Academy of Country Music (ACM) Video of the Year (1989, 1988, 1985); ACM Entertainer of the Year (1988, 1987, 1986)

MICHELLE ◆ WRIGHT

Sultry-voiced Michelle Wright may have attained country music stardom in a relatively short time, but the journey to Music City from her native Canada was long and often trying. Reared in the Canadian farming community of Merlin, Ontario, Wright grew up in a household in which country music was a way of life. Both her parents were country enter-

Michelle Wright has won numerous country music awards in her native Canada.

tainers. In fact, one of the singer's first memories is of her father dressed in cowboy stage attire.

Wright began performing in nightclubs upon graduating from high school. After attending college for a year, she attracted the attention of an American booking agent who promptly put her to work for an entire summer doing every gig that could be booked. Plans for a college degree promptly went out the window as that summer turned into eight years on the road and great success in Canada.

Wright found that there were both pros and cons to performing as a way of life. The daughter of an alcoholic, Wright slipped into the pattern of nightlife overindulgence that has destroyed many a music career. A recovering alcoholic since 1988, the singer has been remarkably candid about her experience. She has been equally open about her past as an abused woman. Wright endured years of physical abuse in a turbulent relationship before ending it.

While performing at an outdoor festival in Canada in 1985, Wright's riveting vocal range, which includes everything from a whisper to full-throated assault, caught the attention of successful songwriter Rick Giles. Giles, collaborating with fellow tunesmith Steve Bogard, promptly cut a demo tape of the singer, then began shopping it around to major Nashville record labels. Though they hit the brick wall of rejection on their first attempt, the team eventually landed

MICHELLE WRIGHT

BORN: July 1, 1960, in Merlin, Ontario, Canada

FIRST HIT: "New Kind of Love" (1990)

OTHER NOTABLE HITS: "He Would Be Sixteen" (1992); "Take It Like a Man" (1992); "A Little More Comfortable" (1992)

BEST ALBUMS: *Now & Then* (1992); *Michelle Wright* (1990)

AWARDS INCLUDE: Canadian Country Music Association (CCMA) Single of the Year (1993, 1992, 1991); CCMA Video of the Year (1993, 1992); CCMA Female Vocalist of the Year (1993, 1992, 1991, 1990); CCMA Entertainer of the Year (1993); CCMA Country Music Person of the Year (1992); CCMA Album of the Year (1991); Academy of Country Music Top New Female Vocalist (1992)

PERSONAL: A recovering alcoholic, Wright speaks openly about her drinking problem—to illuminate her own life choices and to help inspire other people.

Wright likes to design and sew her own stagewear.

a contract in 1989 with the newly formed Nashville division of Arista Records, headed up by Tim DuBois.

Two critically acclaimed albums followed: the groundbreaking self-titled debut, which includes such hits as "New Kind of Love" and "He Would Be Sixteen," in 1990 and *Now & Then,* which includes Wright's signature song, "Take It Like a Man," in 1992. The video for this song—featuring the fit singer in a slinky black cat suit—became one of Country Music Television's most requested videos.

A bona fide star in Canada, Wright won the prestigious Female Vocalist of the Year award from the Canadian Country Music Association from 1990 through 1993. She also won the Top New Female Vocalist award from the Academy of Country Music for 1992.

A dynamic entertainer onstage, Wright has maintained a hectic touring schedule, opening for such big-name entertainers as Randy Travis, Alabama, Diamond Rio, and Kenny Rogers. Wright has consistently shown herself to be a performer grittily determined to fulfill her musical dreams while remaining true to her integrity and values.

TAMMY · WYNETTE

Perhaps no style in country music is more manipulative than that of Tammy Wynette. While Patsy Cline used vocal control and expression to gain her pop-crossover appeal, Wynette's from-the-heart style has always been aimed straight at country ears.

Wynette's best-known hits, "Stand By Your Man," "D-I-V-O-R-C-E," and "Take Me to Your World," are

Tammy Wynette's best songs are characterized by her remarkably effective interpretation of emotional lyrics.

characterized by lavish string arrangements and the cries of pedal steel guitars that cling to the pain in her voice. The delicate balance between sublime orchestration and soft vocals is what shapes Wynette's personality and image as a survivor.

The country star has been married five times (Wynette's current husband-manager, George Richey, was the organist at her fourth wedding), undergone 17 operations for abdominal adhesions (leaving her with a dependency on pain pills, which she since has kicked) and a gallbladder operation, endured death threats, and survived a mysterious 1978 beating and kidnapping.

Wynette was born Virginia Wynette Pugh on May 5, 1942, in a tar-paper shack on her grandfather's cotton farm in Itawamba County, Mississippi. Wynette's father was a farmer and guitarist who died of a brain tumor when Tammy was just eight months old. She was raised by her grandparents while her mother worked in a defense plant in Birmingham, Alabama.

Singing became an emotional escape from the work Wynette had to do on her grandfather's farm. "As far back as I can remember I was singing," Wynette said in a 1989 biography published by her record company. "I dreamed of being a singer, but I also wanted to be a housewife and a mother, like my girl friends. I wasn't single-minded in my goals."

As a young woman, Wynette became a licensed cosmetologist. She still keeps her license up to date.

Seven years after it's American release, Wynette's "Stand By Your Man" became a huge hit in England.

But Wynette quickly discovered that marriage was one way to get off the farm. She got married just before finishing high school in Fremont, Mississippi, giving birth to two daughters in three years. Wynette became a licensed beautician and moved to Birmingham, where she had a third daughter, who suffered a near-fatal attack of spinal meningitis before she was four months old.

In 1992, Tammy recorded the dance tune "Justified and Ancient" with the Scottish rappers KLF.

Her marriage began to fall apart. Just as when she encountered trouble on the farm as a child, Wynette's thoughts turned to song. She auditioned for the *Country Boy Eddie* television show in Birmingham. That led to a small role in a 1965 ten-day traveling revue featuring country star Porter Wagoner (before he had hooked up with Dolly Parton). Quickly gaining confidence, Wynette scooped up her three kids and moved to Nashville.

Wynette was in Nashville just a year when she scored her first hit, a cover of Johnny Paycheck's "Apartment No. 9," released in October 1966. The honky-tonkin' "Your Good Girl's Gonna Go Bad" followed in February 1967 and made it to the country top five.

In July of that year, Wynette did an about-face with a heart-tugging duet with David Houston entitled "My Elusive Dreams." Backed by producer Billy Sherrill's sea of vocals and strings, the song became her first number-one single in a long line of hits. Her follow-up hit, "I Don't Wanna Play House," earned her a Grammy. Wynette hit her stride with "Stand By Your Man," which she cowrote with Sherrill. This 1968 anthem became her signature song and earned her a second Grammy. Wynette's 1979 autobiography of the same title spawned a television movie in 1981. The irony is that as Wynette was enjoying the success of "Stand By Your Man," she married restless heart George Jones, and Jones and Wynette became the King and Queen of country music. Their kingdom included several hit records, [high-strung narratives such as "(We're Not) The Jet Set" in 1974 and "Let's Get Together (One Last

Time)" in 1977], one daughter, and lots of headlines. They were divorced in 1975, although they continued to record together. Other Wynette hits in the years that followed included "Good Lovin'" (1971), "Woman to Woman" (1974), and "Womanhood" (1978).

Wynette's material became more pop-oriented during the early 1980s, as was evident in such tunes as "Sometimes When We Touch" (with Mark Gray, 1985). She seemed to be searching for a niche in the country music of that period. By the late 1980s, with the industry's return to tradition-based styles, Wynette was more at home. Her albums *Higher Ground* (1987), in which she dueted with Ricky Skaggs, and *Next to You* (1989) are closer to her original sound.

Ever the adventurous survivor, Wynette ushered in the 1990s by appearing in a British pop-music television series produced by Dave Stewart of the Eurythmics.

She also released a *Best Loved Hits* collection, proving her career was far from over. The ten songs on the album served as a bridge for the singer who celebrated 25 years with Epic Records. In 1992, she proved her versatililty by recording "Justified and Ancient" with top European rappers KLF. That same year, she released a 67-track retrospective entitled *Tears of Fire*, which chronicled the illustrious career of this Mississippi farm girl who became the First Lady of Country Music.

TAMMY WYNETTE

REAL NAME: Virginia Wynette Pugh

BORN: May 5, 1942, in Itawamba County, Mississippi

FIRST HIT: "Apartment No. 9" (1966)

OTHER NOTABLE HITS: "Justified and Ancient" (1992); "We're Strangers Again" (with Randy Travis, 1991); "You and Me" (1976); "'Til I Can Make It on My Own" (1976); "We Loved It Away" (with George Jones, 1974); "D-I-V-O-R-C-E" (1968); "Stand By Your Man" (1968); "Your Good Girl's Gonna Go Bad" (1967)

BEST ALBUMS: *Honky-Tonk Angels* (with Dolly Parton and Loretta Lynn, 1993); *Next to You* (1989); *Higher Ground* (1987); *Womanhood* (1978); *Your Good Girl's Gonna Go Bad* (1967)

AWARDS INCLUDE: Grammy, Best Country Female Vocal Performance (1969); Grammy, Best Country & Western Female Solo Vocal Performance (1967); Country Music Association Female Vocalist of the Year (1970, 1969, 1968); Academy of Country Music Top Female Vocalist (1969)

·TRISHA·YEARWOOD

Considered by many to be a role model for female independence and success, Trisha Yearwood has gone from self-proclaimed small-town tomboy to country star, touring with such powerhouses as Garth Brooks, Randy Travis, and Vince Gill. Possessing a voice of pure emotion and power, Yearwood rose to the top of the charts with her story song "She's in Love With the Boy," written by John Ims. The song held at number one for two weeks—no small feat for the first single from an unproven young artist. By the time her fourth single was released, the poignant "Woman Before Me," her self-titled debut album—with its million-plus sales—was certified platinum.

The daughter of a banker and an elementary school teacher in the tiny farming town of Monticello, Georgia (self-proclaimed "deer capital of the world"), Yearwood has been singing since she could talk. Reared in a music-loving household filled with the sounds of Patsy Cline, Kitty Wells, George Jones, and Merle Haggard, she began singing along with her musical heroes. By her teens, she had come to appreciate the music of contemporary acts such as Emmylou Harris, Linda Ronstadt (with whom she has been favorably compared), and the Eagles.

Arriving in Nashville in 1985, after two years of junior college, she enrolled at the esteemed Belmont College in pursuit of a music business degree. Upon graduation, Yearwood took a receptionist job with the now defunct MTM Records (Mary Tyler Moore's label), hoping to get a foot in the industry door. Buoyed by growing

Trisha Yearwood favors songs about strong women who make their own choices—good or bad.

praise for her powerful voice and uncanny interpretative skills, she began singing on demo tapes as well as doing background vocals on master sessions. Yearwood caught the attention of producer Garth Fundis, and soon landed a recording contract with MCA Records.

236

With the help of such high-powered talents as Garth Brooks (who chose her as the opening act for his 1991 tour) and Vince Gill, Yearwood and Fundis created a powerful debut album. The disc featured the hits "That's What I Like About You" and "Like We Never Had a Broken Heart" (written by Pat Alger and Garth Brooks) and propelled the singer to instant stardom.

The whirlwind success of Yearwood's first album put her personal and business life in a state of flux. The singer separated from her husband, publishing executive Chris Latham (the two had known each other since college), and there was a parting of the ways with managers Bob Doyle and Pam Lewis. Divorced amicably from Latham in 1991, Yearwood is married to Robert Reynolds of the Mavericks (whose vocalist, Raul Malo, performed on her second album).

Yearwood also signed with Ken Kragen, the powerhouse manager behind the successful careers of Kenny Rogers and Lionel Richie. Kragen recommended a drastic image makeover, introducing a sleeker, more glamorous Trisha Yearwood.

Following her career-making debut disc, Yearwood once again teamed up with Fundis to record her sophomore effort, *Hearts in Armor*, a diverse and stylish album as startlingly fresh and unique as its predecessor. The singer again drew on the talents of her superstar friends. *Hearts* boasted background vocal support from the likes of Garth Brooks (Yearwood sang backup on his blockbuster album *No*

Fences), Emmylou Harris, and rock superstar Don Henley. (Henley had professed his admiration for the singer after she performed at a benefit concert he organized, and Yearwood promptly asked him to lend his voice for her second album.)

The singer also reaped praise for her contribution to the *Honeymoon in Vegas* soundtrack with her remake of the Elvis Presley classic "(You're the) Devil in Disguise," pegged as the strongest cut on the project. In addition, she made her screen debut, playing herself in Peter Bogdanovich's underrated film *The Thing Called Love*.

In 1993, Yearwood released her most mature collection yet. Mixing introspective ballads with songs of independence, *The Song Remembers When* once again teamed Yearwood with Fundis. In addition, Yearwood allowed *Forbes* magazine senior editor Lisa Gubernick to chronicle a year of her life, both onstage and off. Gubernick received rare access to the singer's personal and business dealings. The result was the unusually candid book *Get Hot or Go Home: The Making of a Nashville Star*, which objectively portrayed Yearwood as not always perfect but always honest and human.

Though only a few years into her professional career, Yearwood has already set a high standard of excellence. Combining her explosive vocal power and innate interpretative skills, Trisha Yearwood has embarked on a musical career that could be boundless.

TRISHA YEARWOOD

BORN: September 19, 1964, in Monticello, Georgia

MUSICAL INFLUENCES: Reba McEntire, Linda Ronstadt, Emmylou Harris, Kitty Wells, the Eagles

FIRST HIT: "She's in Love With the Boy" (1991)

OTHER NOTABLE HITS: "The Song Remembers When" (1993); "Wrong Side of Memphis" (1992); "Walkaway Joe" (1992); "That's What I Like About You" (1992); "Like We Never Had a Broken Heart" (1991); "The Woman Before Me" (1991)

BEST ALBUM: *Hearts in Armor* (1992); *Trisha Yearwood* (1991)

AWARDS INCLUDE: Academy of Country Music Top New Female Vocalist (1991)

PERSONAL: Prompted by her burgeoning popularity, Revlon came out with a Trisha Yearwood signature fragrance, "Wild Heart." Yearwood is married to Robert Reynolds of the Mavericks.

· DWIGHT · YOAKAM

Dwight Yoakam has a country boy's background, a college intellectual's vocabulary, and a Southern California angle. He's a modern-day rebel who fought to revive an old-fashioned musical style. He has accumulated many victories, and he has left some enemies in his wake.

Dwight Yoakam broke into the business by playing to the post-punk crowd and roots-rock fans of Los Angeles.

Yoakam roared his way into the country music kingdom with his first album, *Guitars, Cadillacs, Etc., Etc.,* which was initially released in 1984 on Oak Records.

The singer and his guitarist/producer, Pete Anderson, raised $5,000 to fund it. Reprise Records scooped up the rights to the recordings, asked Yoakam to add a few more songs, and distributed it nationwide in 1986. The first song, a kicking remake of Johnny Horton's "Honky-Tonk Man," established Yoakam as a new musical force. However, the young singer's outspoken criticism of the Nashville music industry made for a less than uniform response. While some admired his courage and agreed with his point of view, others were offended, especially a few leading executives who weren't accustomed to verbal blasts from newcomers.

Yoakam comes from independent stock. He was born on October 23, 1956, in Pikeville, Kentucky, a small town in the hills and just a hike from Butcher Hollow, the birthplace of Loretta Lynn. An impoverished rural area, this part of Kentucky is home to hard-working coal-mining people.

While Yoakam was still an infant, his parents moved 90 miles north to Columbus, Ohio. His father owned a Texaco service station. On most weekends, his family traveled back to the hills of Kentucky to visit relatives. Yoakam is haunted by vivid memories, both powerful and comforting, of his Kentucky heritage. He remembers his grandfather, Luther Tibbs, rolling on the ground to shake the coal dust from his lungs so he could sit upright without coughing violently. And, he remembers singing bluegrass and gospel songs on the front porch. He remembers the passionate a cappella singing at the local Church of Christ.

Yoakam wrote his first song at age eight. By 1976, just a year out of high school, he was performing throughout the Ohio Valley region. Yoakam put in two years at Ohio State University and then went to Nashville, ready to dedicate himself to the style of music he loved. But the capital of country music told him his music was "too country." Rather than compromise, he

In the 1980s, Yoakam raised eyebrows when he referred to Nashville's country-pop music as "Nash trash."

moved to Los Angeles, where he drove an airport freight van by day while singing in working-class, suburban honky-tonks at night.

Four years later, he met Pete Anderson, an educated young man dedicated to the raw, traditional forms of American music. With Anderson's help, Yoakam's vision became more defined, his attitude more uncompromising. Before long, Yoakam was attracting more attention. The hard-core country singer from a Kentucky hollow found his audience in the punk and roots-rock clubs of Los Angeles.

Nashville finally took notice of the reams of positive press Yoakam was drawing on the West Coast. Yoakam found favor fast. He followed up his debut album with *Hillbilly Deluxe* in 1987, *Buenas Noches from a Lonely Room* in 1988, *Just Lookin' for a Hit* in 1989, and *If There Was a Way* in 1990. Each album went either gold or platinum. Along with Randy Travis, Reba McEntire, and the Judds, Yoakam helped pump life back into country music at a vital point, when sales had slumped to a dismal low.

By the time Yoakam released his sixth album, *This Time,* in 1993, country music was experiencing a widespread growth in popularity. The album proved a critical and popular success and spawned the hit "Ain't That Lonely Yet".

Yoakam's music pays tribute to the past, both that of his family and that of country music. He has written about his coal-mining legacy, about the state highways that people in the rural south took north to find work in industrial centers, and about the mystery and dangers of rural mountain life.

For outside material, he usually looks to the past as well. Yoakam has put his own spin on classics by Johnny Cash, Elvis Presley, Stonewall Jackson, Lefty Frizzell, Roger Miller, and Gram Parsons. He is credited with helping to bring legendary singer Buck Owens out of retirement. As Owens tells it, the young singer simply showed up at Owens's Bakersfield office unannounced one afternoon. Yoakam then invited his idol to perform with him that night at a fair. Owens agreed, launching a comeback that would include a number-one duet with Yoakam ("Streets of Bakersfield") and two albums for Capitol Records.

Behind the scenes, Yoakam displays a similar devotion to the pioneers of the country music industry. He has developed a close friendship with Minnie Pearl, the country humorist who is a cornerstone of the Grand Ole Opry. When Pearl celebrated her 50th anniversary as a member of the Opry, Yoakam sent her 50 roses.

Yoakam has also taken up acting recently, pursuing an interest he has had since he was in high school. He appeared in the 1993 film *Red Rock West,* starring Nicolas Cage and Dennis Hopper. With his friend Peter Fonda, he produced a play in which Yoakam starred as an inmate at a mental institution.

Dwight Yoakam seems a mass of contradictions: He paved the way for country's new sounds by returning to its traditions; he criticized the Nashville industry while celebrating its performers; he has become hip by embracing the past. In doing so, he helped revitalize country music for a younger generation.

DWIGHT YOAKAM

BORN: October 23, 1956, in Pikeville, Kentucky

MUSICAL INFLUENCES: Buck Owens, Hank Williams, Bill Monroe, Creedence Clearwater Revival, John Fogerty, Emmylou Harris

FIRST HIT: "Honky-Tonk Man" (1986)

OTHER NOTABLE HITS: "Ain't That Lonely Yet" (1993); "You're the One" (1991); "Turn It On, Turn It Up, Turn Me Loose" (1990); "Streets of Bakersfield" (with Buck Owens, 1988); "Little Sister" (1987); "Guitars, Cadillacs" (1986)

BEST ALBUMS: *This Time* (1993); *Buenas Noches from a Lonely Room* (1988); *Guitars, Cadillacs, Etc., Etc.* (1986)

AWARDS INCLUDE: Academy of Country Music (ACM) Top New Male Vocalist (1986)

ACHIEVEMENTS: Starred in and produced the play *Southern Rapture,* directed by Peter Fonda, in L.A.; appeared with Nicolas Cage and Dennis Hopper in *Red Rock West*